Analysing Newspapers

Analysing Newspapers

An Approach from Critical Discourse Analysis

John E. Richardson

palgrave
macmillan

First published 2007 by
PALGRAVE MACMILLAN
Houndmills, Basingstoke, Hampshire RG21 6XS and
175 Fifth Avenue, New York, N.Y. 10010
Companies and representatives throughout the world

PALGRAVE MACMILLAN is the global academic imprint of the Palgrave Macmillan division of St. Martin's Press, LLC and of Palgrave Macmillan Ltd. Macmillan® is a registered trademark in the United States, United Kingdom and other countries. Palgrave is a registered trademark in the European Union and other countries.

ISBN-13: 978–1–4039–3565–6
ISBN-10: 1–4039–3565–3

This book is printed on paper suitable for recycling and made from fully managed and sustained forest sources.

A catalogue record for this book is available from the British Library.

Library of Congress Cataloging-in-Publication Data
Richardson, John E., 1974–
    Analysing newspapers:an approach from critical discourse analysis/
    John E. Richardson.
        p.   cm.
    Includes bibliographical references and index.
    ISBN 1–4039–3565–3 (pbk.)
    1. Journalism—Objectivity. 2. Newspapers—Language. 3. Discourse
    analysis. I. Title.
    PN4784.O24R53 2007
    302.23′22—dc22   2006048541

10   9   8   7   6   5   4   3   2   1
16   15   14   13   12   11   10   09   08   07

Printed in China

Contents

List of Tables and Figures

Tables

Figures

Acknowledgements

All academic work is collaborative. Those who argue that it is an individual pursuit, I can only assume, are self-financing, self-publishing hermits. I am none of these things. This book could not have been written without the help, encouragement and support of a great many people, though I remain, as ever, the only person to blame for its contents.

First, the vast majority of this book was written during my time in the Department of Journalism Studies, Sheffield University. My Head of Department, Peter Cole, was particularly supportive of my efforts to write this book; thanks Peter. The accumulation of headline data (summarised in Chapter 7) was funded by the Sheffield University Devolved Fund. I'd like to thank Sharon MacDonald for her advice that helped secure this funding and Tuulia Sipila (the most conscientious researcher I've ever met!) for her assistance collecting and coding data.

Second, a book needs a publishing home, and the people at Palgrave have been wonderful. From Catherine Gray, who originally invited me to submit a book proposal, through Beverley Tarquini, and, most recently, Emily Salz, they gave me the time and space necessary to write the book and the editorial support I needed to make it read and look better. Emily, in particular, has been an outstanding editor: hortative and critical but always supportive of what I was trying to do with the book.

Third, thanks are due to Andrew Parkes (of Newsquest-Gannett) for giving permission to reproduce copyright material from *News Shopper*, 28 May 2003.

Fourth, for four years I tested out this book's ideas and approach to journalism on a variety of people. Primarily, these were students at Sheffield University taking my 'Language and Journalism' module and I am very grateful for their feedback and support – particularly Georgina Turner whose input during her time at Sheffield, and encouragement of my work since, has been greatly appreciated. Tony Bastow, Tony Harcup, Steve Huckerby, Peter Jones and Alistair Tice were all good enough to read earlier drafts of chapters and provide helpful comments and suggestions – I hope you are not too offended that I have ignored some of your advice! I also owe thanks to friends, family and colleagues – chiefly Meryl Aldridge, Albert Atkin, Chris Blackmore, Joseph Burridge, Martin Conboy,

David Deacon, Frans van Eemeren, Bob Franklin, Mark Hanna, Jackie Harrison, Steve Huckerby, Romana Majid, Liz Poole, Brian Price, Paul Whiston and the members of the Language and the New Capitalism listserv (especially Robert de Beaugrande, Peter Ives, Phil Graham, Kandace Nuckols, Robert Phillipson and Ian Roderick) – who've engaged with my ideas and offered advice over the last two-or-so years. Thank you all very much.

Finally, none of it would be worth it without Kirsty, whose support keeps me going.

Introduction: Newspaper Discourse

This book is aimed at producing more critical language users. In it, I introduce an approach to the critical analysis of the language of journalism, with the aim of encouraging you to engage with and criticise newspaper discourse. Journalistic discourse has some very specific textual characteristics, some very specific methods of text production and consumption, and is defined by a particular set of relationships between itself and other agencies of symbolic and material power. These three sets of characteristics – that is, the language of journalism, its production and consumption and the relations of journalism to social ideas and institutions – are clearly inter-related and sometimes difficult to disentangle. In other words, 'they are different elements but not discrete, fully separate elements' (Fairclough, 2000: 122). Specifically: the sourcing and construct of the news is intimately linked with the actions and opinions of (usually powerful) social groups; it is impossible to select and compose news without a conception of the target or intended audience; and, while *possible*, I believe that it is flawed to consider issues such as contemporary democratic politics, social values and the continuing existence of prejudice and social inequalities without reference to the formative influence of journalism. Each of these three points represents key themes of this book that I will revisit when discussing the structures, functions and power of journalism.

This book represents an analysis of newspapers from the perspective of Critical Discourse Analysis (CDA). CDA is a perspective on critical scholarship: a theory and a method of analysing the way that individuals and institutions *use* language. Critical discourse analysts focus 'on social problems, and especially the role of discourse in the production and reproduction of power abuse or domination' (van Dijk, 2001: 96). CDA starts by identifying a social problem, 'chooses

1

the perspective of those who suffer most, and critically analyses those in power, those who are responsible and those who have the means and the opportunity to solve such problems' (van Dijk, 1996, cited in Wodak, 2001: 1). In response to social inequality and the abuse of power, CDA demands 'politically involved research with an emancipatory requirement' (Titscher *et al.*, 2000: 147). Such an approach inevitably means that CDA takes an overt moral and political position with regard to the social problem analysed – a characteristic of CDA that some scholars (particularly within the more descriptive tradition of Conversation Analysis) have objected to. However, we should recognise that all scholarly discourse is produced in social interaction, is part of a social structure and context, and hence is socio-politically situated whether we like it or not: research which takes a neutral or impartial approach to social injustice does not solve the problem, indeed it could be argued that academic neutrality contributes to the perpetuation of such injustice.

Given the power and significance of news journalism to contemporary society, it should come as no surprise that the discourse of newspapers has been, and continues to be, scrutinised (Fairclough, 1995a; Fowler *et al.*, 1979; Fowler, 1991; Richardson, 2001a, 2004; Richardson and Franklin, 2004; van Dijk, 1991). In line with the three characteristics of newspaper discourse referred to above, I argue that the analysis of how newspapers may (re)produce iniquitous social relations needs to be focused at three levels: on the material realities of society in general; on the practices of journalism; and on the character and function of journalistic language more specifically. Clearly, each of these three levels of analysis is enormous, attracting the attention of many, many scholars; hence I could not hope to attempt to portray them fully. It is nonetheless necessary at this stage to briefly introduce a number of key assumptions that this book makes of each of these three subjects.

This book's view of society

The contemporary world is characterised by the pre-eminence of capitalism; there are very few, if any, places in the world that are not affected by capitalist social relations. Certainly, capitalism affects different parts of the world in different ways. To this extent, I agree with Blommaert's (2005: 36) argument that CDA has been rather slow to recognise that the way late modernity has taken shape 'in First-World societies is very particular, and a majority of the people in the world live in conditions closer to those of villagers in Central Tanzania than to those of inhabitants of Manchester or Vienna'. However, I would nevertheless argue that the social relations that characterise both contemporary Manchester and Central Tanzania are similarly the product of the structuring influence of capitalism.

To say that a society is capitalist is to make a claim about the mode of production and the division of society into classes who are defined by their relationship to the mode of production. In essence, 'a class society is structured in such a way as to enable one set of people to live off the labour of others' (Shaikh, 1986: 73). Under a capitalist mode of production, workers are paid less for their labour than it is worth. As we are all aware, workers are rewarded for their labour (insofar as they are paid a wage) but only for *part* of the working day; for the rest of the working day 'labour is working free for capital' (Wayne, 2003: 11). To take a simplistic example: workers from the 'village in Central Tanzania' referred to above (see Blommaert 2005: 36) may carve a soapstone figurine and be paid 50p for a day's labour; the owner of the company they work for may then sell this figurine to a distribution company for £2; this means that the worker, in effect, worked three quarters of a day for free.[1] This is referred to as surplus labour, since (from a Marxist perspective) it is viewed as labour in addition to that which the labour force needs to survive. Surplus labour forms the basis of capitalist profit. The surplus (£1.50 in the case of our Tanzanian example) is appropriated by those who own the means of production – the company – which, in turn, 'keeps the capitalist class willing and able to re-employ workers' (Shaikh, 1986: 74). By Marx's (1998: 25) great turn of phrase, in a capitalist system 'those who work do not gain and those who gain do not work'.

In a little more detail, from a Marxist perspective, 'classes are defined by their social relations of production' – and the 'social' aspect of this relation needs to be stressed (Wayne, 2003: 17). Economically, there are only three classes: those who buy labour power (the bourgeoisie), those who sell their own labour power (the proletariat) and small-scale craftsmen/women and entrepreneurs (the petit bourgeoisie) who either create a product themselves or purchase a commodity and re-sell it for a profit. However within the proletariat, there are wide disparities in the *social* relation to the means of production – in other words, between those who have a degree of labour autonomy and those who do not, between those who have social control over the labour of others (managers, 'teamleaders', foremen, etc.) and those who do not. The middle classes are a special case within this social formation, being those groups within the proletariat 'who sell their labour power and therefore effectively cede control over the production apparatus *as a whole* to capital, while at the same time retaining some real if limited and variable control over their *own* labour' (ibid.). Take journalists as an example: journalists sell their labour to news organisations – a relation that places them in the proletariat class, an identical economic relation as cleaners who do the same. However the journalist's *social* relation to capital is clearly not the same as the cleaner: their labour is more profitable (produces a higher surplus value) and hence they are paid more; and they (historically at least) have a greater degree of autonomy over their labour. Depending on their professional status, journalists may be able to leave the office, talk to others, eat when they want, write and file their copy from outside the office and not be watched or directly supervised for much of their working day. The same cannot be said of the cleaner, who will have to turn up at a given time, perform the same chores, will often be supervised and as a result feels a greater sense of alienation from their labour. These material differences have significant effects on class subjectivities – that is, middle- and working-class perceptions of capitalism and their social position within a capitalist system. In short, the middle-class journalist may have a more positive view of capitalism because he or she is better insulated from the more obvious injuries of class experienced by the working classes.

Defenders of capitalism often claim that the exchange of labour for a wage is acceptable since both parties enter into the contract freely: both the worker and the owner are free to withdraw from the exchange, both gain from the contract (in the form of a wage or profit) and hence the system is acceptable. McNair (2005: 155), for instance, defends capitalism by arguing that inequality is no longer a factor in advanced capitalist societies, 'where living standards for the great majority have improved steadily since the Second World War'. However, workers and owners do not benefit equally from the system, in terms of wealth, health or 'free time' (i.e. time spent getting ready to go to work, returning from work or recovering from work). The 'trickle down theory' of McNair's argument, in which inequality is taken to be tempered because the wealth of the richest is imagined to permeate down and enrich the poorest, belies a more significant truth: that in a capitalist system, as the wealth of the worker increases, the wealth of the owner increases *exponentially*. This is an economic reality that even the *Washington Post* has recently acknowledged. An editorial from this paper, published 12 March 2006, read:

> In the 25 years from 1980 to 2004, a period during which U.S. gross domestic product per person grew by almost two-thirds, the wages of the typical worker actually fell slightly after accounting for inflation. [. . .] Between 1980 and 2003, total after-tax income for the bottom fifth of households rose 8 percent, and the second-bottom fifth gained 17 percent; in other words, all boats did rise, albeit by less than 1 percent per year. But it's hard to celebrate such modest gains when the top fifth advanced 59 percent over the 24-year period. [. . .] after a quarter-century of disappointment, the struggles of Americans in the bottom half of the income distribution cannot be viewed as temporary.[2]

Unfortunately, the editorial drew back from the necessary conclusion that systemic change is required, not piecemeal measures. Indeed the newspaper's misunderstanding of capitalism was revealed by its stated desire for a policy on class poverty that 'would reduce inequality without damaging growth'. Under a capitalist system, as profits and the wealth of the owners (or shareholders) increase, the *comparative* wealth of the workers must necessarily *decrease*, because the wealth of the bourgeoisie is taken directly from the labour of the proletariat. This relation is true as much of national labour markets as it is of international trade and labour markets (see Hubbard and Miller, 2005). What this therefore means is that *capitalism is inherently exploitative*.

However, this system is neither permanent nor, as some have claimed, the best and final method of organising and administering society (Fukayama, 1992). In fact, *capitalism is inherently unstable*. People do not appreciate being exploited and hence there is always the potential that the working classes will become conscious of the nature of their relation to the means of production and revolt. Therefore, the capitalist class who benefit from *their* relation to the means of production have to fight to conceal the true nature of capitalism from the workers that they exploit. As Chomsky (2005: 19) puts it, the concentrated power centres of capital

> [. . .] realise that the system of domination is fragile, that it relies on disciplining the population by one or another means. There is a desperate search for such means: in recent years, Communism, crime, drugs, terrorism, and others. Pretexts change, policies remain rather stable.

The methods of 'disciplining' the working classes are many and varied, but essentially they fit into one of two inter-related techniques: *misguiding* the proletariat into accepting current social relations as natural, necessary or even enjoyable and *marginalising* and subduing dissent. While material in focus and effect, each of these techniques may be conceptualised as a discourse process achieved communicatively. The language used in newspapers is one key site in this naturalisation of inequality and neutralisation of dissent.

As stated above, CDA is an approach to language use that aims to *explore* and *expose* the roles that discourse plays in reproducing (or resisting) social inequalities. Given this objective, and the fact that 'class remains a fundamental structuring principle of every aspect of life in late capitalism' (Murdock, 2000: 7–8), it is strange that the discursive reproduction of class inequalities remains an under-developed issue for CDA. While previous CDA has examined 'marketising' economic discourse (Fairclough, 1995b) and globalisation (Chouliaraki and Fairclough, 1999), it has yet to analyse the role that newspaper discourse plays in indexing and (re)producing class inequality. This book aims to tackle this deficiency, discussing such issues at greater length in Chapter 2 and especially Chapter 5.

This book's view of journalism

The following question lies at the heart of all analysis and critique of journalism: *What is journalism for?* How we answer this will, in turn, shape the kind of additional questions we ask of journalism, and specifically the ways that we test journalism to see if it is 'measuring up' to the roles we think it ought to be fulfilling. Some may feel that journalism exists to entertain us – indeed that it is simply part of the 'entertainment industry'. Such a view is highly simplistic. While journalism displays features common to many forms of entertainment – comedy, novels and popular music to name but three – it is different to all of them. If journalism were comparable to these 'other' forms of entertainment, then why do governments and other powerful sections of society place so much stock in trying to control the work of journalists? Why are journalists manipulated, bullied and killed simply for attempting to do their job?

Alternatively, some have argued that journalism exists to disseminate – literally to broadcast and propagate – the views of the powerful. Again, I disagree. The circulation and promotion of the views of the powerful is better described as propaganda, and while journalism is often shaped by the agenda of such propagandists, it remains distinct and separate from them. Indeed, there is sometimes considerable resistance to the work of PR within journalism. That such resistance is not always successful is an unfortunate outcome of this 'dance' between journalism and its sources, not a foregone conclusion. Third, many have argued that journalism is a business, that newspapers exist purely to make profit and this single observation explains their contents. Of course this is true up to a point – newspapers are businesses that must make money in order to continue to exist. But what does this observation actually solve? The film industry must also 'make money in order to continue to exist', but it is clearly different (in focus and scope) to journalism. Does concluding that 'newspapers need to make money' get to the bottom of the differences between journalistic genres (or between, say, *The Times* and the *Guardian*) or of the structure of news or, indeed, the influence of journalism? In the words of Murdock and Golding (1977: 18):

> It is not sufficient simply to assert that the capitalistic base of the 'culture industry' necessarily results in the production of cultural forms which are consonant with the dominant ideology. It is also necessary to demonstrate how this process of reproduction actually works by showing in detail how economic relations structure both the overall strategies of the cultural entrepreneurs and the concrete activities of the people who actually make the products the 'culture industry' sells.

In short, detecting that newspapers are businesses should only ever be the starting point of analysis, not the conclusion.

Each of these critiques of journalism, I think, misses the bigger picture. This book is founded on the assumption that *journalism exists to enable citizens to better understand their lives and their position(s) in the world.* Journalism's success or failure – in other words, the degree to which it is doing what it should or is letting us down – rests on the extent to which it achieves this fiduciary role: does journalism help you to better understand the world and your position within it? At this point we can reintroduce the three different approaches to journalism listed above: journalism as entertainment, as a loudhailer for the powerful and privileged and as a commodity produced by profit-seeking businesses. It is evident to all that journalism is often entertaining, it regularly reproduces the opinions of the powerful and (with the exception of a handful of outlets) is a saleable commodity.

In fact, one could argue that each of these three functions – reporting the actions and activities of the powerful and doing so in a form that is entertaining and readily consumable – are necessary to fulfilling the informational needs of the citizen. But when the work of journalists emphasises entertainment, or the activities and opinions of the powerful, or the pursuit of profit *in themselves* or *above* the primary function of journalism – to help citizens to understand the world and their positions within it – *it stops being journalism.*

Of course, this argument is still partial. Other genres of communication, for instance the novel, music, feature films, can also help us to understand the world (though I recognise that they are predominantly fictional and therefore do so in a completely different way to the predominantly factual stories of journalism). In addition to questioning the *function* of journalism, we also need to ask questions about the *form* and *content* of the messages that journalism conveys, and the discourse processes through which such messages are produced and consumed. Most of us can identify the meanings of texts, the meaning of a news report or what the journalist may be trying to make us think. But identifying exactly *how* this occurs is a little more difficult. If we take a relatively straightforward example: how do you tell the difference between different forms of writing? It is immediately obvious that there are certain differences: 'Sports commentary, for example, will predictably be different from the language used in an interview, and the language of advertising will be different from the language of [news reporting]. This much is obvious. Given this observation, however, it is not always easy to [. . .] pin down what makes a text of a particular type identifiable as such', nor is it always easy to pin down exactly 'how it achieves its purpose' (Delin, 2000: 2).

If we take a rather complex example – the issue of bias. Most of us think we can identify biases in news, or those instances when the journalist seems to have an agenda that they're pushing. It is much harder to be able to identify exactly *why* you come to this conclusion; *why* you think that a particular article is biased. Take this excerpt from an interview, for example, which analysed interviews with television viewers about the way in which they deconstructed TV news broadcasts:

> *Barb*: . . . there was that story about the Muslims and about how they were holding neighbourhood watches or something. . . and people do that all the time and they're telling about how these people, they turn violent, but they're really stressing that these

people are Muslim, and it was like because these people are Muslim they were doing this and I don't know, I didn't see the connection about, like, what liberty do they have in making the connection that these people were violent because they were Muslim? Or that these people are wrong because they are Muslim?

Res: okay, did you see the news making that connection?

Barb: yeah

Res: okay, how were they making that connection?

Barb: well, it was like in, every time they referred to these people, and what they did it was because they were, it was just like, Muslim, and these Muslim people live in, it just seemed like they were making that connection. Like between the people group, and the, everyone that is like that act that way. (Hacker *et al.*, 1991, cited in Fairclough, 1992: 193)

Hacker *et al.* suggest that this extract shows that although 'Barb' could identify some aspect of a news story that she disagreed with – she could identify what she thought was bias or an objectionable agenda of some kind – she still found it difficult to explain *how* she came to this opinion. The second passage, in which Barb tries to explain exactly *how* the journalist is making a connection between 'being Muslim' and 'being violent', is noticeably less fluent, less confident than the first, in which she suggests that there is a connection. In essence, what she is saying is:

[*Barb*: the reporter suggests there is a link between violence and being Muslim]

[*Res*: how is this connection made?]

[*Barb*: I don't know, it just seems there's a connection]

This book doesn't just cover that 'what' of the messages communicated by newspapers – for instance, *what* journalists write about the working class, *what* journalists write about war or write about Muslims – it also covers the 'how' of newspaper communication. In other words, *how* journalistic discourse is produced; *how* journalistic texts function; *how* arguments are made and convincingly supported; and *how* newspaper texts may be implicated in the production and reproduction of social inequalities. In doing so, it'll hopefully provide you with a vocabulary for describing and accounting for language and methods of analysis and critique, which will enable you to become more critical of newspaper discourse. These issues and others are discussed in greater length in Chapter 4 on the discursive practices of journalism and Chapter 6 on argumentation and readers' letters.

This book's view of language

This book examines the language use – or discourse – of newspapers, and is based on five fundamental assumptions about language. First, language is *social*. Language is central to human activity; indeed it is one of the things that make us human. It is through the use of language that we grant meaning to our actions; equally, it is through our use of language that we can attempt to remove meaning from our actions. As Blommaert (2005: 10–11) puts it:

> [. . .] there is no such thing as 'non-social' language [. . .] Any utterance produced by people will be, for instance, an instance of oral speech, spoken with a particular accent, gendered and reflective of age and social position, tied to a particular situation or domain, and produced in a certain stylistically or generically identifiable format.

Language use exists in a kind of dialogue with society: language is produced by society and (through the effect of language use on people) it goes on to help recreate it. Language *first* represents social realities and *second* contributes to the production and *re*production of social reality or social life. This 'social-ness' of language is revealed in a number of ways: for example, the way in which people speak to each other is in part a product of social context. You wouldn't speak to someone in a pub the same way as you would in a court of law (unless you wanted to be found in contempt). As well as the physical and the institutional setting, language use reflects 'speakers' identities, expectations as to what speakers intend to accomplish in a particular act of communication, elements of the wider social structure in which speakers are caught, and so on' (ibid.: 11). And language use doesn't just reflect 'the way things are done'; it goes on to recreate these social and sometimes institutional expectations – expectations that we all have when we pick up a newspaper or a magazine, that it will be written in a particular way.

In addition, those involved in a conversation, or any kind of communicative act, don't just hold these large-scale expectations about the general nature of the interaction (e.g. how to speak in an interview or how to speak in court); they also hold assumptions and presuppositions about the world, that are drawn upon in conversation. Take arguments, for instance, which for the moment I'll rather loosely define as the expression of opinions and reasoning within a context of disagreement. A lot of arguments draw on presuppositions that the audience are required to fill in themselves in order for the argument to seem plausible. For example, take this two sentence readers' letter printed in *Time* magazine (November 1997):

> It was clear from last time that Saddam Hussein wouldn't back down. Now is the time to put an end to all this.

There are so many assumptions in this argument that I hardly know where to begin: What happened last time? What was it that Saddam Hussein didn't back down from? Why was it *clear* that he wouldn't back down? What is the 'all this' that the arguer wants to 'put an end to'? What does the arguer mean by 'ending' it? And so on, and so on. These are all assumptions that you, the reader, would have to provide yourself in order to make this argument coherent. If you didn't think that the above argument was coherent when you first read it (i.e. you didn't understand it), this is most probably because you lacked the required assumed background knowledge.

Related to the belief that language is social is this book's second assumption: language use enacts *identity*. What this means is that people project themselves as a certain type of person, and that the identity that a person projects relates, in part, to the activities that they're attempting to accomplish. For instance, you probably wouldn't speak to your parents in the same way as you would to your friends, and this relates, in part, to the way that your parents and friends see you and the way you *want* them to see you. Equally, the way I talk to students in a classroom is different to the way I talk to them should I see them in a pub or out socially.[3] The meanings of an utterance, an argument, a newspaper text or whatever are intimately related to the identity of the producer responsible for its content and the context of its articulation. Therefore in order to fully appreciate communication you have to recognise these identities and the activities that are being acted out. Put another way, our understanding of a communicative act is shaped, in part, by who is speaking/writing and the context in which this occurs. While this may appear straightforward, these aspects of communication can be open to a certain degree of interpretation (which is what makes them interesting). For instance, I might read a readers' letter and describe it as 'Mr X's opinion on public services', but you, having a little more knowledge about this kind of thing, may describe it as 'the opinion of Conservative Party election campaigners on public services, just with Mr X's name at the bottom'. Here we're debating *who* is actually responsible for the text and therefore the way that we should interpret it. Given the widespread public distrust of politicians, using the ostensibly non-partisan views of members in the general public (in this case, Mr X) is an ideal way for political parties to disseminate their arguments. Assumed authorship (in this case of a readers' letter) has a profound impact on the implicit meanings communicated by the text – either as the view of a non-aligned member of the public or the self-interested electioneering of a political party (see Richardson and Franklin, 2004). Relating to assigning context to communication: imagine an article on the website for the British National Party (BNP), where the Party accuse Ariel Sharon of being a war criminal responsible for killing Palestinian refugees at Sabra and Shatila. I might say 'this is the BNP sticking up for Palestinian refugees', but you again having a little more knowledge about this kind of thing, may say 'no, this is the BNP being anti-Semitic. They've used this incident to attack Sharon and make a wider point about a Jewish conspiracy which ensured he has gone unpunished.' Here we're debating the context of the communicative act: *what* the BNP is speaking *on* and perhaps *why*. In this case, these speculations relate directly to the Party's identity – specifically their identity as the largest neo-fascist party in the UK whose leader at the time (Nick Griffin) had a previous criminal conviction for anti-Semitic racial hatred.

This example brings me onto this book's third assumption about language and perhaps the most important one to grasp: language use is always *active*; it is always directed at *doing* something; and the way in which language achieves this activity is always related to the context in which it is being used. For instance, journalists may use language to *inform* us of an event, or to *expose* wrongdoing, or to *argue* for or against something. Each of these verbs – inform, expose and argue for – demonstrates the active nature of communication in these cases. Going back to the last example, which actually *was* taken from a real article on the BNP's website, we may say that the overall function, or *global speech act*, of their argument was either *supporting* refugees or *attacking* Sharon. Hence, language use is not just talk; language use should be regarded as an activity or as a *social action*.

Related to this is this book's fourth assumption: language use has *power*. However, the power of language use isn't flat or democratic in the way that it operates. Clearly, some people's speech is more powerful than others; the opinion of certain people is taken to be more credible and authoritative than the opinion of others; why and how this is achieved is a matter of keen academic and social interest. Equally, some *ways* of speaking or communicating have more power than others; certain genres of communication have more potential effects on social life than other forms of communication do – in terms of both positive and negative effects. Journalism is precisely such a powerful genre of communication. The power *of* journalistic language to *do* things and the way that social power is indexed and represented *in* journalistic language are particularly important to bear in mind when studying the discourse of journalism. Journalism has social effects: through its power to shape issue agendas and public discourse, it can reinforce beliefs; it can shape people's opinions not only of the world but also of their *place* and *role* in the world; or, if not shape your opinions on a particular matter, it can at the very least influence *what* you have opinions on; in sum, it can help shape social reality by shaping our *views* of social reality. For these reasons, and many more, the language of the news media needs to be taken very seriously.

Taking this point a little further, this book's fifth assumption is that language use is *political*. This is perhaps the logical outcome of assuming that language use is social and has power – there isn't any way that language use couldn't be political, given the combination of these two assumptions. However, there is still a prevailing assumption that language is 'clear' and acts as a neutral window on the world, and that the objects and structures of a language exist as a kind of an apolitical structure, like numbers do for mathematics. Such a view of language also meshes quite well with prevailing assumptions about journalism: that it is neutral and 'factual'. These assumptions need to be contested because they can be quite dangerous. Orwell (2004 [1946]) demonstrated this in his classic essay 'Politics and the English Language'. In this essay, he argues two basic points: first, that ugly or offensive thoughts corrupt language; and second, that language can corrupt thought. Being a socialist, Orwell does not suggest that language *in itself* can shape material reality; on the contrary, 'the decline of a language must ultimately have political and economic causes' (p. 102). Hence, language is an instrument that is shaped according to material circumstances and the purpose that we want it to serve. However, 'an effect can become a cause, reinforcing the original cause and producing the same effect in an intensified form' (ibid.). Thus, language is a medium of power that can be used to sediment inequalities of power and legitimate iniquitous social relations. In one frequently quoted section of this essay, Orwell wrote

> political speech and writing are largely the defence of the indefens-ible. Things like the continuance of British rule in India, the Russian purges and deportations, the dropping of the atom bombs on Japan, can indeed be defended, but only by arguments which are too brutal for most people to face, and which do not square with the professed aims of the political parties. Thus political language has to consist largely of euphemism, question-begging and sheer cloudy vagueness. Defenceless villages are bombarded from the air, the inhabitants driven out into the countryside, the cattle machine-gunned, the huts set on fire with incendiary bullets: this is called *pacification*. Millions of peasants are robbed of their farms and sent trudging along the roads with no more than they can carry: this is called *transfer of population* or *rectification of frontiers*. [. . .] All issues are political issues, and [. . .] When the general [political] atmosphere is bad, language must suffer. (Ibid.: 114–116)

The relevance of this argument for contemporary politics, charac-terised by euphemism, dishonesty and the outright debasement of terms such as 'democracy', 'freedom' and 'human rights' (see Collins and Glover, 2002; O'Byrne, 2003) cannot be denied. As Cox (2004: 312) puts it, under current political discourse, the 'terms 'democracy' and 'liberation' have become transformed to mean open markets and military occupation'. Such debasement, and their horrendous polit-ical consequences, need to be resisted.

These assumptions provide us with a starting point for the analysis of the language of journalism. Each of them – that language is social, that it enacts identity, that it is active, that it has power and that language is political – raise a significant number of subsequent questions and provide us with interesting avenues of research and investigation. In addition, these insights into the way language func-tions provide a set of *tools* to apply to the study of journalism that I discuss at greater length in Chapters 2 and 3.

Analysing Newspapers: Context, Text and Consequence

Problems in studying 'content'

Until relatively recently in media research, 'empirical qualitative studies were consigned to the margins of research activity and graduate training' (Delia, 1987, cited in Lindlof, 1995: 8). This view has been steadily challenged, with media research gradually opening up to more interpretative, contextual and constructivist approaches to data collection and analysis. Critical Discourse Analysis, the theory and method of newspaper analysis that this book advocates, is one such interpretative, contextual and constructivist approach. What this means is that critical discourse analysts: offer *interpretations* of the meanings of texts rather than just quantifying textual features and deriving meaning from this; situate *what* is written or said in the *context* in which it occurs, rather than just summarising patterns or regularities in texts; and argue that textual meaning is *constructed* through an interaction between producer, text and consumer rather than simply being 'read off' the page by all readers in exactly the same way. Lindlof (1995: 22) argues that '[o]bjectivist science and quantitative methods have been insufficient to perform these tasks – not because these modes of inquiry are faulty, but because they advocate views of the world that do not value the study of situated, emergent and reflexive human phenomena'. To explain these shortfalls, we need to take a step back and examine in greater detail what quantitative content analysis of newspapers actually *is*.

Berelson (1952) offered a definition that has subsequently been widely adopted as *the* definitive description of quantitative content analysis:

> Content analysis is a research technique for the objective, systematic and quantitative description of the manifest content of communication. (p. 263)

In addition, Berelson provides a specific description of the 'content' that he believes should be the focus of this objective and systematic quantification of communication:

> [...] content analysis is ordinarily *limited to the manifest content* of the communication and is *not* normally done directly in terms of the *latent intentions* which the content may express nor the latent responses which it may elicit. Strictly speaking, content analysis proceeds in terms of *what-is-said*, and not in terms of why-the-content-is-like-that (e.g. 'motives') or how-people-react (e.g. 'appeals' or 'responses'). (p. 262; emphases added)

Subsequent to this definition of the method of quantitative content analysis, Berelson (1952) provides a critical and reflexive account of *three assumptions* that underpin this approach to analysing newspapers. Again it is helpful to quote him at length:

> 1. Content analysis assumes that inferences about the relationship between intent and content or between content and effect can validly be made, or the actual relationships established. [...] Content analysis is often done to reveal the purposes, motives and other characteristics of the communicators as they are (presumably) 'reflected' in the content; or to identify the (presumable) effects of the content upon the attention, attitudes or acts of readers and listeners. (p. 264)

Take, for example, a past piece of my work that analysed the representation of Muslims in British broadsheet newspapers. One aim of this research was to reveal the 'purposes, motives and other characteristics' of the elite communicators as they are 'reflected' in the content of their newspapers. Should these elite newspapers represent (and therefore presumably *regard*) Islam and Muslims negatively – as violent, as threatening, as lascivious, as 'Other' – then this may signal potentially negative effects for Muslims due to the effects of this content on readers. These relationships between purposes, content and effects are, as the quotation suggests, only inferred or suggested in content analysis, since it only studies 'the *manifest content* of communication', not any social or contextual factors outside of, or subsequent to, the text itself.

Second, Berelson states that

2. Content analysis assumes that *study of the manifest content is meaningful*. This assumption requires that the content be accepted as a 'common meeting-ground' for the communicator, the audience and the analyst. That is, the content analyst assumes that the 'meanings' which he ascribes to the content, by assigning it to certain categories, correspond to the 'meanings' intended by the communicator and/or understood by the audience. (p. 264, my emphasis)

In other words, content analysis assumes that when you and I read the same paper we not only understand it in the same way but also understand it in the way intended by the producer of the text. This is a controversial assumption which Berelson later hedges, stating that such an assumption is only really valid in the case of denotative, as opposed to connotative, meaning (see Chapter 3). For this reason content analysis usually attempts to keep the coded categories (or *variables*) focused as much as possible on evident or unmistakable features of the texts. Questions thought to be appropriate usually include the following – In what newspaper is the text printed? On what page is the text printed? How large (centimetres) is the text? In what country is the text located? What sources are referenced in the text? Are they quoted? and others – depending entirely on what the study is about and the kind of questions that the researcher wants to ask.

Despite the apparently 'straightforward' nature of these questions, some will inevitably produce different 'readings' of meaning and therefore potentially different coding. Consider my study of the representation of Muslims in British broadsheet newspapers, for example: Should 'Palestine' be coded as a country? While some may think that it to be a progressive gesture to code Palestine as a country, doing so entails that it *is* a sovereign state and so may inadvertently imply that the struggle for Palestinian self-determination has been realised. Should a reference to Bethlehem be coded as being set in 'Palestine', 'Israel' or 'Jordan' (since it is in the occupied West Bank)? Should a reference to Irbil or Rawanduz always be coded as a report from 'Iraq', or could/should it be coded as 'Kurdistan'?

These are significant questions, since although the suggested options may arguably be as *accurate* as each other, they do not 'mean' or connote the same place. Methodological problems such as these highlight the political implications of 'naming', especially in the case of nations and perhaps particularly in the case of the examples mentioned above.

The third assumption, which Berelson suggests underpins the methods of content analysis, is:

> 3. Content analysis assumes that *the quantitative description of communication content is meaningful*. This assumption implies that the frequency of occurrence of various characteristics of the content is itself an important factor in the communication process. (p. 265; emphasis added)

Thus content analysis assumes that if a word is used 20 times in one newspaper and only twice in a different newspaper, this is of significance. In the context of my research on the representation of Islam: where negative references (e.g. 'violence', 'threat', 'terrorism') are included more frequently in articles that cite Islam as influential than in articles which do not, there may be grounds for arguing that Muslims are being linked, intentionally or otherwise, to negative social action. Tests of statistical independence could be employed to confirm or refute the truth of this claim: that the semantic domain 'Islam' is persistently co-located with negative semantic domains in broadsheet newspapers. Similar claims have been made of the frequency of 'negative topics' in the reporting of ethnic/racial minority communities more generally, or the reporting of homosexuality, or trade unions, or wealth of other marginalised social groups. On first inspection this appears plausible, but this assumption of content analysis, like the second, is rather controversial and requires further explanation.

First, although textual co-location is both interesting and potentially important, the frequency with which 'negative' words and topics are included in articles 'about Islam' is perhaps not as important as the *agency* of this negative social action. In other words: *Who* is being 'violent'? *Who* is being 'threatening'? It is entirely possible that articles reporting the conflict in Bosnia and the conflict in Israel/Palestine could mention 'Islam' and 'violence' as frequently as each other, yet in one context Muslims are represented as the victims of violence and in other as the perpetrators of violence. This problem can, to some extent, be alleviated through increasingly detailed coding, but at some point the codes recording exactly 'how' words, phrases, concepts and arguments are employed in texts will be so complex that they become unworkable.

Gerbner (1958) argued for expanding media analysis from an exclusive focus on formal characteristics of content (the *what-is-said* of Berelson's definition), towards regarding content 'as expressive of social relationship[s] and institutional dynamics, and as formulative of social patterns' (p. 480). Rejecting both of the labels 'quantitative' and 'qualitative' in favour of the term 'critical' media research, Gerbner's contention was

> not so much that inherent physical characteristics of media as such, or that elements of style, vocabulary, syntax, are themselves of profound and direct significance. Rather [. . .] that the nature and consequences of these elements and characteristics can be understood best if content is viewed as bearing the imprint of social needs and uses. (p. 481)

From this perspective, 'consequential meaning [as opposed to explicit or manifest meaning] is far from being an "arbitrary" convention' (ibid.: 487) as Berelson and other traditional content analysts suggest. Rather, consequential meaning 'is the property of a specific event or system of events' (ibid.) which surround the production of media communication. The coding and quantification of categories does, however, remain central to Gerbner's methods of critical content analysis, serving 'as shorthand devices to *label*, *separate*, *compile* and *organise* data' (Charmaz, 1983: 111, cited in Lindlof, 1995: 220) derived from a durable record of communication: texts. However, in critical research this is only ever a starting point, and Gerbner (1958) argues that further questions need to be asked of the data compiled:

> In what ways does this material reflect physical and social qualities of communicating agencies (publishers) and their relationships to other systems such as markets, advertisers, audiences and their world of events? What points of view about life and the world as [the communicator] sees them are implied and facilitated? What social arrangements of ownership and control of communicative means and facilities are revealed by the prevalence of this material? [. . .] What might be the consequences [. . .] of social relationships and points of view mediated through this content as a social event system? (p. 488)

It is for these reasons that my project examining the representation of Islam in broadsheet newspapers quickly evolved into an examination of the discursive representation of Islam (see Richardson, 2001a,b, 2004). In other words, it developed from quantifying the patterns across a sample of texts (content analysis) into a project aimed at examining meaning *within* texts and relationships between these meanings and the wider processes of newspaper production and consumption; it developed from summarising *what* newspapers write about Islam to a project aimed at analysing *how* newspapers write about Islam: in short, it became CDA. The assumptions and methods of CDA adopted in this book are introduced in a later section of this chapter.

Second, although the 'occurrence of certain characteristics of content' may be important, the recording of texts' manifest content must *necessarily* ignore textual absences, even when these absences are systematically under-used stylistic alternatives to the coded content. The work of critical linguists, such as Kress (1983, 1994) and in particular Trew (1979a,b), have revealed the important role which syntactic structures play in the ideological (re)construction of social reality (see Chapter 3). The importance of such transformations is ignored by content analysis since their importance lies in textual *absence*. More specifically, the most contentious aspect of content analysis concerns how the coded categories (or *variables*) are first constructed by the researcher(s). Deacon *et al.* (1999: 117) warn that content analysis is 'an extremely directive method: it gives answers to the questions you pose'. Lindlof (1995: 219) states that coding is 'integral to the task of interpreting communicative phenomena', demanding that 'the analyst decide what is worth saving, how to divide up the material and how a given incident of talk or behaviour relates to other coded items'. What this means is that you could start a content analysis with a certain list of variables to count but could miss a significant aspect of the newspapers you've chosen to study because you have asked the wrong questions.

Third, recording the content – the '*who* says *what* to *whom* and with *what effect*' of Lasswell's (1949) formula – ignores the very important issues of *context* that surround the formation of *content*. Even when pragmatic or illocutionary function of text is coded – for example, the text contains an argument, or an accusation, or an order, etc. – the context in which such an illocutionary act is performed often goes uncoded. This is no doubt primarily due to the unsuitability of content analysis in summarising context: context is an extra-linguistic or extra-textual feature and therefore difficult to record and summarise. But, as Gerbner (1958) has stated, *'what is said by who* depends also on his [*sic*] role' (p. 484). This has been captured in Austin's (1962) notion of *felicity conditions*, or 'the conditions that must obtain for an utterance to have force as a certain speech act (accusing etc.). For example, an imperative statement can only be an [effective] order if uttered by someone with authority over the hearer' (Woods and Kroger, 2000: 5). Similarly, a promise can only be effective as a promise if uttered by someone who is trusted by the hearer. It is doubtful that codes could be developed which record all the contextual conditions granting an individual or group the power to speak, in addition to recording the conditions which endow their words with social force for all the sampled texts.

Of course, there *are* benefits to quantitative content analysis: with this method you can capture a sense of patterns or frequencies of meaning across a large sample of texts, and to achieve this initial task it is still a useful method to use. But these benefits come 'at a cost. By looking at aggregated meaning-making *across* texts, the method tends to skate over complex and varied processes of meaning-making *within* texts; [their] latent rather than the manifest levels of meanings' (Deacon *et al.*, 1999: 117). These are tasks for which the methods of CDA are particularly well suited. But to explain what *Critical* Discourse Analysis is, we first need to step back again and examine *Discourse Analysis.*

Discourse Analysis

The terms 'discourse' and 'discourse analysis' (DA) are vigorously contested concepts whose definition, it often seems, are even beyond the scope of discourse studies itself. Methodologically, theoretically and analytically, the field of DA is extremely diverse (see Blommaert, 2005; Brown and Yule, 1983; Cameron, 2001; Phillips and Jørgensen, 2002; Weiss and Wodak, 2003; Wodak and Meyer, 2001). Discourse is a very trendy word referring to a very trendy concept. It is one of the most well-used (some would say *over-* or *mis*used) words in academia today. Reading around this subject, students (like the rest of us) often come across authors using different – and sometimes *radically* different – accounts of what discourse 'is' and the way that the term ought to be used. Readers should therefore be aware that the following account of 'discourse' – specifically what it is, how the term has been and is applied, and what this means for the study of journalism – is only part of the story.

Schiffrin (1994) has argued that, contrary to the extensive (and sometimes rather impenetrable) debates in DA, there are two general approaches to the definition of discourse. First, there are those who define discourse as a particular unit of language, specifically, as a unit of language 'above' (larger or more extended than) the sentence. Since this approach to discourse focuses on the form which language takes – and specifically how discourse attains the quality of being unified and meaningful – it is called the *formalist* or *structuralist* definition of discourse. Cameron (2001: 10–11) suggests that 'Linguists treat language as a "system of systems", with each system having its own characteristic forms of structure or organisation. [. . .] If discourse analysis deals with "language above the sentence", this means that it looks for patterns (structure, organisation) in units which are larger, more extended, than one sentence.' Theorists who adopt this first definition of discourse tend to look at the features which link sentences together; the formal features which make two sentences 'a discourse' rather than just two unconnected phrases. Cameron (2001) gives the following example, taken from an article by the conversation analyst Harvey Sacks rather than a newspaper:

The baby cried.
The mommy picked it up.

Cameron's discussion of this two-sentence sequence introduces some of the key issues that occupy formalist discourse analysis. She suggests that this sentence demonstrates four characteristics central to formalist accounts of discourse: cohesion, narrative, causality and motivation. Taking each in turn, Brown and Yule (1983: 24) suggest that cohesion between elements in connected sentences exist when 'one word or phrase is linked to other words or phrases'. Here, we have the pronoun 'it' in the second sentence. The conventional approach to pronouns approaches them as a syntactic substitution – that is, they substitute another word or words occurring elsewhere in discourse. From such an approach, in this example 'it' in the second sentence substitutes 'the baby' in the first. A more productive approach is to consider pronouns in terms of reference – what they *refer* to. From such a perspective, pronouns are co-referential semantic forms: they refer to someone (or something) in the same way as proper nouns. That is, 'he' refers a particular man in the same way as his proper name 'John Smith' does. The difference is that pronouns cannot be interpreted in their own right and instead 'direct the hearer/reader elsewhere for their interpretation' (ibid.: 192). It is this co-reference – in this case, the way that both 'the baby' and 'it' refer to the same thing – that creates *cohesion* between the two sentences and therefore a structure above or larger than a single sentence.

Second, we can consider this two-sentence discourse in terms of its narrative structure. It appears almost natural to impose a *narrative*, or a story, onto the sequence in which the events occur chronologically and in the same setting. In other words, it is common sense to assume that 'the baby cried' and then immediately afterwards 'the mommy picked it up'. In fact, the baby could have cried in Singapore and the mommy picked it up two years later when they were in London. There is nothing in these sentences to contradict this reading, but it is certainly not the most conventional interpretation. In fact in this case Cameron (2001) wrote that we are likely to further impose a *third* principle, that of *causality* onto the sequence. In other words, we infer '*because* the baby cried the mommy picked it up'. This is because the sequence fits with a schema, or script, we have of babies crying and them being picked up to be comforted. A script is a portion of knowledge, often shared unconsciously 'within a group of people and drawn upon in making sense of the world' (Fowler, 1991: 43). Therefore, it is precisely at this point where social, historic and perhaps cultural knowledge starts to creep into what may have previously been considered a predominantly structural issue. Fourth, Cameron (2001) suggests that the majority of readers go a stage *further* than causality, into *motivation*, concluding that 'The mommy' is in fact the baby's *own* mother. However, if we look back to the text, this is not necessarily the case; the text states that '*The* mommy picked it up', not using a possessive pronoun such as '*her*', '*his*' or even '*its* mommy'. This shows the *detail* of the script that we are using to interpret the sequence: the first guess of most people in the West would not be that a crying baby was picked up by a woman who just happens to be the mother of some other child.

What this suggests is that we make sense of discourse partly by making guesses – usually unconsciously – based on social knowledge (ibid.). If this is true, then perhaps the first definition of discourse as 'language above the sentence' is not completely adequate: it misses, or underestimates, the social ideas that inform the way we use and interpret language. This social aspect of language understanding is reflected in the second broad definition of 'discourse' – the *functionalist* definition – that argues discourse should be studied as 'language in use'. Brown and Yule (1983) go as far as to state

[...] the analysis of discourse is, necessarily, the analysis of language in use. As such, it cannot be restricted to the description of linguistic forms independent of the purposes or functions which these forms are designed to serve in human affairs. (p. 1)

Here we see why it is known as the functionalist definition of discourse: functionalists assume that language is active, and discourse analysis is the analysis of what people *do* with language. Cameron (2001: 13) suggests that theorists who adopt this definition of discourse are interested in '*what* and *how* language communicates when it is used *purposefully* in particular instances and *contexts*'. Research which adopts this definition of discourse assumes that language is used to *mean* something and to *do* something and that this 'meaning' and 'doing' are linked to the context of its usage. In other words, in order to properly understand discourse we need to do more than analyse the inter-relations of sentences and how they hang together as a cohesive and coherent text. To properly interpret, for example, a press release, or a newspaper report or an advert, we need to work out what the speaker or writer is *doing* through discourse and how this 'doing' is linked to wider inter-personal, institutional, socio-cultural and material contexts.

In written and broadcast journalism, *meaning* is constantly tied to *context*, and this occurs primarily in two ways – in the *assigning of sense* and in *the assigning of reference*. Errors or word play in each of these two processes can cause confusion, misunderstandings or humour as demonstrated by the examples below. First, journalists need to assign sense. That is, the meanings of the words themselves need to be fixed, given that a single word can 'mean' different things. In English, the meaning and function of a word is usually implied by grammar, or the manner in which it is used. Take the word 'foil', for instance: whether the author used this word as a verb (to baffle or frustrate) or a noun (thinly hammered metal) is usually determined by the words that surround it in a sentence. However, there are many examples in the press where the assigning of meaning has misfired; take these headlines from the Internet (which *claim* to be genuine examples):

Prostitutes Appeal to Pope

Here the double meaning of the headline is obvious and more likely to create humour rather than cause misunderstanding. We are far more likely to conclude that the sub-editor intended *appeal* to mean 'to plead' or 'to request' rather than its alternative meaning, 'to attract' or 'to tempt'. But take this example:

Juvenile Court to Try Shooting Defendant

This misfire plays on two double meanings: 'to try' can mean 'to put on trial' or 'to attempt'; and 'shooting' which can either be a verb or a noun. In this case, 'shooting' is used to modify the head noun 'defendant' to give a compound noun 'shooting defendant', instead of fully spelling out that this person is a 'defendant of a shooting'. But in this example it initially appears that 'shooting' is part of the *verb* phrase of the clause: 'to try shooting [somebody]'. This is a problem of equivocation – or vagueness or ambiguity in language – and *context* is usually central in deciding which meaning the writer meant us to read. Again, it is highly unlikely that most readers would think a juvenile court would be considering firing a gun at a defendant!

Second, we need to look at *the assigning of reference* – or what an utterance *refers* to. Reference is an issue which obviously cannot be looked at outside of context, since terms like *here, there, this, yesterday, me, you, I,* and names like *the Prime Minister* and *the Bishop of Bath and Wells* are only meaningful when you know what or who they refer to. For example, the following retraction was printed in *The Dunnoon Observer*, a Scottish local newspaper:

Correction
The 'old pouffe' which started the fire at 7, Douglas Cottages, as reported last week, referred to an item of furniture and not to the owner, Mr Donnie McArthur.

Issues of reference are of rather obvious importance to news given, not only potentially libellous references such as in the report that the above example corrected, but also the influence that the reporting context can have both for the production of news and for audience understanding.

As may have already been implied, this book assumes that discourse analysis is the analysis of what people *do* with talk and text. Language is used to *mean* things and to *do* things that relate not only to the immediate context of speaker–text–audience but also to the wider socio-political, cultural and historic contexts which bound the communicative act. In addition to the functions that certain words, sentence constructions, arguments, etc. play in communication, discourse analysts also assume that language use itself performs much wider meta-functions. Discourse exists in a kind of dialogue with society: 'language simultaneously *reflects* reality ("the way things are") and *constructs* (*construes*) it to be a certain way' (Gee, 1999: 82). Accordingly, language represents and contributes to the production and *re*production (which discourse analysts usually label 'the (re)production') of social reality. I will say more on this in the later section on the dialectical character of discourse.

Critical Discourse Analysis

Critical Discourse Analysis (CDA) represents a growing body of work that adopts the functionalist definition of discourse. However, in addition to accepting that discourse is language in use, the overall aim of CDA 'has been to link linguistic analysis to social analysis' (Woods and Kroger, 2000: 206). Critical discourse analysts argue that if we accept Gee's (1999) suggested general principle of functionalist discourse analysis – that language use contributes the (re)production of social life – then, logically, discourse must play a part in producing and reproducing social inequalities. In response, CDA 'seeks to have an effect on social practice and social relationships' (Titscher *et al.*, 2000: 147), particularly on relationships of disempowerment, dominance, prejudice and/or discrimination. Critical analysis of this kind may be focused 'at different levels of abstraction from the particular event: it may involve its more immediate situational context, the wider context of institutional practices the event is embedded within, or the yet wider frame of the society and the culture' (Fairclough, 1995b: 62). Titscher *et al.* (2000), using the work of Wodak (1996), summarise the general principles of CDA as follows:

- CDA is concerned with social problems. It is not concerned with language or language use *per se*, but with the linguistic character of social and cultural processes and structures.
- Power-relations have to do with discourse, and CDA studies both power in discourse and power over discourse.
- Society and culture are dialectically related to discourse: society and culture are shaped by discourse, and at the same time constitute discourse. Every single instance of language use reproduces or transforms society and culture, including power relations.

- Language use may be ideological. To determine this it is necessary to analyse texts to investigate their interpretation, reception and social effects.
- Discourses are historical and can only be understood in relation to their context. At a metatheoretical level this corresponds to the approach of Wittgenstein, according to which the meaning of an utterance rests in its usage in a specific situation. [. . .]
- Discourse analysis is interpretative and explanatory. Critical analysis implies a systematic methodology and a relationship between the text and its social conditions, ideologies and power-relations. [. . .] (Wodak, 1996: 17–20, cited in Titscher *et al.*, 2000: 146)

In seeking to accomplish these goals, CDA investigates, and aims at illustrating, 'a relationship between the text and its social conditions, ideologies and power-relations' (ibid.). From this, we can identify four key themes of CDA which require further discussion: the constituted and (re)creative character of discourse; power and social relations in discourse; ideology; and hegemony.

Discourse, idealism and materialism

A tension between Idealism and Materialism runs through the theory of CDA – a tension between structure and agency, or the extent to which discourses create or are constituted by 'the objects of which they speak' (Foucault, 1972: 49). The Romantic movement of the early nineteenth century 'laid emphasis on the way in which we invest the world with our own meanings' and argued 'that human beings collectively and individually created their own reality in response to changing circumstances' (McLellan, 1986: 7). In this mode of thinking – labelled *Idealism* – there is thought to be a movement from ideas to material reality; in other words, social consciousness is taken to determine social being. The corollary of such a position, of course, is that we only need to alter the way that people think in order to do away with exploitation, prevent racism or discontinue domination. Opposing such a position is the *Materialist* view of social practice. Those who adopt a materialist perspective suggest that this determining relationship is predominantly the other way around, from material reality to ideas. As Jones (2001: 231) puts it:

The materialist perspective [. . .] proceeds consistently from the premises of basic realism. Human experience proves to us that material reality exists, demonstrating that the inherent properties of material reality, including its existence outside of, prior to and independent of us, are in principle knowable and can be discovered through experience.

In other words, a world exists independent of human beings, and it is this material existence (and specifically our social relations) that determines our consciousness. Critiquing the Idealistic philosophical position, Marx argues it is 'a mistake to start from human consciousness and to proceed from this to an investigation of material reality. The correct approach [is] the other way around. The origin of the problem was not mistaken ideas, but the misshapen nature of social reality which generated mistaken ideas' (McLellan, 1986: 12).

CDA maintains that discourse (language in use) should be viewed

> [. . .] as a form of social practice. Describing discourse as social practice implies a *dialectical* [or] a two-way relationship: the discursive event is shaped by situations, institutions and social structures, but it also shapes them. (Fairclough and Wodak, 1997: 55; emphasis added)

Critical Discourse Analysis therefore appears to adopt elements of both Materialist and Idealist perspectives on social structure: language use is shaped by society and goes on to (re)produce it. Unfortunately however, despite claims to the contrary, the dominant approach in CDA has been to separate language use from language users; to treat discourse as a thing that *in itself* can include or exclude, reproduce social inequalities or effect social change. This line of argument has, to a greater extent, been encouraged by the dominance of a linguistically based analysis in CDA, which (whilst acknowledging the socially constituted character of discourse) has tended to start from 'the text' and to 'argue forward' to imputed social effects. Indeed Fairclough (1992: 6) has gone as far as to suggest that contemporary social changes are 'constituted to a significant extent by changes in language practices'. Such an approach slides precariously close to an Idealistic conception of social reality, in contrast to Fairclough's declared commitment to Marxist social theory. Take Fairclough's (2000) critique of Tony Blair's representation of the global economy, for instance (analysed in Jones and Collins, forthcoming). Here, Fairclough argues that in Blair's speech, 'alternative ways of organising international economic relations are excluded from the political agenda *by these representations*' (p. 129; emphasis added). As Jones and Collins point out:

> [. . .] all the excluding and marginalizing, within mainstream politics and media, not just of forthright anti-capitalist critique but even sustained and honest factual examination of political events and their history, is being done not by '*these representations*' but *by people*. (p. 23; original emphasis)

Materialists would argue that language use – even powerful forms of language in use such as journalism – cannot *in itself* alter the course of society. Racism, for instance, is not something that can be isolated as a 'thing' in a text, but exists as a relationship between the text, its producers and inequalities in society. To be clear, social change is only possible through people acting upon the world. Therefore, the approach to CDA that I adopt 'conceives at once of a *subject* who is produced by society, and of a *subject* who acts to support or change that society. [. . .] this human subject is constituted in ideology, and at the same time acts to make history and change society' (Coward and Ellis, 1977: 61). Language use is one way in which subjects – *people* – may act upon society. Journalistic discourse, in particular, is one active element in bringing about such change through shaping understandings, influencing audience attitudes and beliefs (particularly through their reinforcement), and transforming the consciousness of those who read and consume it. To slightly adapt Marx's famous maxim, journalists can make history but not in circumstances of their own choosing. To understand how this may occur, we now need to develop a more comprehensive understanding of power and of relations of power in society.

Power and social relations in discourse

Titscher *et al.* (2000: 151) suggest that when tackling CDA, '[q]uestions of power are of central interest' since 'power and ideologies may have an effect on each of the contextual levels' of production, consumption and understanding of discourse. CDA engages with, analyses and critiques social power and how this is represented and, both explicitly and implicitly, reproduced in the news. But what *is* social power? Power is another incredibly slippery concept and the subject of seemingly endless academic discussion about what it exactly *is* and what it exactly *means*. Indeed, along with discourse and ideology, power is an essentially contestable concept – a concept whose meaning and application is inherently a matter of dispute (Gallie, 1955). In accordance with Steven Lukes' (1974) brilliant monograph on the subject, I feel that it is useful to consider three conventional approaches to the study of power. Lukes reveals the distinguishing features of three views – or what he calls *faces* – of power: 'the view of the pluralists (which I shall call the one-dimensional view); the view of their critics (which I shall call the two-dimensional view); and a third view of power (which I shall call the three-dimensional view)' (p. 10).

First, Lukes suggests the first face of power, as exemplified by the work of Robert Dahl. Dahl's 'intuitive' idea of power is an interesting but ultimately rather crude conceptualisation which suggests: 'A has power over B to the extent that he can get B to do something that B would not otherwise do' (ibid.: 11–12). In political research by adopting this one-dimensional view of power, 'an attempt is made to study specific outcomes in order to determine who actually prevails in community decision-making' (Polsby, 1963, cited in Lukes 1974: 12). The person, or group, who swings the decision to their favour most frequently, is portrayed as the 'most powerful'. As Dahl (1961: 66) puts it, a 'rough test of a person's overt or covert influence is the frequency with which he [*sic*] successfully initiates an important policy over the opposition of others, or vetoes policies initiated by others'. This model therefore focuses on behaviour, on outcomes and in the making of decisions on which there is observable conflict.

This one-dimensional view of power is simplistic because it emphasises the importance of *conscious* initiation and explicit decision-making. It therefore takes 'no account of the fact that power may be, and often is, exercised by confining the scope of decision-making to relatively "safe" issues' (Bachrach and Baratz, 1970: 6). They continue:

> *Of course* power is exercised when A participates in the making of decisions that affect B. Power is *also* exercised when A devotes his energies to creating or reinforcing social and political values and institutional practices that limit the scope of the political process to public consideration of only those issues which are comparatively innocuous to A. (Ibid.; emphases added)

This second 'face' of power therefore brings in the notion of the 'mobilisation of bias' into the definition of power, and critiques how those who benefit from the 'rules of the game' 'are placed in a preferred position to defend and promote their vested interests' (ibid.: 43). This is particularly important in understanding how journalists and the news media in general are *used* by social groups with power. The two-dimensional view also shows us how power is instrumental in making 'non-decisions'. Bachrach and Baratz (1970: 44) point out that the power to make non-decisions is 'a means by which demands for change in the existing allocation of benefits and privileges in the community can be suffocated before they are even voiced; or kept covert; or killed before they gain access to the relevant decision-making arena'. For example, the decisions to press release only *certain* stories or to foreground certain policy decisions over others, which 'results in [the] suppression or thwarting of a latent or manifest challenge to the values or interests of the decision-maker' (ibid.). Therefore, this two-dimensional view of power retains the behaviourist focus of the one-dimensional view, but expands its analysis to allow 'consideration of the ways in which decisions are prevented from being taken on potential issues over which there is an observable conflict of (subjective) interests' (Lukes, 1974: 20).

However, the third 'face' of power – and Steven Lukes' own model – suggests that this second 'face' does not go far enough and that power should be viewed as a more *systemic* phenomenon. In Lukes' view, the second face of power 'gives a misleading picture of the ways in which individuals and, above all, groups and institutions succeed in excluding potential issues from the political process. [. . .] the bias of the system can be mobilised, recreated and reinforced in ways that are neither consciously chosen nor the intended result of particular individuals' choices' (ibid.: 21). In other words, individuals and groups gain power from their social relation to others and their position in a hierarchical social system. The structural biases of the system are 'not sustained simply by a series of individually chosen acts, but also, most importantly, by the socially structured and culturally patterned behaviour of groups and practices of institutions' (ibid.: 21–22). To put this account of power in the format adopted above:

> [Of *course*] A may exercise power over B by getting him to do what he does not want to do, but he also exercises power over him by influencing, shaping or determining his attitudes, beliefs, and very wants. (Ibid.: 23)

The *second* face of power assumes that if 'the observer can uncover no grievances, then he must assume there is a "genuine" consensus on the prevailing allocation of values' (ibid.: 24). But this ignores 'the crucial point that the most effective and insidious use of power is to prevent such conflict from arising in the first place' (ibid.: 23) and, instead, to promote the acceptance of social conditions that are not in the interests of broad segments of the population. In summary, Lukes (1974: 34) argues that '*A* exercises power over *B* when *A* affects *B* in a manner contrary to *B*'s interests'. So how does this occur? I suggest that it occurs through discourse and, specifically, in the ability of language to act ideologically.

Ideology and ideological work

As suggested above, ideology is an essentially contestable concept and, as such, it makes little point to describe what it 'really' means. Instead we should trace the history of the concept and how it is used. The term 'ideology' was originally coined by Antoine Destutt de Tracey in the years after the French Revolution to refer to 'a new science of ideas, an idea-logy, which would be the ground of all other sciences' (McLellan, 1986: 6). De Tracey argued that the ideas we hold are not the product of God or nature but are generated by our social environment as perceived through our physical senses. 'A rational investigation of the origins of ideas, free from religious or metaphysical prejudice', he argued, 'would be the foundation of a just and happy society' (ibid.). Hence, ideology in this first instance seems positive and progressive, referring to the 'study of how ideas are formed based on experience' (Gee, 1990: 4).

Marx developed this approach to ideology, arguing that 'the history of ideas demonstrate[s] that the products of the intellect are refashioned along with material ones' (Marx, 1998 [1848]: 27). However the relation between ideas and experience is further refined and focused in Marx's account, to reveal that our ideas and beliefs are not the product of 'experience' *per se*, but rather 'alter according to their *economic* circumstances' (ibid.; emphasis added) and therefore stand as a reflection of these circumstances – as a reflection of social relations. More specifically, they stand as a reflection of the circumstances of the *ruling* class and their desire to maintain their class privilege. Contrary to the psychological (and, in Marxist terms, bourgeois) perspective of de Tracey, Marx demonstrated that ideology is more than individual ideas formed through experience: ideology and its signs develop 'through the process of social interaction [and are] defined by the social purview of the given time period and the given social group' (Vološinov, 1973 [1929]: 21).

Gee (1990: 6) suggests that ideology under Marx 'is an "upside-down" version of reality. Things are not really the way the elite and powerful believe them to be: rather, their beliefs invert reality to make it appear the way they would like it to be, the way it "needs" to be if their power is to be enhanced and sustained.' Callinicos labels this interpretation of Marx an *epistemological* conception of ideology:

> Here, ideology is conceived as a set of false beliefs, constituted by a dual relation, first, to the reality of which it is an inverted reflection, and, secondly, to the true, scientific knowledge of that reality. [. . .] The obverse, of course, is that another minority, this time an enlightened one armed with the truth, can free the masses from these deceptions by the power of reason alone. (Callinicos, 1983: 128)

'The knowledge driven economy' is a classically ideological phrase representing an 'upside-down' version of reality. The noun phrase (itself a nominalisation of an active process) suggests that it is 'knowledge' which shapes or dictates the character and direction of the 'market'. In fact the reverse is the case: the social relations that characterise the economy (and specifically the forces and relations of production) direct and shape knowledge. This is observable at an ontological level – equating to Foucault's oft-expressed maxim that 'knowledge = power'; it is observable at the level of language use – for instance, the way that many academics at British Universities discuss (i.e. discursively *construct*) students to be consumers and departments to be producers; and it is observable at a level of policy and practice – for instance, the introduction of variable tuition fees in line with classic demand–supply economic logic. At all points, the reality is the reverse of that suggested by the noun phrase 'the knowledge driven economy'.

Certain cruder interpretations of Marx's position suggest that such ideological work is one-way traffic: that the economic relations of society simply *create* false ideas which are held often contrary to people's true interests. Such interpretations fail for two reasons. First (as suggested above), they fail to realise how ideology does 'not just reflect "reality" but partially help[s] to create, to constitute it' (Gee, 1990: 8); second, Marx's point about ideology relates not to issues of 'logical or empirical falsity but of the superficial or misleading way in which truth is asserted' (McLellan, 1986: 18). Taking the second point, this means that the 'falsity' of capitalist ideology (if one can discuss ideology in such terms) is due not to its empirical status but rather to its origins and functions in concealing the relations of production behind an 'appearance of free exchange' (ibid.: 16). It is on this basis that Callinicos (1983: 129) suggests that there is 'a second "pragmatic" dimension to Marx's conception of ideology: the illusions generated by the 'historical life-process' serve the interests of the ruling class by smoothing over and concealing the contradictions of class society'. This occurs because '[t]he ideas of the ruling class are in every epoch the ruling ideas [...] the class which has the material means of production at its disposal, consequently also controls the means of mental production, so that the ideas of those that lack the means of mental production are on the whole subject to them' (Marx and Engels, 1974: 64). Ideologies are 'practices which function symbolically' (Callinicos, 1983: 135) or, in Thomson's (1990) rather neat turn of phrase, 'meaning in the service of power'.

Ideology, then, 'is not just any system of ideas of beliefs but ways of thinking in which historically transient exploitative forms of social organisation are represented as eternal, natural, inevitable or "rational"' (Jones, 2001: 227). The question of how this occurs – how ideological ideas help conceal exploitation and therefore (re)produce inequitable social realities – has been most fruitfully broached by neo-Marxist scholars.[1] Althusser (1971), for instance, 'sought to examine the ways in which bourgeois social relations are reproduced through ideology's ability to shape, and indeed to perform the conscious desires and beliefs of individuals' (Callinicos, 1983: 127). Pêcheux (1994: 142), building on the work of Althusser, underlined his argument that 'the ideological state apparatuses are not the expression of the domination of the ruling ideology, i.e. the ideology of the ruling class [...] but are the site and the means of realisation of that domination'. What this means is that ideological formations, such as the press, are themselves a site of class struggle, and 'constitute simultaneously and contradictorily the site and the ideological conditions of the transformation of the relations of production' (ibid.). Of all the developments of a Marxist theory of ideology, Gramsci's (1971) theory of hegemony – and more specifically the distinction between force and consent – has arguably been the most enduring and perhaps the most productive, and it is towards this theory that we now briefly turn.

Hegemony

Hegemony may be described as the process in which a ruling class persuades all other classes to accept its rule and their subordination (ibid.). Put another way, hegemony is 'a condition in which the governed accept or acquiesce in authority without the need for the application of force. Although force was always latent in the background, hegemony meant leadership rather than domination' (Cox, 2004: 311). With the successful institution of hegemony, the subordinate classes consent to the leadership of the ruling class and the dominance of their institutions and values. In short, this equates with consenting to unequal class relations. When successful, the ruling class can implant its values with the minimum of force since the ruled acquiesce to the power and political legitimacy of the rulers. In the words of Gramsci:

> The 'normal' exercise of hegemony [...] is characterised by the combination of force and consensus which vary in their balance with each other, without force exceeding consensus too much. Thus it tries to achieve that force should appear to be supported by the agreement of the majority, expressed by the so-called organs of public opinion – newspapers and associations. (*Quaderni del Carcere*, p. 1638, cited in Joll, 1977: 99)

Thus, a hegemonic ruling class is one that gains support for itself from other classes. This is achieved: first, by the ruling class taking into consideration 'the interests and tendencies of the groups over which hegemony is to be exercised' (Gramsci, 1971: 161). Second, any concessions to public demands should be publicised in order to 'demonstrate' the ruling class' probity and hence their moral and political leadership. That the ruling classes are increasingly required to take the working classes into consideration cannot be denied. McNair (2005: 157), for instance, uncritically celebrates the fact that 'the steady global expansion of liberal democracy in recent decades [...] has made governing elites, ruling classes and dominant groups everywhere responsive to mass opinion'. Such 'responsiveness' is only part of the story of course, and Gramsci (1971: 161) reminds us that 'such sacrifices and such compromises cannot affect what is essential', that is the maintenance of the ruling class' economic privilege. The basic reality that 'responding' to 'mass opinion' in no way disrupts the privilege and dominance of the ruling classes is implicit in McNair's celebration of capitalism: the elites continue to govern and the 'masses', while listened to, should know their place in the scheme of things.

Third, hegemony is maintained by the ruling class teaching their ideas and their values in the general public, particularly their central claim to political legitimacy. Education, therefore, lies at the heart of hegemony – indeed Gramsci argues '[e]very relationship of hegemony is necessarily a pedagogic relationship' (ibid.: 350). Given that capitalism is inherently exploitative, we need to ask: Why has a revolutionary movement failed to develop in the West? Why don't the working classes revolt, lose their chains and win the world? Essentially, Gramsci suggests, they have been *taught* not to; they have been taught that capitalism is the 'natural way of things'; that the ruling political classes are better at 'running things' than they would be; and their everyday compliance confers political legitimacy to class rule. As Cox (2004: 310) puts it:

> Legitimacy or illegitimacy characterise the relationship of government to the governed – or, more broadly, the nature of authority. The relationship is legitimate when people in general accept the institutions and procedures of authority and the decisions which emerge, even if they do not like them. When that general acceptance becomes eroded, when there is no general acceptance that decisions have been properly arrived at, the relationship becomes illegitimate.

The work of mainstream journalists mediates the relationship between ruling class ideology and news content (Murdock, 2000) and supports the hegemony by naturalising, or taking for granted, the inequalities of contemporary capitalism (Gitlin, 1979). Journalists, having internalised 'commonsensical notions of who ought to be treated as authoritative', 'accept the frames imposed on events by officials and marginalise the delegitimate voices that fall outside the dominant elite circles' (Reese, 1990: 425). However, it should be noted that such elite ideological dominance arises 'as a property of the system of relations involved, rather than as the overt and intentional biases of individuals' (Hall, 1982: 95). In short, the current practices of journalism play an essential role in maintaining the class authority within the political system. However, this class rule by consent 'is always a partial, precarious and fragile state of affairs [. . .] For that reason, the extent to which ideological means of dominance and control will be effective in deflecting, disarming or containing resistance and opposition in particular circumstances is always an open question' (Jones and Collins, forthcoming: 9).

Fairclough's method of critical discourse analysis

The approach to CDA that I feel most satisfied with is that of Norman Fairclough (1995a,b, 2000, 2003). For Fairclough, in contrast to the social psychological approach of Wetherell and Potter (1992), the social-cognitive model of van Dijk (1993, 1998, 2001) and the discourse-historic method of the Vienna School (Reisigl and Wodak, 2001; Wodak, 1996, 2002; Wodak *et al.*, 1999), CDA means

> the analysis of relationships between concrete language use and the wider social cultural structures. [...] He attributes three dimensions to every discursive event. It is simultaneously text, discursive practice – which also includes the production and interpretation of texts – and social practice. The analysis is conducted according to these three dimensions. (Titscher *et al.*, 2000: 149–150)

Fairclough's model of CDA, in my view, provides a more accessible method of *doing* CDA than alternative theoretical approaches. He argues that to fully understand what discourse is and how it works, analysis needs to draw out the form and function of the text, the way that this text relates to the way it is produced and consumed, and the relation of this to the wider society in which it takes place. As suggested above, CDA approaches discourse as a circular process in which social practices influence texts, via shaping the context and mode in which they are produced, and in turn texts help influence society via shaping the viewpoints of those who read or otherwise consume them. This process is relatively straightforward to grasp theoretically: the idea that newspapers are the product of specific people working in specific social circumstances and that, in turn, the news can have social effects are commonsense assumptions. However, these assumptions are more difficult to apply in analysis: the circular and reinforcing nature of discourse can appear like a spinning roundabout, difficult to jump onto; how do we distinguish cause and effect when effects become causes? To depict and explain how Fairclough proposes that we actually *do* CDA, I feel that it is best to start with the text itself, gradually building outwards to include more complex discursive and social practices.

Textual analysis

Textual analysis involves the analysis of the way propositions are structured and the way propositions are combined and sequenced (Fairclough, 1995b). Figuratively, textual analysis can be represented as given in Figure 2.1.

```
Text
Representations (ideational function)
Identities & social relations (interpersonal function)
Cohesion and coherence (textual function)
```

Figure 2.1 Textual analysis

Content analysis is one form of textual analysis that, when applied as the *sole* research method, is an analytically inadequate way to examine the role that journalism plays in maintaining and/or transforming social inequalities, for the reasons described above. The difference with a more interpretative (and some would say *critical*) textual analysis is that the analyst examines the text in terms of what is present and what *could* have been but is *not* present. We assume that every aspect of textual content is the result of a 'choice' – the choice to use one way of describing a person, an action or a process over another; the choice to use one way of constructing a sentence over an alternative; the choice to include a particular fact or opinion or argument over another, etc.[2] In more detail, the analysis of these choices in texts

> [...] covers traditional forms of linguistic analysis – analysis of vocabulary and semantics, the grammar of sentences and smaller units, and the sound system ('phonology') and writing system. But it also includes analysis of textual organisation above the sentence, including the ways in which sentences are connected together ('cohesion') and things like the organisation of turn-taking in interviews or the overall structure of a newspaper article. (Fairclough, 1995a: 57)

Texts should therefore be analysed at various levels. However, textual analysis, from the perspective of CDA, doesn't simply involve looking at the linguistic form and content of texts. As Gerbner put it, we shouldn't consider elements of vocabulary, grammar, semantics (and so on) to be of profound and direct significance in themselves; rather it is the *function* that such elements serve in the moment of their use that is of interest. Therefore, we must examine the traditional forms of linguistic analysis listed above *in relation to* their direct or indirect involvement in reproducing or resisting the systems of ideology and social power. For instance, van Dijk (1999), sharing much of Fairclough's analytic perspective and methods, states that when adopting a textual analysis, discourse should 'be analysed at various levels or along several dimensions. [...] Each of these may be involved directly or indirectly in discriminatory interaction' or biased discourse against disempowered individuals and groups (p. 4). Chapter 3 provides a lengthier discussion of some of these levels of analysis and their significance for the analysis of newspaper discourse.

Discursive practices

Second, we need to consider the discursive practices of news discourse. On this point, Fairclough (1995a: 58) states that

> The discourse practice dimension of the communicative event involves various aspects of the processes of text production and text consumption. Some of these have a more institutional character [e.g. the editorial procedures of the *Independent* compared to *The Times*] whereas others are discourse processes in a narrower sense [the 'decoding' of texts by the reader/viewer].

It is at this stage that analysis becomes *discourse* analysis rather than *textual* analysis. Discourse analysis involves an analysis of texts as they are embedded within, and relate to, social conditions of production and consumption. Again, I have attempted to represent this figuratively (Figure 2.2).

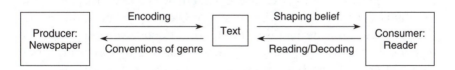

Figure 2.2 Discourse Analysis

This aspect of CDA remains the most under-developed. Indeed Jones and Collins (forthcoming: 4) go as far as to argue that although the critical interpretation and interrogation of discourse

[...] can only be supplied by experienced, well-informed and critically minded participants in the relevant field [...] this principle has been ignored or set aside in CDA in favour of a view in which detailed historical, theoretical and practical knowledge of the relevant spheres is deemed unnecessary to understanding political and ideological aspects of discourse.

At this point in the theoretical literature, this is undoubtedly a salient argument. Cotter (2001: 428), for instance, argues that current research has not analysed news texts as the '*outcome of a discourse process* [...] A process- or practice-orientated approach would allow new insights into the integrated examination of news practice, news values and audience role.' More forcefully, Verschueren (1985: vii) has argued that too much discourse analysis of journalism is ignorant of the 'structural and functional properties of the news gathering and reporting process'. Clearly CDA needs to address these lacunae.

In one sense, an analysis of the discursive practices of journalistic discourse appears to emulate Hall's (1980) model of the encoding and decoding of media texts: the meaning in media texts being 'encoded' by their producer(s) and the reader/viewer 'decoding' a meaning from the intersection of the text itself and the context in which the text is 'read'. But in another sense, CDA requires us to go a step further than this model, since the meanings encoded/decoded in texts are the result not only of producer intensions but also of 'the outcome of specific professional practices and techniques, which could be and can be quite different with quite different results' (Fairclough, 1995a: 204). These professional practices are 'based in particular social relations, and particular relations of power' (ibid.), which inevitably leave their residue in the product of the communicative event, the text.

As Figure 2.2 suggests, at each point of discursive mediation – between producer and text and between text and consumer – the discursive practices are a two-way street. Clearly, and most obviously, the producer and the mode of production encode meaning into the text (choosing one story over another, choosing to foreground one view rather than another, choosing one word over another, etc.); but the text also acts on the producer, shaping the way that information is collected and presented due to the conventions of the text-genre under construction. For instance, one can imagine a news report and an editorial written by a journalist in a particular news organisation encoded with the same ideological message, but the radical differences between these two text-genres demand that the information which carries this encoded ideological message must have been collected and presented in very different ways: the producer shapes the text but the text, and its conventions, shapes its production too. Similarly at the point of consumption the discursive practices occurring are also a two-way street. First, the messages of the text (which may or may not be ideological) attempt to shape the understandings of the reader; this observation is widely taken as read, and forms the basis of much political critique of 'the media'. However, reading is an activity in which readers 'do not simply receive messages; they decode texts' (Condit, 1989: 494). When a text is consumed, this is done by readers who have perspectives, agendas and background knowledge that may differ radically from that encoded in the text. Hence, the reader of a newspaper may resist, subtly counter or directly misunderstand the encoded meaning of the report. Hall (1980: 54) argues that the meanings produced through encoding and decoding – and specifically how similar they are – depend on the degree of

> [. . .] asymmetry between the codes of 'source' and 'receiver' at the moment of transfiguration into and out of the discursive form. What are called 'distortions' or 'misunderstandings' arise precisely from the lack of equivalence between the two sides in the communicative exchange.

To complicate matters a little further, discursive meaning is not simply the result of encoding and decoding of the manifest content of texts: our assessment of the 'meaning' of a text is often affected by our judgement of who produced it, given that we tend to believe the testimony of people (or institutions) we trust, or believe those with practical knowledge. Similarly, the production of texts (and the encoding of textual meaning specifically) always has at least one eye on the imagined or target consumer and the kind of texts that they prefer to read. As Cotter (2001: 428) argues, 'a deeper knowledge of the practitioner's focus on his or her readership or audience would allow a more nuanced discussion of media practice and its relation to audience or the communities that are covered' (ibid.). The complexities of these processes are discussed in greater depth in Chapter 4.

Social practices

Third, and following from the acknowledgement of 'social relations of power' mentioned above, Fairclough suggests that a fully rounded critical discourse analysis should involve an analysis of the text's 'socio-cultural practice' or 'the social and cultural goings-on which the communicative event is part of' (Fairclough, 1995a: 57). This level of analysis 'may be at different levels of abstraction from the particular event: it may involve its more immediate situational context, the wider context of institutional practices the event is embedded within, or the yet wider frame of the society and the culture' (ibid.: 62). For instance, we could ask what does this text say about the society in which it was produced and the society that it was produced for? What influence or impact do we think that the text may have on social relations? Will it help to continue inequalities and other undesirable social practices, or will it help to break them down? It is at this point that discourse analysis becomes *critical* discourse analysis, as represented in Figure 2.3.

In essence, CDA involves an analysis of how discourse (language in use) relates to and is implicated in the (re)production of social relations – particularly unequal, iniquitous and/or discriminatory power relations. Analysis retains the details of both *textual* analysis (the analysis of prepositional content) and *discourse* analysis (the analysis of text production and consumption), but now these insights are expanded and viewed in relation to the wider society. Specifically, the form–content–function of texts, as well as their production and consumption, are subject to *critical analysis* – that is, subjecting discourse to ethical and political critique, challenging the features that contribute to the perpetuation of structured inequalities, 'exposing power abuse and mobilising people to remedy social wrongs' (Blommaert, 2005: 25). This can *only* take place when texts, and their (ideological) claims, 'are analysed against the facts – the reality' of social practices and relations of power more specifically (Jones, 2001: 245). In other words, the 'analysis of the "internal" conceptual structure of [texts] can [*only*] become a useful tool in ideological analysis when informed by and positioned within a social theory (e.g. Marxism) capable of illuminating the "external" connections between ideas and social practice as a whole' (ibid.: 247).[3] As Luke (2002: 102) argues

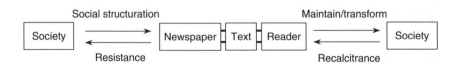

Figure 2.3 Critical Discourse Analysis

[. . .] what texts 'do' in the world cannot be explained solely through text analysis or text analytic language. To reiterate, the actual power of the text, its material and discourse consequences, can only be described by reference to broader social theoretic models of the world.

As before, each point of discursive mediation – between society and discourse and between discourse and society – is characterised by a dialectical relation. First, society and the social formation – that is, the historic, economic, political and ideological features of society – forms a backdrop that both structures and enables the work of journalists. However, we should not think of the social formation as a 'thing' outside of ourselves, moulding our lives as a potter moulds a lump of clay. Rather, the social formation is a 'structure-in-process' (Coward and Ellis, 1977: 62), 'constituted by unequal elements that are in contradiction with each other: movement and change are provided by the struggle between elements' (ibid.: 63). Specifically, Coward and Ellis (1977: 63) argue that a Marxist account of capitalist social structure takes into account three practices through which 'the social formation is produced and transformed'. First,

> [. . .] economic practice, the production and reproduction of the material means of subsistence, and of 'the specific historical and economic production relations'. [. . .] Second, political practice produces the 'mutual relations' of social groups, the forms of social organisation and the relations of dominance and subordination between these forms. [. . .] Third, ideological practice produces positions which enable subjects to act within the social totality.

As discussed in the introduction, the economic practice of capitalism may be characterised by the production of surplus value by the workers which is then appropriated by the capitalist classes. However, such economic practice cannot exist on its own, requiring political form and ideological rationalisation. While political practice is constituted by the contradiction between classes, this 'takes place, not as two monoliths facing each other, but through various groups, fractions of classes, alliances, etc. [. . .] it is the realm of the State' (ibid.: 66). Echoing Pêcheux's (1994: 142) earlier point about ideological state apparatuses, Coward and Ellis (1977: 66) argue that the State (with its legislative and repressive branches) 'does not express the interest of a given economic class' in a direct and literal way (although it does do this on occasion). Rather, it ensures the perpetuation of *the context* in which such an interest – the appropriation of surplus labour by the ruling classes – is achieved. The third social practice – ideological practice – I have discussed above, concluding that it acts to smooth over the contradictions of class society, providing 'the way in which the individual actively lives his or her role within the social totality' (ibid.). Each of these three social practices exist prior to, and are constituted by, the work of journalism.

However these social practices do not 'write the news'. As stated in the Introduction, journalists enjoy a degree of autonomy in their work (albeit of a relative kind) and there is a good degree of resistance, manipulation and transformation of such practices in newsrooms. As O'Neill has argued, 'while the market may undermine the constitutive values of journalism such as truth telling, this process is neither uncontested nor totally successful' (from Harcup, 2002: 108). Criticism of the misuse of power remains at the top of news agendas, whether of the conduct of the British Government during the Hutton Enquiry, the culpability of Army Officers in the fallout of the Abu Ghraib prison scandal or 'alleged governmental deceit, lies, betrayal, lack of trust and immorality' more generally (McNair, 2005: 156). Similarly, at the core of journalism's code of professional ethics is a commitment to independence. And, while such a commitment is too often merely an aspiration rather than a reality (see Chapter 4), there *are* 'journalists who fly the flag for freedom of information and for the right of citizens to be informed, even at the cost of embarrassing the state' (Harcup, 2002: 102). For instance, Harcup cites several recent examples, including 'Martin Bright, a reporter on *The Observer* who in 2000 defied police attempts to get him to hand over notebooks, emails and other material concerning a security service whistleblower' (ibid.). Nevertheless, from a materialist position, it is impossible to conceive of individuals or institutions outside of the structuring influence of social practices, and while journalists currently 'enjoy a certain amount of independence' they nevertheless remain 'determined in the last instance by the economic needs of capital, and the reproductive requirements of the capitalist mode of production viewed more broadly' (McNair, 2005: 152).

Summary

Critical Discourse Analysis may be described as a 'shared perspective on doing linguistic, semiotic or discourse analysis' (van Dijk,

1993: 131) as opposed to a homogenous method, school or paradigm. Such research aims to link linguistic analysis with social analysis: language ought to be analysed in relation to the social *context* in which it is being used and the social *consequences* of its use; and, more specifically, the relationship(s) between discourse and its social conditions, ideologies and power relations needs to be examined. In relation to the discourse of journalism, CDA maintains that social practices and the discursive practices of the production of journalism exist as a dialectical (i.e. a two-way) relationship. Similarly, there is a dialectical relationship between the consumption of journalistic texts and social practices: readers decode the meanings of texts using knowledge and beliefs of the world, and these texts go on to shape (through either transformation or reproduction) these same readers' knowledge and beliefs. Central to each of these discourse processes is *power*: the power of social practices on production; the power of texts to shape understandings; the power of readers to resist such management; and the power of people to reproduce or transform society. Often such transformations are to the benefit of the capitalist elite – the minority of already powerful individuals and groups – but this need not be the case. As Lukes (1974: 54) puts it:

> To use the vocabulary of power in the context of social relationships is to speak of human agents, separately or together, in groups or organisations, through action or inaction, significantly affecting the thoughts or actions of others (specifically, in a manner contrary to their interests). In speaking thus, one assumes that, although the agents operate within structurally determined limits, they none the less have a certain relative autonomy and could have acted differently. The future, though it is not entirely open, is not entirely closed either (and, indeed, the degree of its openness is itself structurally determined).

Lukes' point, therefore, 'is that to identify a given process as "an exercise of power", rather than as a case of structural determinism, is to assume that it is *in the exerciser's or the exerciser's power* to act differently' (p. 55). Another world *is* possible. It is the point of CDA to show how discourse conceals this from us, normalising inequalities and closing down the possibility of change.

Analysing Texts: Some Concepts and Tools of Linguistic Analysis

Introduction: levels of analysis

In this chapter I examine textual analysis as a first level in our analysis of newspaper discourse. Specifically, I introduce some linguistic concepts and tools and discuss them in relation to actual newspaper texts. My introduction is unavoidably selective and misses out some notable and important concepts. The contribution of linguistics to textual analysis is huge, so readers are recommended to seek out other texts, such as Fowler (1991), van Dijk (1997a,b), Bell (1991), Fairclough (1995b) and others to fill in these inevitable gaps in the discussion. This chapter also aims to introduce three key issues developed throughout the rest of the book: first, the inter-related nature of textual form and textual content, such that texts written or laid out in different ways *mean* different things. (What *I* mean by this will hopefully become clearer as you read on.) Second, the notion of levels of analysis. In the words of Fairclough (1995a: 104), there are two major aspects of texts to consider during analysis: 'the first has to do with the structuring of propositions, the second with the combination and sequencing of propositions'. The first of these aspects concerns the representation of individuals and other social actors, and the analysis of *clauses* representing actions, processes and events. The second aspect concerns the *organisation* of these single clauses into a coherently structured whole. Our linguistic analysis of news-text should therefore move from the small-scale (micro-) analysis of words, through sentences and onto larger-scale analysis of the organisation of meaning across a text as a whole. This progression can be represented schematically, thus:

Structuring of propositions	Words (lexis)	Micro-textual analysis
	Sentences 1 (syntax and transitivity)	
	Sentences 2 (modality)	
	Presupposition	↓
Combining propositions	Rhetoric	
	Narrative	Macro-textual analysis

Third, texts are multi-functional, performing simultaneous tasks. In accordance with the theory of Systemic Functional Linguistics, I assume that texts simultaneously fulfil an *ideational* function, an *inter-personal* function and a *textual* function. Taking each of these meta-functions in turn, texts 'simultaneously represent aspects of the world (the physical world, the social world, the mental world); enact social relations between participants in social events and the attitudes, desires and values of the participants; and coherently and cohesively connect parts of texts together' as a united whole (Fairclough, 2003: 27).

Lexical analysis: the choice and meaning of words

The analysis of particular words used in a newspaper text is almost always the first stage of any text or discourse analysis. Words convey the imprint of society and of value judgements in particular – they convey connoted as well as denoted meanings. All types of words, but particularly nouns, adjectives, verbs and adverbs carry connoted in addition to denoted meanings. Take this text, published in the *Guardian Weekly*, which examined the words used by journalists during the 1991 war against Iraq (cited in Allan, 2004: 162–163):

They have	**We have**
A war machine	Army, Navy and Air force
Censorship	Reporting restrictions
Propaganda	Press briefings
They	**We**
Destroy	Suppress
Kill	Eliminate
Kill	Neutralise

They launch	**We launch**
Sneak attacks	First strikes
Without provocation	Pre-emptively
Their men are	**Our men are**
Troops	Boys
Hordes	Lads
Saddam Hussein is	**George Bush [Snr] is**
Demented	At peace with himself
Defiant	Resolute

The alternatives in each of these pairings could, arguably, have been used to refer to the same person, people or action, but the ideological constraints (felt particularly at time of war) meant that they very rarely were. The words used to communicate the message(s) of a text – whether about an individual, a group of people, an event, a predicted or *expected* event, a process, a state of affairs or any of the other subjects and themes of newspaper texts – frame the story in direct and unavoidable ways. And in newspaper reporting of the 1991 US-led war against Iraq, the framing of these texts achieved through such choices demonstrates 'how a racialised "us and them" frequently underpinned some journalists' choice of descriptive terms' (ibid.: 161).

Elements of such racialised reporting practices remain in the 2003 invasion of Iraq. For instance:

> **British in battle to liberate Basra** (London *Evening Standard*, 26 March 2003)
>
> British troops were poised to enter Basra today after an uprising by the local population against Iraqi army units led to a bloodbath. The Iraqi soldiers shelled rioting crowds with mortars, fought hand to hand battles and used machine guns to cut down unarmed protesters.
>
> Thousands had taken to the streets in a revolt against troops resisting the advance of coalition forces. [. . .]

It is important to state, first, that the actual event reported here did not take place. Although 'British forces claimed that there had been a popular uprising' in Basra, these reports 'were later revealed (notably by al-Jazeera inside the city) to be untrue' (Lewis and Brookes, 2004: 139). Aside from this fact, look in the above excerpt at how the action of Iraqi soldiers are described and compare these to the actions of British soldiers: the violence of the Iraqis is referred to directly, spelled out in specific terms (they 'shelled rioting crowds with mortars, fought hand to hand battles and used machine guns to cut down unarmed protesters') and their after-effects clearly stated: they led to 'a bloodbath'. The British soldiers, on the other hand, are represented only in terms of movement: they 'advance' and 'were poised to enter Basra'. Any sense that the British troops were also shelling and killing – often inno-cent Iraqis – is conveniently glossed over, through the choice of verbs. The invasion of Iraq is examined in greater depth in Chapter 7.

Naming and reference

The way that people are named in news discourse can have significant impact on the way in which they are viewed. We all simultaneously possess a range of identities, roles and characteristics that could be used to describe us equally *accurately* but not with the same *meaning*. The manner in which social actors are named identifies not only the group(s) that they are associated with (or at least the groups that the speaker/writer *wants* them to be associated with) it can also signal the relationship between the namer and the named. As Blommaert (2005: 11) explains:

> Apart from referential meaning, acts of communication produce *indexical* meaning: social meaning, interpretative leads between what is said and the social occasion in which it is being produced. Thus the word 'sir' not only refers to a male individual, but it *indexes* a particular social status and the role relationships of defer-ence and politeness entailed by this status.

You the reader, for example, may be female, as well as being a student, and a barmaid, and British, and a Muslim, and autistic, and so on adding many other categories. Journalists *have* to provide names for the people in the events they report and this naming always involves choice. And logically, by choosing one social category over another, they include them within a category and exclude them from other different categories – or perhaps, choose to fore-ground one social category over other equally accurate alternat-ives. Reisigl and Wodak (2001) have called these naming options a text's 'referential strategies', and have illustrated that choosing to describe an individual (or a group) as one thing or as another 'can serve many different psychological, social or political purposes [. . .]

on the side of the speakers or writers' (p. 47). For example, a social actor may be individualised ('Paul Edwards went...') in order to emphasise his ordinariness or 'every man' qualities; or else collectivised under a broad range of groupings, each with different explicit and implicit meanings (see van Leeuwen, 1996). With a little effort, we can imagine someone who could as accurately be labelled 'a father', or 'a Sheffield man', or 'an ex-policeman', or 'a Kurd', or 'a drunk', or 'an asylum seeker', or 'a foreigner', or 'a Communist' or by using a range of other collectivised terms. But there are significant and clearly apparent differences between the explicit (denoted) and implicit (connoted) meanings of these terms. Take this very interesting example: in an article reporting the (temporary) defeat in the House of Lords of New Labour's attempt to introduce indefinite house arrest (**Lord Irvine joins rebellion as peers inflict defeat on anti-terror Bill**, *Independent*, 8 March 2005), the Conservative Earl of Onslow is quoted asking:

> Why, if the Home Secretary thinks Mohammad el-Smith wants to do something and is planning to do something and has talked to others about doing something nasty, that is not a conspiracy?

While the Earl makes a persuasive point regarding the redundant nature of the Government's Terror Bill given existing conspiracy laws, it is the name 'Mohammad el-Smith' that interests me here – what does this referential strategy imply? The name is a clever variation on the name 'Joe Bloggs' or the American 'John Doe': this is the hypothetical 'average man', or in this case, the hypothetical 'average terrorist'. Here, Smith – the most common family name in Britain – is combined with Mohammed, a name understandably associated with Islam. It is through the use of 'Mohammad' as a first name that the Earl implies (or perhaps *lets slip*) he believes the hypothetical average terrorist suspect to be Muslim.[1]

The chosen referential strategies perform a function within the text. Not only do they project meaning and social values onto the referent, they also establish coherence relations with the way that *other* social actors are referred to and represented. Clark (1992), for example, has examined the way in which the tabloid *Sun* newspaper reports incidents of sexual violence, such as rape. Clark argues that when reporting a crime of this type, the news article holds up one of the participants as being to blame for the incident – literally as 'the victim' – and this is reflected in the way that they're named.

So, if *The Sun* 'decides' that the *man* was to blame for the attack, he is referred to as a 'maniac', a 'monster', a 'fiend', a 'beast' and other terms which suggest sub-humanity, depravity and animalistic abandon. On the other hand, if *The Sun* decides that it was the *woman's* fault, that she 'led the man on' or invited the attack, then she is referred to as 'a lolita', 'an unmarried mum', 'a divorcee', and using adjectives which draw attention to her physical shape or her appearance, like 'busty——', 'shapely——' or 'blonde——'. In the discourse of *The Sun*, 'Busty divorcees' are never attacked by fiends; instead, the men who attack 'Busty divorcees' are represented as blameless and are described by name or using respectable terms, like 'family man' or proximate colloquial terms like 'hubby'. And when the man *is* a fiend, the women attacked are, by contrast, referred to in ways which suggest innocence or sexual purity, like 'bride', 'school girl', 'mother of three', 'daughters', etc. So you get a *squared* relationship, where

Bad men [sex fiend]	*attack*	innocent women [Mum, daughter]
Bad women [busty divorcee]	*provoke*	innocent men [hubby]

Related to this is the work of Teun van Dijk. In a series of studies, he has developed a conceptual tool called 'the ideological square', which he suggests determine choices between referential strategies (indeed discourse in general). He suggests that the ideological square is characterised by a *Positive Self-Presentation* and a simul-taneous *Negative Other-Presentation*; it is a way of perceiving and representing the world – and specifically 'our' and 'their' actions, position and role within the world. The ideological square predicts that 'outsiders' of various types will be represented in a negative way and 'insiders' will be represented in a positive way. This occurs by emphasising (what is called foregrounding) 'their' negative charac-teristics and social activities and de-emphasising (or backgrounding) 'their' positive characteristics and social activities. Conversely, 'our' positive characteristics and social activities are foregrounded and 'our' negative characteristics and social activities are backgrounded. This ideological square is observable across all linguistic dimensions of a text. Starting with referential strategies, positive terms are used to refer to 'Us' and 'Our country' and negative words being used to refer to 'Them', 'Their country', Their values', etc. Take this headline, for example: **This illegal immigrant drink-driver killed a boy in an uninsured motor. The sentence is 8 weeks**

(*Sun*, 2 March 2005). In this headline, the sub-editor working for the *Sun* decided that 'drink-driver' wasn't enough to convey the wickedness of the person responsible for this unfortunate accident – he was an *immigrant* and an *illegal* one at that. Without even knowing the full facts of this man's case, there are clearly many other ways that he could have been referred to. One alternative is actually provided in the penultimate paragraph of this 26-paragraph article. Here, the journalist grudgingly acknowledges the alternative referential strategy of a 'Home Office insider', who said that the perpetrator 'is entitled to stay in this country until the full appeals procedure is exhausted. In those terms we would not call him an illegal immigrant – he is an overstayer.' Lacking the combined negative impact of 'illegal' (strategy: *criminalisation*) and 'immigrant' (strategy: *de-spatialisation*), it is clear why the *Sun* passed over the Home Office's more accurate legal definition.

Predication

Clearly, referential strategies bear the imprint of value judgements. Also of relevance to the analysis of news texts is the choice of words used to represent more directly the values and characteristics of social actors. Reisigl and Wodak (2001) call these descriptions a text's predicational strategies, or 'the very basic process and result of linguistically assigning qualities to persons, animals, objects, events, actions and social phenomena' (p. 54). It is through predicational strategies that

> persons [etc . . .] are specified and characterised with respect to quality, quantity, space, time and so on. [. . .] Among other things, predicational strategies are mainly realised by specific forms of *reference* (based on explicit denotation as well as on more or less implicit connotation), by *attributes* (in the form of adjectives, appositions, prepositional phrases, relative clauses, conjunctional clauses, infinitive clauses and participial clauses or groups), by *predicates* or *predicative nouns/adjectives/pronouns*, by *collocations* or explicit *comparisons, similes, metaphors* and other *rhetorical figures* [. . .] and by more or less implicit *allusions, evocations* and *presuppositions/implications*. (Ibid.)

For example, in one celebrity filler (*Sun*, 25 February 2005), the actress Tina O'Brien is described as 'Coronation babe Tina O'Brien' and 'the pint-sized stunner' – two predicational strategies that clearly associate physical appearance with desirability. A marginally more serious article about a celebrity (**Natalie's film clinch shocks Jerusalem**, *Daily Express*, 25 February 2005) reports that Natalie Portman has been criticised by Orthodox Jewish groups for filming a kiss near to the Western ('Wailing') Wall in Jerusalem. The report describes her in two complimentary ways: as 'the porcelain-skinned Portman' and as 'the Israeli-born Star Wars actress'. The first of these is a physical predicate typical of the way tabloids describe women; the second is more interesting. Here, the paper implies that she is Jewish, and is therefore aware of Jewish religious sensitivities. This subtle referential strategy therefore undermines the rhetorical position of her detractors.

Finally, predication is also used to criticise, undermine and vilify certain social actors, sometimes with potentially dangerous consequences. Take the way that Maxine Carr (a woman convicted for conspiring to pervert the course of justice when she provided a false alibi for her boyfriend, Ian Huntley) is described in these following cases (all from 25 February 2005):

"Soham liar Maxine Carr" (*Daily Mirror*)
"Soham liar Maxine Carr; the former fiancé [*sic*] of child killer Ian Huntley" (*Daily Express*)
"Soham killer's ex-girlfriend" (*Daily Mail*)
"Soham killer Ian Huntley's ex-girlfriend" (*The Sun*)

The striking thing about these predicational strategies is their similarity. First, all lack the definite article (i.e. '*the* Soham liar...'). Bell (1991) calls this determiner deletion, and it is a syntactic style typical of the red-top and, to a lesser extent, mid-market British tabloids. Dropping the definite article in such a way 'confers on the descriptive NP [noun phrase] something which it did not previously have: title-ness. It moves from the category of common count nouns and takes on a status akin to titles such as *President Bush* or *Lord Lucan*' (ibid.: 196). In this case, all the titles conferred are clearly negative ones. Second, for the *Sun* and the *Daily Mail*, Carr is not even described in her own terms and instead is the object of a possessive construction: as an '[agent's] ex-girlfriend'. For the *Daily Mail* it was enough to label this agent '[the] Soham killer', while the *Sun* felt it necessary to qualify the noun phrase further with the addition of 'Ian Huntley'. These four negative predicational strategies were all then used in the service of these newspapers' editorial position on Carr – that she does not deserve anonymity and legal protection – disregarding the plain fact that it is *because* of her continued vilification by these same newspapers that she needs this legal protection in the first place.

Sentence construction: syntax and transitivity

Transitivity describes the relationships between participants and the roles they play in the processes described in reporting. Mills (1995: 143–144) argues that 'The study of transitivity is concerned with how actions are represented; what kind of actions appear in a text, who does them and to whom they are done' – in short, the '*who* (or what) does *what* to *whom* (or what)'. As such, transitivity forms the very heart of representation, describing the relationships between participants and the roles they play in the processes described in reporting. Central to the study of transitivity is the realisation 'that in producing texts there is a range of choices to be made, and every text which has been produced could have been produced differently' (ibid.). That is, choices in the way to represent an event's participants (referential and predicational strategies, covered above) and choices in the way that the event itself is represented, as reflected in the principal verb of the clause. As Simpson (1993: 88) demonstrates, in any process, there are three components that can be changed:

1. The *participants* involved in the process. These roles are typically realised by noun phrases in the clause.
2. The *process* itself, which will be expressed by the verb phrase in a clause.
3. The *circumstances* associated with the process, normally expressed by adverbial and prepositional phrases.

In the above section on lexicon, I have already suggested some of the ways the denoted and connoted meaning of clauses (or whole texts) can change, by using different referential or predicational strategies to refer to people. By Simpson's (1993) terms, these are changes to the way that the *participants* involved in the process are named and described.

Second, there is the *process* itself. In English there are four principal types of verbs, and therefore four different types of process that a sentence can use. First, *verbal* processes, such as speaking, shouting or singing. Second, verbs can be *mental* processes such as thinking, dreaming and deciding. Third, *relational* processes of being, such as have, seem and be (or is), which involve an agent and an attribute (e.g. 'You are *x*'; 'I have *y*'). And fourth, *material* processes, which can be further divided into *transitive* action involving two or more participants – the agent and the object of the action (e.g., 'He kicked her', 'I pushed you'); and *intransitive* action with only one participant (e.g., 'She ran', 'Aristotle flew', etc.).

In addition, we need to consider the construction of the process. To explain what this means, I'll take a frequently used example of transitive action: 'John kicked the ball.' This is called an *active* construction: the verb 'kicked' is in its active form since the subject, or actor (John), comes before the object (ball). This same process can be transformed into a *passive* construction: 'The ball was kicked by John'. Here we still have transitive action, but the verb takes a passive form and the object (ball) comes before the subject (John). This transformation can be taken further – the actor can be deleted leaving a passivised verb without agent: 'The ball was kicked.' Reading this process, we now don't know who kicked the ball. Of course, in this case this information may not be important, the news is that a ball was kicked (*'Ball was kicked shock!'*); on other occasions the deletion is highly significant. We can represent this transformation figuratively (Figure 3.1).

This transformation – in which a transitive action (kicking, pushing, attacking, etc.) is changed so the agent is deleted – appears *very* frequently in newspapers. In addition, active agent deletion does not only occur with transitive action processes; the agent can just as easily be deleted when representing a verbal process ('he alleged...' → 'allegations were made') or a mental process ('he considered the proposal' → 'the proposal was considered'). Any transformation of this kind removes a sense of specificity and precision from the clause. Take, for example, the lead sentence from a report printed in the *Guardian* (19 July 2003; my emphasis): 'The government

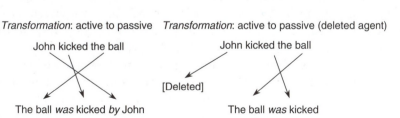

Transformation: active to passive   Transformation: active to passive (deleted agent)

John kicked the ball   John kicked the ball

[Deleted]

The ball *was* kicked *by* John   The ball *was* kicked

Figure 3.1 Syntactic transformation

found itself facing similar *accusations of spin* this week following the release of some confusing crime statistics.' Here, the journalist deletes the people actually accusing the government of 'spinning' from the clause. At this initial stage in the news report, the journalist considered 'accusations of spin against the government' to be a more important aspect of the story than who was actually doing the accusing; to discover who the accusers were, you had to read on.[2]

While this may seem rather fixed, with neatly demarcated types of verb processes, in fact the English language allows us to describe the *same* event in many *different* ways. Thus, we may choose to represent an event as a transitive action process (e.g. 'the IMF is changing the international economic order') or as a relational process (e.g. 'the international economic order is in a state of change'). Each of these options carries significant connoted meanings. Indeed, successive studies of journalism have shown that there is often social or ideological significance between these choices (Fowler, 1991; Richardson, 2004; Trew, 1979a,b). For instance, Fairclough (2000) shows that transforming an *active* process into a *relation* or 'state of affairs' can remove important (perhaps uncomfortable) political implications. He quotes a passage from New Labour's (1998) White Paper 'Building the Knowledge-Driven Economy':

> In the increasingly global economy of today, we cannot compete in the old way. Capital is mobile, technology can migrate quickly and goods can be made in low cost countries and shipped to developed markets.

The second sentence of this excerpt contains three processes. Taking each in turn: 'capital is mobile' transforms a transitive action process – 'companies move capital around the globe' – into a relation or 'state of affairs' and hence lacks agency. This transformation echoes exactly a point made by Marx in 1848: that in a 'capitalist society it is capital that is [represented as] independent and personalised, while the living individual is dependent and depersonalised' (ibid.: 25). Capital, as a social relation, cannot have an existence independent of people – a fact that the process 'capital is mobile' implicitly denies. Second, 'technology can migrate quickly' ascribes agency to technology itself rather than something that is acted upon by multinational companies – in addition, the movement of technology is represented metaphorically as migration, a *natural*, seasonal process. Third, 'goods can be made in low cost countries' and '[goods can be] shipped to developed markets' are transitive action processes without agents. We need to ask ourselves: Who is doing the making? Who is doing the shipping? As in the example from the *Guardian* discussed above, these are passive sentences without agent. Fairclough argues that New Labour is able to simultaneously acknowledge but camouflage the active role of multinational companies in dominating the global economy. Through transforming the processes involved, the active roles that multinationals play in maintaining globalised economic inequalities are backgrounded, deleted or transformed into a depoliticised and 'natural' relation.

Third, by Simpson's (1993) terms, we can change the *circumstances* associated with the process either by additional contextualisation (in the form of adverbial or prepositional phrases) or through the structuring or framing of a process' meaning relations. For instance, Montgomery *et al.* (2000: 92) show that during the 1983 British Miners' strike, the *Daily Mail*, which was generally supportive of the Conservative government position, 'described events on the picket line using sentences such as the following':

> 41 policemen had been treated in hospital
> police horses and their riders were stoned
> [. . .] pickets bombarded the police

In terms of transitivity, the police are represented here as the objects (or the 'afflicted') of violent transitive action, while the pickets appear as the agents of this violence. In contrast, the left-wing newspaper the *Morning Star* represented the events on the picket lines in the following way:

> police attacked isolated groups of miners
> several miners were hit by truncheons
> [. . .] 3,000 pickets yesterday gathered outside Cortonwood Colliery

Here, the miners shift to become the objects of the police's violent transitive actions and where the miners are represented as active agents, 'it usually involves processes of non-violent [intransitive] movement' (ibid.).

Given that transitivity forms the very basis of representation, transitive choice cannot be overlooked in any linguistic analysis of journalism. That said, it is important that analysis doesn't overstate the effect that a choice from the transitivity system can have on textual meaning – in particular, it is important not to fixate on an individual passive structure and the meaning that it (arguably) realises. Take this constructed example, in which Widdowson (2004: 31) adapts a much-quoted newspaper lead analysed by Trew (1979a):

> Police opened fire on African demonstrators in Salisbury today as ANC leaders were meeting. Eleven Africans were shot.

Here, in the second sentence, the agency of the police is removed through the use of a passive verb phrase ('were shot') with a deleted agent. The absence of agency in this second sentence is revealed by asking: *shot by who?* However, as Widdowson (2004: 31) points out, 'It would surely be perverse in this case to interpret the passive ideationally as representing the event as happening without agentivity, since the agentivity is explicitly described in the preceding clause.' Viewed in the context of the surrounding sentences, it seems 'reasonable to suggest that this [second sentence] is not a case of reference evasion, but reference avoidance [. . .] The agent is deleted because it is redundant' (ibid.). In other words, because agency is ascribed in the first sentence, it doesn't need to be stated in the second. With discourse analysis, the unit of analysis is the text (as a whole) and hence analysis should ideally combine a discussion of what the *text* represents and excludes – or, how the *textual meaning* is communicated through relations of presence and absence – rather than on a sentence-by-sentence basis. Take this Press Agency report for example, printed in the main section of the *Sunday Telegraph*:

Jenin clashes
Five Israeli soldiers and a Palestinian were wounded after Israeli forces entered Jenin on the West Bank. (5 January 2003)

This above quote, which represents the *complete* report of this event, contains two significant *transitive action* verb processes. Taking each in turn: the first clause states 'Five Israeli soldiers and a Palestinian were wounded.' Here a transitive action process – 'to wound' – is expressed as a passive construction without an agent. Such a transitive choice always involves a degree of ambiguity, but in this case it results in a degree of imprecision so acute that the clause is almost useless. This clause fails as adequate journalism because only one half of a transitive action process (which always involves at least *two* parties) is recoverable from the text: we are only told about the affected subjects, not the active agent(s), of the reported event. We are not even sure whether the 'five Israeli soldiers and a Palestinian' were wounded as a result of a single or multiple actions. This choice may have been taken for reasons of space. In other words, the soldiers and the Palestinian were wounded by different people (each other?) but to provide any more details about who the active agents were in each case would take up space which the editor had decided this report didn't deserve (see Chapter 4 for a discussion of 'news values'). The chosen construction implies that the afflicted subjects were wounded at the same time and in a way that was linked to the event described in the prepositional phrase – an implication that, due to the extreme brevity of the report, we are not able to evaluate or interrogate. If the process, or processes, were expressed in an active way – thus as 'X wounded five Israeli soldiers and a Palestinian', or 'X wounded five Israeli soldiers and then Y wounded a Palestinian' – then the text would have provided a better account of the reported action.

The second verb-clause – 'Israeli forces entered Jenin' – is more ideological. First, it is highly unlikely that Israeli forces could 'enter Jenin' without significant resistance from armed Palestinian groups but the author chose to represent the event as involving Israelis moving *into* Jenin rather than acting *upon* its Palestinian population. Second, the author chose to use the rather benign verb 'enter' rather than a host of alternatives, such as 'invaded', 'over-ran' or 'attacked' that generate significantly different connoted meaning. These altern- ative transitive processes would have retained the violent nature of the reported action in a way that 'enter' did not.

Sentence construction: modality

Modality forms the counter-part of transitivity, referring to judge- ments, comment and attitude in text and talk, and specifically the degree to which a speaker or writer is committed to the claim he or she is making. As Simpson (1993: 47) puts it, 'modality refers broadly to a speaker's attitude towards, or opinion about, the truth of a proposition expressed by a sentence. It also extends to their attitude towards the situation or event described by a sentence.' Modality provides a further step in our analysis, showing that there are not only links between *form* and *content*, but also between *content* and *function*. Modality is usually indicated via the use of modal verbs (such as *may, could, should, will* and *must*), their negations (*may not, couldn't, shouldn't, will not* and *must not*) or through adverbs (*certainly*). Modal verbs and adverbs such as these are a regular feature of more 'opinionated' genres of journalism such as the edit-orial and the column – genres of journalism that do not simply *report* an event (information) but also provide a *judgement* of an event (eval-uation, comment). So you may have someone write: 'he could have been more forceful' or 'he should have been more forceful' – very different ways of describing not only an event but also the writer's view of the event.

More specifically, modality may be expressed in two principal forms: truth modality and obligation (or duty) modality. Truth modality varies along a scale of options from the absolutely categorical ('This war *will* be stopped if the people intervene in the political process') through to varying degrees of hedging ('This war *can* be stopped if the people intervene in the political process') and reduced certainty ('This war *could* be stopped if *only* the people intervened in the political process'). Obligation modality refers to future events and, specifically, the degree to which the speaker/writer believes that a certain course of action or certain decisions *ought* or *should* be taken. Again, this modality can be expressed in categorical terms ('chil-dren's rights *must* take precedence over the profit motive of private-sector companies') or more cautiously ('children's rights *ought to* take precedence over the profit motive of private-sector companies').

Categorical modal truth claims (*will, must, certainly, necessarily,* etc.) appear more authoritative than hedged claims and therefore tend to be used more frequently, particularly in more sensationalised or more vigorously argued copy. However, a lower degree of commit-ment can also have striking effects on shaping our understanding of an event or a possible event. For example, the lead sentence in a news report printed in the *Daily Mail* reads:

> Britain *could* suffer a Madrid-style terrorist attack in the run-up to the Royal Wedding and General Election, the country's most senior police officer warned yesterday. (25 February 2005; emphasis added)

The ambiguity of such a modal claim (combined with the verb 'to warn') paradoxically heightens the sense of dread and threat. When we see such claims, we should ask: 'of course Britain *could* suffer a Madrid-style terrorist attack [note the referential strategy], what is the like-lihood that it *will*?' Clearly a great many things *could* happen, but journalism should not be used to fly the kites of the security state in such an uncritical way. This propagandistic technique is not a new one, of course. During the build-up to the 1998 Desert Fox cruise missile attack on Iraq, for example, the claims made regarding the 'threat' of Iraq were so often couched, hedged and mitigated to be almost devoid of any real content. An article printed in the *Independent* head-lined **Britain warns of Saddam's timebomb** (19 November 1997) for example, quoted a British 'intelligence assessment' which stated:

> Provided it still has key components – and that is unclear – Iraq *could* within a few months build, with little risk of detection, missiles capable of hitting Israel and key targets in Saudi Arabia. (emphasis added)

What this assessment actually states is that Iraq *may* be able to produce missiles *providing* it has certain key (i.e. essential) compon-ents, the likelihood of which is unclear; in other words, it doesn't state very much. However, through the collocation of Iraq, weapons and risk it nevertheless contributed to the growing sense that 'some-thing should be done' about Iraq and Saddam's 'bad bombs'.

Readers should note, however, 'that speakers also have the option of expressing the basic proposition in its 'raw' form; or in other words as a categorical assertion' – that 'you are', 'he or she is' or something 'was' (Simpson, 1993: 49). In such cases, adding a modal verb – even a categorical one like 'must' – actually results in an epistemically *weaker* claim than if the journalist chose not to modalise the verb. Simply put, while it may seem a little counter-intuitive, 'You are right' is a stronger claim than 'You *must* be right' (ibid.) even though 'must' is a categorical modal verb. For example:

> Top environmentalists warned yesterday that a population explosion among Britain's deer *is* playing havoc with woodland birds. [. . .] The BTO [British Trust for Ornithology] review, carried out for Government wildlife advisers, says that deer *are* playing a key role in wrecking the habitat for many species. (**Bambi turns killer**, *Daily Express*, 25 February 2005; my emphases)

Here, the journalist uses a non-modal categorical assertion – a deer population explosion *is* having a certain effect – and modalising this claim would diminish its argumentative force. However, looking to how this BTO review was reported in other newspapers reveals entirely different judgements of these 'Top environmentalists' conclu-sions. The *Independent*, for example, claims that the review of bird populations offers 'seven possible causes which *may be* behind the decline' (**Mystery of the silent woodland birds**, 25 February

2005; my emphasis). One of these was 'intensified habitat modification by deer, which eat the woodland bushes'; others included climate change, reduction in insect numbers and predation by grey squirrels and crows; but the report states that even 'these possibilities are *speculative*'. On this evidence, it appears that the *Express* chose to single out the deer and categorically claim their responsibility purely in order to justify their sensationalist headline!

At this point, to some readers, modality may seem to be a rather peripheral area of study. But consider the recent 'dodgy dossier' story, and specifically the claim that the Iraqi military were able to deploy chemical or biological weapons within 45 minutes of being given the order to do so, that eventually resulted in the Hutton Inquiry. Aside from the fact that the bigger picture – a democratically elected government mislead the public about the case for starting a war – was largely ignored, the standoff basically boiled down to modal truth claims. First, in a letter to John Scarlett, the chairman of the Joint Intelligence Committee, Alastair Campbell suggested that the words 'may be' be replaced by the word 'are' in a sentence about Iraq's ability to deploy chemical and biological weapons: instead of reading 'Iraq *may be* able to deploy . . .' it was changed to 'Iraq *are* able to deploy . . .', which is a considerable shift in truth modality. Second, when Andrew Gilligan now famously first reported this in a two-way broadcast on 29 May 2003, he said he'd been told by 'one of the senior officials in charge of drawing up the September dossier that the government *probably* knew the 45-minute figure was wrong'. By the ITN 10 o'clock news that same day, Gavin Hewitt was claiming: 'in the final week before publication, some material *was* taken out, some material put in. His [source's] judgment, some spin from No 10 *did* come into play.' Again, we see a considerable shift in truth modality from 'probably' to 'was' and 'did'.

In sum, modal choices like these are an indication of the attitudes, judgements or political beliefs of the writer/speaker. As such, they constitute 'a major exponent of the interpersonal function of language' (Simpson, 1993: 47), provide a window into the political functions and, particularly in this case, the potential political *effects* of the language of journalism.

Presupposition

Much of the discussion so far has focused on the relations between form and content – or how the meaning of what is written is related

to the way in which it's written. However not all meaning is immediately 'there' in a text to be simply read from the manifest content;
there are also *hidden* or *presupposed* meanings in texts. A presupposition is a taken-for-granted, implicit claim embedded within the
explicit meaning of a text or utterance. Presuppositions are marked
in a variety of ways in texts. Reah (2002: 106) lists three linguistic
structures common to presupposed meaning. First, certain words,
such as change of state verbs (stop, begin, continue) or implicative
verbs (manage, forget) invoke presupposed meaning in their very use:
'stop' presupposes a movement or an action; 'forget' presupposes a
great deal, including an attempt to remember. The classic example
of such a presupposition is the sentence 'Have you stopped beating
your wife?' It is impossible to answer 'yes' or 'no' to this question
without confirming the presupposition: that you have, at some time
in the past, beaten your wife. In a similar way the question 'Do
you think military attack is the best way of *ending Iraqi belliger-
ence?*' – aired on the BBC's flagship Newsnight programme in the
build up to the 2003 invasion of Iraq – presumes that Iraq is *being*
belligerent.

Second, the definite article ('the——') and possessive articles
('his/her——') trigger presuppositions. For example: 'the challenge
facing the modern world' not only presupposes *a* challenge exists but
also that *a* modern world does too (see Fairclough, 2000: 27; 163).
Journalistic examples are not difficult to find. The *Independent* of
12 March 2005 refers to: 'the Mourinho look' (presupposes that such
a thing exists); 'the revelation [. . .] that Britain went to war on the
basis of one page of legal advice' (presupposes this is a 'revelation'
and not a 'fact'); 'the women's vote' (presupposes that it exists as a
thing, and not simply as a consequence of an activity); and many,
many others.

Third, presuppositions are present in 'wh- questions', such as 'why',
'when', 'who', etc. So, a politician asked 'Who is responsible for
the poor state of the National Health Service?' is actually being
asked two questions: the explicit request to name someone; and the
presupposed question 'Is someone responsible for the poor state of
the National Health Service?' which remains implicit. The technique
is also frequently used in print journalism. For example: 'Why do
Islamist terrorist groups like al-Qaeda and Hamas want to crush the
West and destroy Israel? Michael Scott Doran unravels the historical
roots of their extremism' (*Guardian*, Saturday Review, 8 December
2001). This wh question presupposes a great deal: first, and most
obviously, it presupposes that Islamist terrorist groups (like al-Qaeda

and Hamas) *do* want to crush 'the West' *and* destroy Israel. But this presupposition, in turn, also relies on the presupposition that both these organisations can be categorised as Islamist terrorist groups and that *both* organisations want to do *both* these things.

Fourth, Reah omits to mention that presuppositions can also be triggered by nouns and adjectives used to qualify (or modify) noun phrases. I refer to these as *nominal* presuppositions. Sometimes nominal presuppositions are largely uncontentious; on other occasions, usually because the noun refers to social or political subjects, the presupposed meaning is more questionable. Take the following headline: **Britain's asylum system takes new hammering** (*Daily Express*, 25 February 2005). The use of the adjective 'new' presupposes that Britain's asylum system has experienced old or past 'hammerings'. This presupposition fits with the political agenda of the *Daily Express*, a newspaper that regularly decries what it sees as a scandalous level of 'abuse' of the British asylum system. Nominal presuppositions can also be embedded in the questions of interviewers:

Q: what's the future if uneconomic pits continue to be around [. . .]?
A: well – as you know Miss Chalmers [. . .] for the last 40 minutes I've been explaining to you that the NCB in Britain is the most efficient and technologically advanced industry in the world. (from Harris, 1991: 85)

In a similar way to the 'wh- question' above, here the interviewer (intentionally or otherwise) embeds the presupposition that *'uneconomic pits exist'* in a question ostensibly about the future of coal mining in the UK. The respondent challenges this presupposition by arguing that coal mining in the UK is nothing less than 'the most efficient and technologically advanced industry in the world'.

Rhetorical tropes

As I have argued elsewhere (Richardson, 2004), I feel that journalism is best approached as an argumentative discourse genre. Similarly, Kieran (1998: 27) states that 'a journalist's news report should aim to persuade the audience that his or her description and interpretation is the rational and appropriate one'. However, given that journalists – like all of us – are unable to provide reports of events that are entirely true and objective, they employ rhetorical strategies aimed 'at persuading others to adopt [their] same point of view' (Thomson, 1996: 6). This is not to suggest that journalism is mere rhetoric (in the pejorative sense of the word), but rather that journalism represents 'opinion statements [. . .] embedded in argumentation that makes them more or less defensible, reasonable, justifiable or legitimate as conclusions' (van Dijk, 1996: 24). The success of this argumentation often rests on the use of rhetorical tropes. Corbett (1990: 426) defines a trope as 'a deviation from the ordinary and principal signification of a word'. In other words, in contrast to a rhetorical scheme, which involves 'a deviation from the ordinary pattern or arrangement of words' (ibid.) (e.g. parallelism, antithesis, etc.), a trope will take words and use them to denote–connote something apart from their ordinary meaning. Such tropes are employed strategically as a 'way of describing things which makes them present to our mind' (Perelman and Olbrechts-Tyteca, 1969: 167) and are 'non-obligatory additional structures in texts that may draw attention, and may therefore indirectly emphasise specific meanings' (van Dijk, 1991: 217).

There are almost literally hundreds of such tropes recognised by rhetorical theory (see Corbett, 1990; Jasinski, 2001). Here I will only introduce five that I feel are useful to the analysis of newspaper discourse.

Hyperbole

Hyperbole is an example of excessive exaggeration made for rhetorical effect. The headline of the article examined above – **Bambi turns killer** (*Daily Express*, 25 February 2005) – is one such example. Such cases reflect the sensationalism, and often the humour, of news reporting in the tabloid press. However it is in the reporting of various social out-groups – 'racial' or ethnic minorities, criminals and mental health patients in particular – that hyperbole can take on a more sinister dimension. Van Dijk (1991) points out that in his study of the reporting of 'race' and 'racial' minorities hyperbole was highly selective: 'disturbances are not merely described as "riots" but even as "mob war" when young West Indians are involved, a policeman is not "stabbed" but "hacked down and mutilated in a fury of blood lust"' when killed by a black man (p. 219). Racist hyperbole persists in some reports. Take this editorial from the *Sun* (2 March 2005), for example, commenting on the same drink-driving death examined briefly above:

Kick him out
Even through his tears, the father of tragic Jamie Mason can see clearly about the wicked driver who killed his son.
"He should not have been in this country, let alone in that car." [. . .] Chisango will be free in a week and will continue his SEVEN-YEAR battle to stay in this country
What the hell are the immigration authorities up to?

In the reporting of this story, the *Sun* reconfigures a traffic accident into an immigration story. This in itself is unwarranted, but it is the hyperbole – specifically choosing to describe the driver as wicked – that interests me, since the facts of this case provided in a *Sun* news report that same day (albeit in a backgrounded form) are hardly indicative of the actions of a 'wicked' man. These show the driver was 1 1/2 times over the legal limit; that the alcohol in his system was a residue from the night before; that the Police found insufficient evidence to charge him with causing death by careless driving; that they failed to prove he was driving without due care and attention; and that he was, in fact, 'going only marginally over the 30 mph speed limit'. In short, the death he caused was an unfortunate accident. The hyperbolic account of this accident should therefore be viewed as an attempt to 'emphasise the aggression or other negative properties of black people' (van Dijk, 1991: 219) and, in this case, to support *The Sun's* wider point that 'Our' immigration system is being abused by 'wicked foreigners'.

Metaphor

A familiar concept to most, a metaphor, in the most general sense, involves perceiving one thing in terms of another. Take the economy, for example. We can talk about an economy being 'overheated' or 'stagnating', 'tiger economies', 'peaks' and 'troughs' in production, 'a financial boom', the 'bubble bursting' or a range of other metaphors which are employed in order to understand financial affairs in terms of something else.

Certain types of metaphor are associated with specific genres of journalism. Metaphors of war are frequently, indeed ubiquitously, employed in sports reporting. In most sports, we talk about 'attack and defence', about 'counter-attack'; we 'shoot for goal' or 'shoot at the goal';

if one side is subject to a prolonged period of pressure they can be said to be 'under siege'; a team can get 'slaughtered' by the opposition, etc. The players in our teams, or the more successful members of our teams, are often labelled 'heroes' or 'our boys'; the less successful are labelled 'villains' or, in the case of Paula Radcliffe, after she dropped out of the 2004 Olympic marathon, a 'casualty of war' (*Daily Mirror*, 23 August 2004). Such a metaphorical framework shapes our understanding of sport as an extraordinary activity – an activity that allows us to abandon reason and sense of proportion. As Sontag (1990: 99) wrote, this is because war 'is one of the few activities that people are not supposed to view "realistically": that is, with an eye to expense and practical outcome. In all-out-war, expenditure is all-out, imprudent – war being defined as an emergency in which no sacrifice is excessive.'

Interestingly, war itself is often reported (and hence understood) using metaphors and metaphorical frameworks. Lule (2004), for instance, shows how during the prelude to the US/UK invasion of Iraq in 2003, news-reporting was dominated by four metaphors: 'the *Timetable*; the *Games of Saddam*; the *Patience of the White House*; and *Making a Case/Selling the Plan*' (p. 184). Explaining each of these metaphors:

> [. . .] the administration had a timetable it was trying to follow, a timetable with a final and inevitable destination: war. The timetable, however, was threatened by the games of Saddam, who adroitly played hide and seek with the weapons [. . .] The White House was losing patience with the process, the UN, and eventually, its allies. Subsequently, the administration was forced to make its case, sell its plan to the American people. (Ibid.)

Other prominent metaphors frequently employed to make war 'understandable' are *war is business, war is politics* and *war is a freedom* (see Lakoff, 1991). Each of these, like the metaphorical frameworks employed to promote the invasion of Iraq, help to hide the true consequences of violent conflict: blood, bones and bodies.

Metonym

Jasinski (2001: 551) writes that metonymy 'is a form of substitution in which something that is associated with X is substituted for X'. More formally, a metonym is a trope in which one word, phrase or object is substituted for another from a semantically related field of reference. Metonymy differs from metaphor, in that metaphors operate through transference of similar characteristics while metonymy oper-ates through more direct forms of association. Reisigl and Wodak (2001: 56–58) detail a number of metonymic replacements:

- the cause or creator is replaced by the product: e.g. 'the Anti-terrorism, Crime and Security Act 2001 criminalises Muslims'
- the user of an object replaced by the object: e.g. 'Rachel Corrie was killed by an Israeli bulldozer'
- people replaced by a place in which these people work/are staying: e.g. 'The White House declared . . .'; 'the detention centre erupted into violence'
- events replaced by the date on which these events occurred: e.g. 'September 11th must never be allowed to occur again'
- a country, or state, replaced by (certain) people living in this country: e.g. 'We cannot let the evil of ethnic cleansing stand. We must not rest until it is reversed' (Tony Blair, 22 April 1999, cited in Fairclough, 2000: 148).

From a discourse analytic perspective, the significance of metonymia, like with all tropes, lies not in their presence in a text but in the ways that they're used. Occasionally, metonyms are used because the actors responsible are unknown. Consider the following headline: **Truck crashes into UK embassy** (*Independent*, 1 April 2003). Here, the user of an object replaced by the object – perhaps partly because the reason why the truck was driven into the embassy building died with the driver, and partly because it was a punchier headline than alternatives (e.g. 'Man drives truck into UK embassy').

On the other hand, metonyms may 'enable the speakers [or writers] to conjure away responsible, involved or affected actors (whether victims or perpetrators), or to keep them in the semantic background' (Reisigl and Wodak, 2001: 58). Consider the following headline, also taken from the *Independent*: **Beside the Tigris, another river carries food, fuel and arms north** (7 April 2003). This metonym involves the *social agent* (the army) being replaced by the *medium* (the river, through which this action is enabled): the text reveals that these materials were carried by the army, using their boats on the river, not in fact by the river itself. This metonym is comparable to saying that 'the wind takes tourists on holiday', rather than pilots using planes. Casting the river as the active agent – and the rather poetic evocation of the Tigris – makes the event seem far more romantic than the reality: the army moving its supplies in order to kill Iraqis more efficiently.

Neologism

A neologism is a recently created (or coined) word, or an existing word or phrase that has been assigned a new meaning. Neologisms are created in a number of ways (see Jasinski, 2001: 551), but in relation to journalism, three are of particular relevance. First, through the addition of prefixes or suffixes to create new words. Perhaps the most prevalent example of this in journalistic discourse is the use of '-gate' as a suffix to designate a scandal. Since the Watergate scandal of 1972–74, in the USA there has been Irangate, Lewinskygate and Rathergate; Camillagate, Cheriegate and Squidgygate in the UK; Hansiegate in South Africa and many other affairs, some of which were decidedly minor.[3] The result has arguably been to trivialise the Watergate scandal itself.

Second, neologisms can be created by shifting word meaning, either through changing grammatical function (e.g. 'Google' and 'ebay' used as verbs rather than as nouns) or by developing a new euphemistic meaning. Examples of this type of neologism are legion, particularly regarding the reporting of war. Euphemisms, such as 'engage' (kill), 'take out' (kill), 'neutralise' (kill), 'theatre' (battlefield), 'friendly fire' (being killed by your own army), 'collateral damage' (unplanned for, but expedient killing of civilians) and others, are consciously used during wartime to background the uncomfortable reality that wars involve killing people.

Third, neologisms can be created through blending two existing words (e.g. smog = smoke + fog; brunch = breakfast + lunch). This is sometimes called a *portmanteau*, and of newspapers only tabloids tend to coin new words in this way. For example, an article on the designer clothes worn by certain British minor celebrities headlined **Aristochavs** (*The Sun*, 16 March 2005) combines 'aristocracy' and 'chav' – itself a derogatory neologism, applied to young adults of white working class or lower middle class origin, and similar to the US epithet 'white trash'. Later in this same article, they reverse the portmanteau and label the 10 women pictured Britain's 'chavistocracy'. Either portmanteau is belittling, but the article also has a wider social function. We do well to remember, 'more than any other class, the middle class must work hard to achieve and maintain class position. The work of the middle class involves the creation and recreation of a lifestyle that is recognisably middle class [. . .] This is tricky business because the signs of "middle classness" are easily appropriated and assimilated by the working class' (Moon and Rolison, 1998: 126). Here, the newspaper is literally putting the identified minor celebrities in their place: that despite their expensive clothes, they are 'chavs', white trash, *working class*. More than this, by labelling the people depicted 'aristochavs' the newspaper implies that they are the *trashiest* white trash. In doing so, the tabloid *Sun* simultaneously attempts to keep its working class target audience 'abreast of exactly what constitutes a middle class lifestyle' (ibid.) and to protect the signifiers of this middle-class lifestyle (expensive fashion) from being appropriated by the working class.

Puns

Finally, for this section, there are puns and other forms of word-play. Puns may be grouped into three main forms: homographic puns that exploit multiple meanings of essentially the same word (e.g. *foil* meaning to baffle and *foil* meaning thin metal); ideographic puns that substitute words of similar but not identical sound (e.g. *merry* and *Mary*); and homophonic puns that substitute words with the same sound but unrelated meaning (e.g. *raised* and *razed*). For example, the headline **Batchelor Pads It Out: Jockey denies misleading investigators** (*Daily Mirror*, 22 June 2004), reporting allegations against the jockey Mattie Batchelor, contains an example of a homographic pun on the word 'pad'.

While some may just view such features as a merely entertaining aspect of (particularly tabloid) news discourse, like all rhetorical features, they often underscore a newspaper's editorial and often political agenda. For example, **My Euro Vision: Blair spells out why he backs Yes vote on new constitution** (ibid.) is a pro-European constitution article printed in a pro-Euro newspaper. A less successful pun, **Beware the bribes of March** (17 March 2005), draws attention to what the conservative *Sun* newspaper considers to be the problems with the Chancellor Gordon Brown's pre-election budget. It is less successful because the ideograph – *bribes* – is a little too far from the word it puns – *ides* – and the literary reference is perhaps not instantly recognisable to a tabloid readership. The *Sun* is usually far better at inventing puns – for example, **Was it a left hook or a right hamza?** (*Sun*, 7 March 2005) reporting a physical assault in prison against the Muslim preacher Abu Hamza. While the report is prejudicial and revels in the criminal attack against this man, the headline is rhetorically successful because it uses both a homographic pun on hook (as a verb or a noun) and an ideographic pun on 'hamza' ('right hander').

Narrative

> Journalists are professional storytellers of our age. The fairy
> tale starts: 'Once upon a time.' The news story begins: 'Fifteen
> people were injured today when a bus plunged...' The journ-
> alist's work is focused on the getting and writing of stories. (Bell,
> 1991: 147)

In essence, the study of news narratives is the study of 'news
stories' – that is, the contents of news stories and the ways that
such stories are presented. Logically, therefore, when considering
news narratives, we first need to distinguish between the narrative
content and the narrative *form* (Montgomery *et al.*, 2000). Narrative
content is the sequence of events as they occurred in the actual
story: in essence, the plot or the structure of actions. The basic
narrative structure, first discussed by Aristotle in his *Poetics* (1962),
develops along the following trajectory: introduction of characters
and setting, rising action, introduction of complication, climax in
which the complication is overcome and the final resolution. Hard
news narratives are very rarely this complete because of their focus
on ever-unfolding social events. Instead, news is often structured
around a simpler plot, constituted by a three-part structure: *setting*,
event and *outcome*, lacking a final resolution. This plot is not only a
sequence of events but also 'an order of *meaning*' (White, 1981: 5;
my emphasis); we need to apply knowledge in order to establish a
coherent link between the situation and the action, or how, given
the complication and the social actors involved, an outcome is
achieved.

Narrative *form* is the sequence in which events are presented to
us. Hard news narratives are organised in relation to the inverted
pyramid or 'climax-first' structure. As Franklin *et al.* (2005: 122)
put it, the inverted pyramid is the 'standardised format for writing
a hard news story which places the most important information at
the head of the story and uses the lead paragraph to answer the
five "W questions": Who? What? Why? Where? And When?' Since
the more significant elements are located at the top of a story, hard
news rarely takes a chronological form (see Bell, 1991). In terms of
the three-part plot structure suggested above, news narrative usually
takes the form: *complication* (the actual reported 'event'), the *setting*
or background and then the *outcome* to the story. The narrative form
of the news report can be shown most easily with an NIB ('news in
brief') story (Table 3.1).

Table 3.1 Narrative

	Five Ws	Chronology
A coroner in Swansea has called for an urgent review of the guidelines on bungee jumping, after	Who; Where; What	3
hearing that Chris Thomas, 22 who weighed 20 stone, died because he was too heavy for his harness.	Why	2
Mr Thomas fell to his death in front of a crowd of 300 people.	Background	1
A verdict of accidental death was returned.	Outcome	4

Laying the story out in such a way reveals the chronology of the story (narrative content) and the particular episodic narrative form of hard news.

Of course, the inverted pyramid is not the only way of structuring news stories. As Blundy (2004: 181) rather forcefully puts it, news can also be written with a 'dropped intro', in which the journalist puts 'all the who–what–why–where–when, that would normally come first, in the second paragraph and a silly incomprehensible piece of rubbish in the first one'. With this more literary form of newspaper journalism, the report invariably starts with a pronoun such as 'it', 'he', 'she' or 'they'. This is called *cataphoric* reference, in which the pronoun refers forward to its co-referent.[4] This is intended to create a sense of anticipation, as the reader does not know who or what the pronoun refers to. In contrast, in the more typical inverted pyramid narrative form, the first mention of an individual provides you with a name or the information necessary to know whom the text refers to. For example, a report may refer to 'Chancellor Gordon Brown' in the lead sentence, then use the pronoun 'He' in the second paragraph (**Secrets and fries**, *News of the World*, 16 January 2005); or may refer to 'John Reid, the Mike Tyson of public life' in the lead sentence then use the pronoun 'He' in the second paragraph (**Reid's £1bn 'cure' has NHS on ropes**, *Daily Mirror*, 25 February 2005). This is called *anaphoric* reference: the pronoun used refers backwards to its co-referent that is included earlier in the text.

Returning to cataphoric pronouns, in the news article **Mystery of the silent woodlands** referred to above, the *Independent* starts the report: 'It has hardly been noticed, but it is another sign of a world going badly wrong.' The reader needs to continue to the next sentence to find out that 'It', used twice in this lead sentence, refers to the plummeting populations of certain British woodland birds. Another story from the *Independent* (**Tiddlywinks goes to pot as students shun the game**, 12 March 2005) opens: 'They are the unsung heroes of British sport, with seven championships lifting 37 world titles since 1985.' Again, the reader would have to continue reading to the second paragraph to find out that the pronoun 'they' refers to 'members of the Cambridge University Tiddlywinks Club' (though the headline does hint at such a referent). In the more extended example below, the cataphoric pronouns are italicised and emboldened in order to better trace their referents:

> *They* had been watching **him** for months, aware that **his** pop star good looks concealed a secret life as one of Europe's new terrorist kingpins. Finally, on a cold winter dawn, *the police* moved in. **Abderrazak Mahdjoub** did not resist as *armed German officers* surrounded **his** Hamburg home and led him away.
>
> For at least a year, *investigators* claim, **the 30-year old Algerian** had been a key part of a network of Islamic milit- ants dedicated to recruiting and dispatching suicide bombers to the Middle East. Several volunteers had got through, wreaking havoc in a series of attacks in Iraq. Many more were on their way, along with bombers focused on targets in Europe. (**Terror cells regroup – and now their target is Europe**, *Observer*, 11 January 2004)

It is interesting, first, that the pronouns and noun phrases refer- ring to both the police and Mahdjoub adopt the same semantic trajectory: both start with a cataphoric pronoun ('they' and 'him'), replace this with a proper noun ('the police' and 'Abderrazak Mahd- joub') that is then modified ('armed German officers' and 'the 30-year old Algerian'). The narrative therefore draws the reader in, providing progressively more information about the participants of the reported action and revealing more about the story. Second, despite this being a news story printed in a broadsheet newspaper, it reads more like the opening of a spy novel. Each sentence is assertive; there is a noticeable lack of modalised verbs resulting in every clause being expressed in a categorical way ('They *had* been . . .'; 'the police moved in'; he '*did not* resist'; 'volunteers *had* got through'; 'Many more *were* on their way', etc.). The only occasion that a more journalistic voice creeps into this opening is where the journalists acknowledge that all of Mahdjoub's activities reported in the second paragraph are only *claimed* by the investigators – and even here, this (some would say *vital*) information is backgrounded in a subjunctive clause. The result is a wholly unwelcome blurring of genres (news and entertainment), authorship (are these the claims of the investigators or journalists?) and 'the relationship between story and actual events', in other words questions of truth (Fairclough, 2003: 85).

As the above discussion perhaps hints at, 'narratives help us impose order on the flow of experience so that we can make sense of events and actions in our lives' (Foss, 1996: 399). Narratives, like history, are not simply 'one thing after another'; narratives 'establish relationships between or among things (e.g. events, states, situations) over time' (Jasinski, 2001: 390). Further, 'stories usually concern noteworthy events' (Ochs, 1997: 192) – or, in the language of news reporting, *newsworthy* events. They 'articulate and sustain common understandings of what the culture deems ordinary' (ibid.: 193) and provide us with a means of organising and therefore comprehending the events of the world around us. Thus, news narratives are, on one level, a reflection and a product of nothing less than our 'general cultural assumptions and values – what we consider important, trivial, fortunate, tragic, good, evil, and what impels movement from one to another' (Martin, 1986: 87). The form of each of these cultural assumptions and values is contestable; so too are the political explanations of cause/effect. Consequently, Martin (1986: 8) writes: 'Narrative, considered as a form of entertainment when studied as literature, is a battleground when actualised in newspapers, biography and history.' To explore this in greater depth, we need to consider the discursive practices of newspapers.

Discursive Practices: Producing Print Journalism

Introduction: what are discursive practices?

As stated in Chapter 2, discursive practices amount to the processes involved in the production and consumption of texts. Phillips and Jørgensen (2002: 69) explain that discursive practices focus on 'how authors of texts draw on already existing discourses and genres to create a text and on how receivers of texts also apply available discourses and genres in the consumption and interpretation of the texts'. In other words, the discursive practices of journalism are the processes through which journalists produce texts, and readers use and understand them. The analysis of discourse, therefore, requires more than the list of text-linguistic concepts introduced in Chapter 3. In more detail, Blommaert (1999: 5–6) states:

> Texts generate their publics, publics generate their texts and the analysis of 'meanings' now has to take into account a historiography of the context of production, the mechanisms and instruments of reproduction and reception, ways of storage and remembering. The fact is that discourses [. . .] have their 'natural history' – a chronological and sociocultural anchoring which produces meaning and social effects in ways that cannot be reduced to text-characteristics alone.

Hence, discourses are always socially situated: discourse occurs in social settings (of production and consumption) and the construction of discourse 'relates systematically and predictably to [these] contextual circumstances' (Fowler, 1991: 36). In the case of mass-mediated communication, discourse is institutionally based. Indeed Kress (1985, cited in Fowler 1991: 42) goes as far as to state: 'Discourses are systematically-organised sets of statements which give expression to the meanings and values of an institution.' It is in this sense that we can refer to *news discourse*: the system (and the values upon which it is based) whereby news organisations select and organise the possible statements on a particular subject. The study of news discourse should consider not only issues which have an influence on the content of news – such as the selection criteria employed to distinguish between 'an event' and 'news' (news values) and the logic which underwrites such selection criteria (costs of news gathering, writing for the audience, partisan commitments) – but also the form, the organisation, the presentation and the consumption of news, both at textual and intertextual levels.

Of course, it goes without saying that journalism produces texts – texts that can be analysed using the same linguistic categories, tools and concepts that can be used to study any other type of text. This observation, alongside the more general and frequently commented upon 'linguistic turn' in social scientific enquiry, has resulted in a swathe of research which implicitly (and on occasion explicitly) suggests that newspaper texts can be studied in the same way as magazine texts, or in the same way as musical lyrics, political speeches or a range of other discourse genres. I object profoundly to such an approach: newspaper journalism is *not* the same as any other discourse genre. Put quite simply (indeed some would say rather crudely): How many singers were hounded, bullied and harassed by military or governmental officials in order to stop them doing their job? How many were killed because of their job? There remains something about journalism that provokes such a reaction. And while I recognise that violence of this kind does not characterise the working conditions of most journalists in 'the West', the same is not true of everywhere in the world.[1] Any analytical approach – particularly from academics who claim to be *discourse* analysts – that 'concertinas' together discursive genres and subjects them to a 'one size fits all' linguistic analysis is not only doing its readers, but also the field of (critical) discourse analysis, a great disservice.

Each discursive genre is the product of a constellation of discursive practices that make it, to the greater extent, unique. Aside from certain differences that can be identified through first-level analysis of newspaper texts (e.g. the unique sequencing of propositions characteristic of news reporting and the somewhat specific representations of events, states and processes), newspaper discourse fulfils particular functions; has been created in accordance with particular production techniques and in specific institutional settings;

is marked by particular relationships between other agencies of political, judicial and economic power; is characterised by particular interpersonal relations between writer and reader; and is consumed, interpreted and enjoyed in ways that are specific. Looking solely at 'news reporting' – one of several text genres that make up newspaper discourse – news 'is the end-product of a complex process which begins with a systematic sorting and selecting of events and topics according to a socially constructed set of categories' (Hall *et al.*, 1978: 53). As Fairclough (1995a: 204) puts it, journalistic texts are 'the outcome of specific professional practices and techniques, which could be and can be quite different with quite different results'. This chapter examines some of these professional and institutional practices of journalism and their relevance to the study of news discourse.

Markets or citizens? Conceptualising the audience

Gandy (2000) shows that there are many different ways that the audience can be theorised. For example, the audience can be conceptualised as 'a public', with rights to information; indeed, this is the view adopted by those suggesting that journalism plays a 'watchdog' role in society. Or, the audience can be conceptualised as a victim, being either directly or indirectly harmed by what the journalists write and say; this is the view adopted by those suggesting that journalism plays a 'lapdog' role. Alternatively, the audience can be viewed in a variety of other ways, for example as a speech community (sub-) culture or diaspora (see Gillespie, 1995; Sreberny, 2000). Here, I'm only going to sketch out two approaches to the audience: the idea of the audience as a consumer and the idea of the audience as a commodity.

The audience as consumer

Of course, we know that newspapers are businesses. The vast majority of news producers exist to make profit and, under the current conditions of capitalism, the continued existence of a news producer hinges on it selling its product (to its identified audience) and doing so in the most profitable manner possible. By such a view, news is a product – a product that must be made attractive or appealing to a market of consumers. And, so the argument goes, this will in turn overly emphasise stories that are amusing, pleasurable and engaging to these identified consumers, since stories that achieve 'audience appeal' form the basic, most fundamental gauge of what to put in the paper (Franklin, 1997). But, of course, there are a variety of consumers with different tastes and different preferences and these audience groups choose to consume different newspapers (within the limitations of the products on offer) on the basis of these preferences. McQuail (1994: 290) calls this kind of audience a 'gratification set', formed on the basis that it satisfies 'some individual need or purpose independent of the media, relating, for instance, to a political or social issue' or a need for specific information. The recognition of such a market engaging in the same consumer behaviour, in turn, encourages the creation and proliferation of options to satisfy these preferences. The effect of this proliferation of news media outlets on the total body of the potential audience has become known as audience fragmentation.

Audience fragmentation is the division of the available audience between ever-increasing numbers of media options. Faced with more and more choices, the audience has a tendency to disperse amongst the different media options, leaving each option with a smaller share of the audience. And, since the amount that advertisers are willing to pay is directly linked with audience share, the fragmentation of audiences has a knock-on effect, reducing revenue and resources. Audience fragmentation has not affected all news media equally; television has been particularly affected. There are now hundreds of channels available via satellite, digital and cable in addition to domestic analogue transmission, each satisfying the preferences of an audience, sometimes quite a niche audience and some doing this more successfully than others. In contrast, newspapers have hardly been touched by audience fragmentation. Although newspapers are currently suffering small year-on-year declines in sales and hence the total number of consumers, the *share* of the readers is relatively stable across and between newspaper titles. Of course, this is due in part to the costs inherent in launching and establishing a newspaper and in part to the fact that most papers are distributed in a specific bounded area. This stability has lead John Honderich, the publisher of the *Toronto Star*, to claim that 'more and more, newspapers are becoming the sole mass medium, particularly for advertising' (www.mediainfo.com) – a point that's especially true in a country like the UK with a genuine national press.

Drawing these two points together, the worry is that greater fragmentation of the audience will adversely affect the quality of journalism. Simply put, advertisers will not subsidise a news producer without an audience. And this pushes journalism towards increasing light, entertaining copy at the expense of more weighty examinations or more expensive long-term investigative reporting. This is because the idea of the audience as a market characterises the relationship between sender and receiver – or between journalist and reader – as 'a "calculative" act of buying or consuming, rather than a normative or social one, narrowing down the range of possibilities for much public communication' (ibid.: 287). Such instrumentalism can have a detrimental effect on journalism, undermining 'the constitutive values of journalism such as truth telling' (Harcup, 2002: 108). Effectively, when journalism becomes simply another 'media product', manufactured according to the bottom line, it leaves little room for ethics, professionalism, objectivity and the things that constitute *journalism*.

The audience as commodity

Of course, the commercial logic of the newspaper market is twofold: newspapers don't just sell copies they also sell advertising space, and the significant links between newspaper titles (and types), capital generated from advertising revenue and the audience cannot be overlooked. Both broadcasters and newspapers 'are in the business of producing *audiences*. These audiences, or means of access to them, are sold to advertisers' (Owen and Wildman, 1992: 3; cited in Gandy, 2000: 48). When journalism is viewed in such a way, the audience shift from being the *consumers* of a product, to being the *product themselves*, particularly within news organisations marketed towards the richer social classes, in which advertising is a more significant source of revenue. As Curran and Seaton (1997: 37) have argued, organisations that conform to the 'marketing requirements of advertisers' obtain large external subsidies that they 'can then spend on increased editorial outlay and promotion in order to attract new readers'.

A more worrying corollary of audience fragmentation, therefore, is this *segmentation* of the audience into more or less attractive audience markets. While audience fragmentation occurs 'bottom–up' as a consequence of increased choice between media options, audience segmentation occurs 'top–down' when media producers attempt to corral a target audience in order to attract advertising revenue. This target audience can be defined in a variety of ways – by age, gender, ethnicity or some other group characteristic – but it is always related to buying power: to *class*. As suggested above, advertisers are not interested in the size of an audience *per se*, or in the share (or 'fragment') of the total audience that a newspaper or television station attracts. The issue isn't that 2 million people buy a particular newspaper, or that 1 million people subscribe to a particular satellite station – numbers are useful but not the be-all and end-all; what matters is the *nature* of the segment that is attracted. Certain products only sell to certain segments of the population and hence only need to be advertised to these segments: BMW cars need only be advertised to the rich, while dodgy loan companies need only be advertised to the poor. What is crucial to understand 'is that not all audiences are equally valued in the market. If particular audience segments that are attracted (or produced) by particular content are undervalued in the market, advertisers will be unwilling to pay the same "cost per thousand" they would be willing to pay for more "desirable" audiences' (Gandy, 2000: 48–49). Schement (1998: 93) argues 'in the calculus of modern media, ethnicity has emerged as a potent determinant for organising media segments'. This is arguably the case, but only to the extent that Black audiences tend to be poor audiences. In every Western country, without exception, Black communities are significantly over-represented in the impoverished and ill-educated social strata, and media organisations earn more money by supplying a product that attracts the richer strata of the audience. This in turn encourages a preponderance of newspapers that satisfy the tastes and preferences of these richer audience segments – the middle and upper classes.

This preponderance of newspapers designed to sell to the richer social classes is made clear if we look at the range of national newspapers on sale in the UK. As most people are aware, broadsheet newspapers tend to sell more within the elite and upper middle classes, the mid-markets tend to sell to the middle and lower middle classes and the red tops tend to sell to the working classes, as shown by Worcester (1998) – see Table 4.1.

This table demonstrates that the five daily broadsheets are predominantly read by those in the old A/B social classes: the *Financial Times'* audience is 57 per cent of these top managerial and professional positions, going down to the lowest, the *Guardian*, which nevertheless boasts 39 per cent. The red top tabloids on the other hand show the opposite pattern, being predominantly read by those in D/E classes (unskilled manual and unemployed) and to a lesser extent, the skilled manual (C2).

Of course, this is evidence for what is already well known. It is more interesting, I think, to consider what else this demonstrates: Why do those in the A/B classes, who make up perhaps 20 per cent of the population, have five daily papers to choose from, whereas the working classes – the C2, D and E classes, who make up about

Table 4.1 Social class of British Newspaper Readerships

	Social class of readerships (%)			
	A/B	C1	C2	D/E
Financial Times	57	28	9	5
The Times	55	27	9	9
Telegraph	47	31	13	10
Independent	45	32	13	10
Guardian	39	33	13	15
Broadsheet averages	**48.6**	**30.2**	**11.4**	**9.8**
Daily Mail	23	32	24	21
Daily Express	22	31	24	21
Mid-market averages	**22.5**	**31.5**	**24**	**21**
Daily Mirror	7	16	37	40
The Sun	6	15	38	41
The Star	4	15	39	43
Red-top tabloid averages	**5.7**	**15.3**	**38**	**41.3**

50–60 per cent of the population – have only 3 dailies? The answer is obvious: wealth. Take these recent figures from the Inland Revenue (UK)[2] – Table 4.2.

This table shows that the richest 25 per cent of the population (in other words, the A/B classes, with a few C1s thrown in for good measure) own 74 per cent of the wealth in Britain. If you exclude housing collateral – in other words, if you only consider disposable income – this rises to 88 per cent. The table also shows the extent to which the massive disparity in the distribution of wealth has increased in recent years. Since 1996 – the year before the

Table 4.2 Relative poverty in the UK, 1986–2002

	%				%		
	1986	1996	2002		1986	1996	2002
Marketable wealth owned by:				Marketable wealth, minus housing owned by:			
Most wealthy 1%	18	20	23	Most wealthy 1%	25	26	35
Most wealthy 5%	36	40	43	Most wealthy 5%	46	49	62
Most wealthy 10%	50	52	56	Most wealthy 10%	58	63	75
Most wealthy 25%	73	74	74	Most wealthy 25%	75	81	88
Most wealthy 50%	90	93	94	Most wealthy 50%	89	94	98

Source: http://www.statistics.gov.uk

assumedly progressive 'New' Labour Party was voted into power in the UK – the affluence of the richest 1 per cent of the population has risen substantially: they now possess 35 per cent of the country's wealth compared to 26 per cent in 1996. Conversely, while in 1996 the poorest 50 per cent of the population owned 6 per cent of the country's disposable income, this has now dropped to 2 per cent by these latest figures. In short, the 25 per cent of the population predominantly buying and reading broadsheets in Britain own 88 per cent of the wealth. On the other hand, the C2, Ds and Es who Worcester (1998) demonstrates predominantly read tabloids – around 50 per cent of the population – own only 2 per cent of the disposable wealth, and hence are a far less attractive market in the eyes of advertisers and newspapers.

As John Westergaard (1977: 103) has argued, in a market system there is a reduction 'in the number and diversity of newspapers on offer, head for head of population, on the steps down from establishment and bourgeois public to wage-earning public'. In other words, the less money you have, the less choice you have when it comes to buying a newspaper written with you in mind. British national newspapers demonstrate this reduction in number and diversity very clearly.

Professional practices

The preceding section is, perhaps, overly pessimistic in its characterisation of the influence of the market on the output of newspapers. While acknowledging the low number of newspapers with a working-class target audience – and the total absence of a radical working-class national press – journalists work 'in a field of conflicting loyalties and duties: to readers, editors, advertisers, proprietors, the law, regulatory bodies, contacts, themselves and other journalists' (Harcup, 2002: 103). As O'Neill (1992: 28) puts it:

> Journalists, like other workers, are not totally passive in their attitude to their own faculties. They also have the capacity to resist the pressures of the market place. The constitutive values of journalism have some power through such resistance, despite the countervailing tendencies of the market place.

One way in which the professional values of journalism arguably resist the economic values of the market is in the development and application of journalism's codes of ethics.

Ethics

Ethics, in the most general sense, is 'the study of the grounds and principles for right and wrong human behaviour' (Sanders, 2003: 15). In relation to journalism, ethics is the consideration (by academics and journalists themselves) of what journalism *should* or *ought* to be doing. As Belsey and Chadwick (1992: 1) remind us, 'journalism remains an honourable profession, because it has an honourable aim, the circulation of information'. This is the proper function of journalism: to provide information to help us understand the world and our position in it, but as indicated above, there are many factors that militate against the quality of information provided by journalism. On this point, Harcup (2002: 103) argues that journalists are torn between an ostensible 'professional commitment to ethics and truth telling while at the same time being expendable employees expected to produce whatever stories are demanded in the marketplace'. Ethical questions focus on precisely this tension: How to enhance the quality of journalistic information in the face of the structural and financial pressures of the market?

While the specifics of journalistic ethics differ between country and profession,[3] all ethical codes contain variations on certain guidelines that aim to inform both an ethical *process* of newsgathering and an ethical *product* in the form of the news itself. Here I'll only discuss the products of ethical news reporting, as prescribed by four basic principles:

1. seeking and reporting truth;
2. acting independently, of sources and other journalists;
3. minimising harm;
4. and being accountable for their work (see Iggers, 1999: 23, 38).

Thus, the British National Union of Journalists states that journalists 'shall at all times defend the principle of the freedom of the press and other media', striving 'to eliminate distortion, news suppression and censorship', 'shall protect confidential sources of information', 'shall not accept bribes' and 'shall neither originate nor process material which encourages discrimination, ridicule, prejudice or hatred.'[4] Similarly, the International Federation of Journalists Declaration of Principles on the Conduct of Journalists states that 'Respect for truth and for the right of the public to truth is the first duty of the journalist', and follows this first clause by declaiming that journalists 'shall do the utmost to rectify any published information which is found to be harmfully inaccurate' and 'shall be aware of the danger of discrimination being furthered by the media', amongst other principles.[5] Other codes of practice also contain specific inter-pretations of these four basic principles.

However, the task of providing quality information, in the form of news reporting, is not as easy as simply 'sticking to these principles'. As Iggers (1999: 35) points out, while these codes of ethics 'are supposed to provide the basis for ethical decision making', in fact 'they embody some of the ambiguities and contradictions at the heart of journ-alism'. Without even going into the complicating details of specific codes, which contain many more clauses and sub-clauses than these four basic defining principles, there are tensions and conflicts even *between these four principles*. Most significantly, the code declaring the 'right to report' invariably goes up against, and sometimes runs in direct opposition to, the requirement to 'avoid or minimise harm'. From the perspective of moral philosophy, the first of these codes – the right to report – is a categorical principle; while the second – the requirement to minimise harm – is a consequentialist principle (see Atkin, 2000). Categorical principles are always argued from the basis of rights, duties and moral absolutes: something is presented as inviol-able or sacrosanct, despite rights always being subject to exceptions.[6] In contrast, consequentialist principles are always argued from the basis that 'morality is judged by its beneficial effects and that prin-ciples should always be weighed against consequences. Thus, we adjust and amend our moral behaviour in accordance with what we perceive are its effects' (Sanders, 2003: 20). An example should illustrate the way that these differing principles can stand in conflict with each other: as a journalist, would your commitment to freedom of speech and reporting the truth extend as far as a story that *may* cause harm? In such a case, would your decision to run the story be swayed by the individual (or *kind* of individual) who may suffer this harm? For example, would you pull a story if it may cause harm to someone in the public eye (say a celebrity), or to a child, or Gypsies, or Abu Hamza? What if the potential harm was a cumulative, and hence harder to detect, social harm – for instance, contributing to a general associ-ation of 'race' and crime or homosexuality and disease? In short, elev-ating the right to report without due consideration of potential harm can result in reporting that encourages social evils such as racism, sexism, homophobia and so on; but elevating minimising harm above the right to report can result in a muzzled or servile press. This is by no means an easy dilemma to resolve, since it goes to the very heart of much broader conceptions of the social responsibilities of journalism.

In addition to these more philosophical concerns, Iggers (1999) also points to problematic aspects of several of these key ethical principles in themselves. I'll only sketch out two of these here. First, take the code that requires journalists to act autonomously and independently of sources. The reality of the newsgathering process 'is an inextricable interdependence between reporters and sources' (ibid.: 40). Gandy (1982) has likened this process to a dance between reporter and source, while MacManus (1994) describes it as a transaction, in which the party with the greater market power 'may be able to dictate the conditions of exchange' (p. 74). Regardless, the process of newsgathering is such that 'Reporters must cultivate sources and are keenly aware that their future access to information depends on how they handle today's story. Sources, in turn, cultivate reporters' (Iggers, 1999: 40). This is particularly the case with local journalism, where the greater proximity of the journalist to the community they report on results in a greater awareness of the potentially negative effects of their work. While some may view this working reality as a positive influence (minimising harm), in fact it can inhibit the work of journalists (report the truth), who may feel a greater pressure not to alienate certain key (usually bureaucratic) sources.

Second, we need to consider accuracy – or, bearing in mind Fairclough's above point about how specific professional practices and techniques can always be different, the particular way accuracy is *interpreted* and *applied* in news reporting. Iggers (1999: 40) presents an example typical of the conventional journalistic interpretation of accuracy:

> A report quoting a Pentagon spokesman on the number of casualties in the invasion of Panama can be simultaneously completely accurate as a representation of what the spokesman said, but quite inaccurate as a representation of what actually happened.

An employee of *BBC Monitoring*[7] recently stated that his organisation operates using precisely this protocol: in translating international speeches and other materials for their customers, accuracy is interpreted as closeness to the original not correspondence with material reality (Chokri, 2005). Therefore, when the Israeli daily *Haaretz* claimed **Bush, Sharon at Loggerheads Over Settlements** the *BBC Monitoring* accurately translated and disseminated this 'fact', regardless of whether President Bush and Prime Minister Sharon were *actually* in dispute over the future of the illegal occupation of Palestinian territories.[8]

This point should not be taken to mean that I advocate inaccuracy on the part of journalists. Molotch and Lester (1974) argue that the news reflects the views and practices of those who have the power to determine the experiences of others – views and practices that *need* to be accurately reported for the news to have any value. However, an awareness of this discursive practice of journalism – that the views and practices of the powerful will be reported *by virtue of the fact* that they are the views and practices of the powerful – presents an opportunity for such powerful groups to use the news media as conduits for their propaganda. I will return to the issue of journalistic autonomy in the later chapter on war reporting.

Objectivity

Objectivity is a key defining value underwriting the practices of modern journalism and hence is an issue of perennial interest for students of journalistic discourse. However, on too many occasions the discussion of this key concept confuses dictionary definitions of 'objectivity' with journalistic definitions of objective reporting. For most dictionaries, objectivity relates to what is external to the mind rather than belonging to the consciousness of the perceiver; relates to outward things, uncoloured by feelings or opinions; and relates to that which is observable or verifiable. Objectivity does not mean this to most journalists, though as Dunlevy (1998: 120) states, 'some of the components of [dictionary definitions] may be built into journalism's definition'. Essentially, to file an objective report a journalist needs to distance him or herself from the truth claims of the report. Distancing oneself from the truth claims of the report is not the same as removing all value judgements from a report. Instead, it requires that the fact and opinion in a news report – that is, the *reported speech*, included in whatever form – needs to be that of people *other than* the journalist. For this reason, columns, editorials and other forms of news analysis will never qualify as 'objective reporting': the voice of the journalist is either too loud or too central for them to be objective.

However, this does not mean that an objective report is the same as a neutral report. Nobody could ever convincingly argue that news reporting (even 'objective reporting') is valueless. Indeed value judgements are built into the process of news making at all stages of the production process, through newsgathering, news writing, story selection, editing and presentation – all, of course, decided against a social and economic backdrop which values richer audiences more than poor ones. For this reason, an 'objective story' will never be one in which, as Hackett (1984) claims, facts are separated from values and journalists act as neutral channels through which messages pass. Indeed, to suggest that this is what journalists *mean* by objectivity is to create a straw man argument.[9] News reporting is inevitably value-laden – and, on occasion, is fundamentally biased – but this does not stop it from being journalistically objective. To explain how this can be the case, we need to explore journalistic objectivity 'by observing what journalists do when they are being objective' (Dunlevy 1998: 120).

As Tuchman (1972) observed, journalists use the practices of objectivity to fend off criticism. Such 'strategic rituals' (ibid.) locate objectivity not in the epistemic (truth) value of a report, but in the 'set of procedures that the reporter uses in order to produce those objectively true accounts' (Iggers, 1999: 92). Specifically, Tuchman suggested four procedures that reporters need to observe in order to construct an objective news report. First, the use of sources in the verbalisation of (competing) truth-claims. For instance, a politician may claim 'the British NHS is the best health service in the world'. Such a view is a judgement, not a verifiable fact, and an objective report would quote another source contesting this opinion. Second, an objective report includes supporting evidence in the form of background or contextualising information. For instance, a report on the threat of nuclear weapons proliferation may provide information on the ranges of specific nuclear ordnance, or their destructive capabilities, or the number of countries in the world with nuclear arsenals, in addition to the views of sources on whether proliferation was a 'good' or 'bad' thing. Third, an objective report will often use 'scare quotes' to indicate a contentious truth claim – or at least that the truth claim is not the reporter's. This strategic quotation is frequently used to ensure that reporting is non-prejudicial, as discussed in a later section of this chapter.[10] Finally, an objective report uses the inverted pyramid structure of news reporting and a narrative style that removes the authorial voice of the journalist. In the terms suggested by Phillips and Jørgensen (2002: 69), the first two of these strategic rituals relate to how reporters draw on already existing discourse, while the latter two relate to the organisation and presentation of their own discourse. Since the narrative structure of news text was discussed in Chapter 3, I will only discuss the use of sources and supporting facts here.

First, and most importantly, we need to consider who gets to speak in the news. Almost every study of news sources concludes that access to the news is a power resource *in itself* (see Cottle, 2000;

Manning, 2001; Richardson, 2006). In the UK, Whitaker argues that there are only ten sources routinely monitored by the news: Parliament, Councils, Police, other Emergency services, Courts, Royalty, Diary events (e.g. Ascot), Airports and other news media groups. Others such as Corporations, Trade Unions, Political Parties, Public Service groups, pressure groups and 'experts' are monitored less regularly, with members of the public coming in a distant third (cited in Fowler, 1991: 21). We should question why this is the case. As Blommaert (1999: 8) puts it:

> If some group or individual does not succeed in having their voices heard (or if, in fact, they don't even seem to have a voice) then the reason for this [. . .] usually has to do with slowly or dramatically emerged forms of inequality sedimented in the differential allocation of speaking rights, attributions of status and value to speaking styles, uneven distribution of speech repertoires and other historical developments.

A relevant factor in this 'differential allocation of speaking rights' is the reliance on the 'information subsidies' (Gandy, 1982) of powerful corporate sources. Such sources anticipate the criteria of inclusion used by journalists, tailor their news releases according to the news outlet targeted and develop news management strategies (including choreographed media events, 'spin' and outright manipulation) in order to gain favourable news coverage (Franklin, 1998). More specifically:

> The conventions of objective journalism have given rise to an entire industry of think tanks and policy institutes whose function is to give representatives of entrenched political or economic interests the credentials they need to serve as authoritative 'knowers'. Having such credentials gives these 'experts' access to the media (Iggers, 1999: 103)

In short, newspaper discourse has tended to be shaped by 'the elements in society that are powerful enough and organised enough to generate press materials, hold press conferences and otherwise garner media attention' (ibid.: 102). And this heavy bias towards 'the coverage of public bodies [. . .] towards the coverage and pronouncements of politicians [. . .] a bias towards the establishment if you will' (Harwood, in Iggers, 1999) is a direct result of the need for authoritative sources in objective reporting.

Second, the selection of supporting evidence in the form of 'facts' demonstrates bias, on two levels. Most obviously, the selection of facts is a subjective process involving choice between alternatives. Such choices tend to be shaped by the actions of propaganda and PR, as outlined above, and are bounded by the editorial policies of different newspapers, such that contextualising facts supporting one political perspective/interpretation tend to be systematically favoured over their opposites. For instance, in the hypothetical 'nuclear proliferation' example I referred to above, it is far more likely that a news report in a Western newspaper on the threat of nuclear weapons would support the idea of this 'threat' by using facts about the arsenals, ranges and destructive capabilities of *Iran's* nuclear weapons rather than those of the USA, the UK or Israel. However, a further more systematic bias is built into the current working practices of journalism. As Dunlevy (1998: 129) states:

> [. . .] because newswork is geared towards tight deadlines, facts must be quickly identified and verified. [. . .] When the facts [reporters] gather challenge commonly accepted views of the world they require higher levels of verification and substantiation. They might demand that each challenging fact be verified by more than one independent source (Tuchman, 1978: 85). Thus facts about the powerful are treated with more care than those about the powerless.

For instance, a story on British human rights abuses abroad will more typically present the facts of the piece as aberrations rather than the norm – as regrettable *exceptions* to the claimed benevolence and promotion of justice rather than as a *direct consequence* of the explicit decisions of Blair and his government (see Curtis, 2003, 2005). In this way, the facts that journalists both include and 'in their caution leave out [. . .] help to legitimate the existing power structure and the existing ways of seeing and doing things' (Dunlevy, 1998: 129).

Organisational practices: writing for the audience

As Iggers (1999: 100) argues, journalistic texts emerge 'from a dynamic that is shaped by a number of competing forces of differing strengths and directions'. One key determining force is the audience. In short, without a sense of the audience, there can be no selection of what to present *as* 'the news'. In the words of DeWerth-Pallmeyer (1997: 5), the audience 'is the backdrop against which reporters and editors consider questions of news value'. The consideration of the audience affects not just the choice of story but also the tone and style of its presentation. For example, one assistant news editor, at a Chicago television station, has said that in presenting the news

> You're trying to make the story meaningful to your viewer, so if you're talking to the economics professor, sooner or later, you're going to have to say in very polite terms, 'Let's cut out the college lecture. Tell my white-collar and blue-collar audience out there in very basic terms how this will affect them.' (Ibid.: 29)

Indeed, 'tacit understandings of the audience are imbedded in the news gathering process, in the news values they use, and in the technology they use' (ibid.: 34). This relationship, between a newspaper and its audience, is 'based on the fulfilment of audience expectations and the validation of past trust relationships, which in turn are dependent on legitimised and institutionalised routines of information presentation evolved over time' (Blumler and Gurevitch, 1995: 13). However, this certainly does not mean that this relationship remains static. Indeed, given the year-on-year decline in readership, there is a 'shared determination' for the press 'to reach out to new constituencies of readers and reverse the decades of decline (and unprofitability) suffered by newspapers around the world since the Second World War' (Peter Stothard, *Guardian*, 16 June 1997). During his time as editor of the *Independent*, Andrew Marr was remarkably open about the methods the paper employed to try to, at the very least, retain its readership:

> Those brightly coloured bits that go around the mastheads of most papers (though not currently us) are basically very simple come-ons. They say: sex, booze, films, cheap, sex, violence . . . and so on. We do something not dissimilar in our little panel below the masthead. The evidence is that these little come-ons work, sending subliminal messages even to people who think that they only buy a newspaper to discover the latest stage of negotiations between the Austrian Finance Minister and the Armenian Refugee Alliance. (*Independent*, 15 November 1997)

Writing from a discourse analytic perspective, Cotter (2001: 428) argues that a 'key aspect in the production of media discourse is the role of *the audience in relation to* the media producer'. Key questions that she suggests need to be asked about this relations include 'What is the role or position of the audience in the practitioner's mind? How does this influence creation of news text? How does it affect discourse structure, style choice, syntax or phonology? Whom is the practitioner writing for?' (ibid.) The relationship between newspaper and audience, between producer and consumer of news will now be explored in greater depth.

News agenda, news values

News values are the criteria employed by journalists to measure and therefore to judge the 'newsworthiness' of events. Whether produced by the *Sun* or the *Financial Times*, the news needs to be interesting or appealing to the target audience. News values are meant to be the distillation of what an identified audience is interested in reading or watching, or the 'ground rules' for deciding what is merely an 'event' and what is 'news'. Journalists use these ground rules to select, order and prioritise the collection and production of news and while they 'may not be written down or codified by news organisations [. . .] they exist in daily practice and in knowledge gained on the job' (Harcup and O'Neill, 2001: 261).

The study of news values has tended to take two broad forms: first, journalists and ex-journalists have provided lists of the kinds of qualities that they believe a news story should possess. For example, Alistair Hetherington (1985), a former editor of the *Guardian*, has suggested: significance; drama; surprise; personalities; sex, scandal and crime; numbers (magnitude of the story); and proximity. Second, lists of news values have been derived by summarising the themes of a sample of news reports and, working backwards, suggesting criteria which events need to show evidence of in order to qualify as 'the news'. The most influential list of this kind was offered by Galtung and Ruge (1965), based on their study of three international crises (Congo, 1960; Cuba, 1960; and Cyprus, 1964). Galtung and Ruge offered 12 news values which, they suggest, are employed in gauging newsworthiness and predicted that the more an event satisfies these criteria, the more likely it is of being reported as news. In turn, these news values were:

1. frequency (daily news needs daily stories);
2. threshold (the scale or intensity of the event);
3. unambiguity (whether the event can be easily described);

4. meaningfulness (the cultural proximity to the story);
5. consonance (events people expect to happen – e.g. violence at football games – or want to happen);
6. unexpectedness (the scarcity or rarity of the event);
7. continuity (follow-up stories);
8. composition (a balance of stories across the paper or news programme);
9. reference to elite peoples;
10. reference to elite nations;
11. personification (about or directly affecting people – human interest); and
12. negativity ('if it bleeds it leads!').

In a recent study of three British national daily newspapers, Harcup and O'Neill (2001) re-tested these news values and found that they were inadequate in certain respects. In agreement with Tunstall's (1971) criticism of the above list, they argued that 'by focusing on coverage of three major international crises, Galtung and Ruge ignored day-to-day coverage of lesser, domestic and bread-and-butter news' (Harcup and O'Neill, 2001: 276). Second, they argue that some of Galtung and Ruge's news values are a product of the way in which events are written about – the way that journalists *construct* news – rather than the characteristics that an event needs to have in order to be reported. Take the news value 'unambiguity', for example: 'most journalists are trained to write unambiguous angles to stories that may be ambiguous, complex or unclear' (ibid.: 277). On the basis of this appraisal, Harcup and O'Neill drew up a restructured list of ten news values which they suggest events satisfy in order to be selected as 'news': reference to the power elite (individuals, organisations and nations); reference to celebrity; entertainment (e.g. sex, human interest or drama); surprise; good news (e.g. rescues or personal triumph); bad news (e.g. tragedy or accident); magnitude; relevance (cultural proximity or political importance); follow-up stories; and the newspaper's agenda (both politically and relating to the structure of the genre).

Of course, these lists of news values suggested by both professionals and academics are very general. The precise manifestation of what these values *mean* to journalists sifting news from mere events is wholly dependent on the (imagined) preferences of the expected audience. Thus, the daily developments of the stock exchange are of significance to certain readers while daily developments in the lives of minor celebrities are thought significant to (perhaps) different readers. With this in mind, most research on news values examines the outputs of the news media and relates this to the target audience. While this research is undoubtedly valuable, it is also important to recognise that textual or journalistic meaning is communicated as much by *absence* as by presence; as much by what is 'missing' or excluded as by what is remembered and present. For instance, a recent report from the Glasgow Media Group (2000) shows that the majority of television news about the developing world concentrated on conflict, war or terrorism or disaster. Out of 137 developing countries, 'there was no coverage of 65 of them. Of the 72 countries that were mentioned, 16 were covered only in the context of reporting visits from westerners, wildlife events, sport or bizarre/quixotic stories (such as a round-the-world balloon travelling over them)' (p. 10).

Finally, we should recognise that news values change over time, with certain longstanding features of newspapers discontinued in line with the changing preferences of the readership. The demise of the 'Parliament page' is a good historic example of this (see Blumler and Gurevitch, 1995; Franklin, 1997; Negrine, 1997). At the start of the 1990s, British broadsheet newspapers printed faithful, albeit not comprehensive, 'Parliamentary pages' on a daily basis. Although coverage of parliament had been in decline throughout the century, the continuing existence of the parliamentary page 'confirmed the importance of parliament and MPs' (Negrine, 1997: 97). *The Times* was the first to jettison the page, and its departure has since been justified by the then editor Simon Jenkins:

> We are not there to provide a public service for a particular profession or, for that matter, for a particular chamber [. . .] Newspapers are about providing people with news. (Ibid.)

The discontinuation of the parliamentary page was self-consciously directed at satisfying the demands of a *particular* audience – perhaps the 'new constituencies of readers' mentioned by Peter Stothard above. The inclusion of the parliamentary page *did* provide 'people with news', just not the *right* people or the right *news*, as implied by the elliptical nature of Jenkins' second sentence: he states 'Newspapers are about providing people with news', thereby implying that 'people do not consider the parliamentary page to be news'. The parliamentary pages of the remaining British broadsheets were also subsequently removed, contributing to a general trend in the reporting of politics. Negrine shows that between 1986 and 1996 the number of political items in both the *Guardian* and the *Daily Telegraph* dropped by 25 per cent (1997: 98), a pattern echoed in both the *Independent* and *The Times*.

Missing the mark

Above, I wrote that news values are the (*imagined*) preferences of the expected audience. I did this for a specific reason: news values are, in a sense, guesswork. Of course they are based, as Blumler and Gurevitch (1995) put it, on a relationship developed over time, but because they *are* guesswork, newspapers can still miss the mark and sometimes spectacularly so. For instance, on 12 September 2001, when all other British newspapers led with the atrocities in America on the previous day, some dedicating over half of the newspaper to the story, the front page of the *Morning Star* read: **Unions Gear Up to Defend Schooling**. This story reported the TUC Congress' support for the National Union of Teachers and their fight 'to defend Britain's comprehensive schools from government attacks'. While no doubt an important issue, it was hardly the story that most occupied the world on that day – including the delegates at the TUC Congress. The story of the attacks on the Pentagon and the World Trade Center was relegated to a quarter page article tucked away on page 2. The editorial that day in the *Morning Star* (**Press Home Union Rights**) was similarly blind to world events. Even allowing for the fact that the paper is poorly resourced, may have already laid-out the page and hence may have found reformatting difficult and costly, this was a wildly eccentric decision presumably made on the basis that the paper is, as its masthead claims, the 'daily paper of the left'.

Similarly, reporting can backfire when the values of the audience are misjudged. For instance, on 23 September 2003, the front page of the *Sun* read **BONKERS BRUNO LOCKED UP**. The story covered the mental health problems of Frank Bruno – the British boxer and now part-time pantomime star – describing him as a 'nut'. The article (and the screaming headline in particular) was not only derogatory about Bruno but attacked the dignity of anyone with mental health problems. The story continued on the inside pages of the paper, under the subhead **Bruno is bonkers**: 'at the weekend it was claimed that he had started believing he was the racing legend Frankie Dettori'. The paper must have been aware that there would be a section of its readership that found the tone of the report offensive, but they completely misjudged the proportion. In fact, the reaction from the *Sun* readership was immediate and highly critical, flooding both the paper and early morning radio phone-in programmes with complaints.[11] In later editions of the paper, printed only hours later, the front page and in fact the whole editorial line on the story had been altered. Bruno was now described as a 'hero' under the headline **SAD BRUNO IN MENTAL HOME**. The following day, the *Sun* was evidently still trying to recover from its mistake. On the front page it announced a charity appeal 'to help people with mental health problems like boxing hero Frank Bruno' (**SUN'S FUND FOR BRUNO: Stars back our charity appeal**, 24 September 2003). As part of their attempts to make the problem go away, they also threw a £10,000 donation into their charity appeal and invited Marjorie Wallace of the mental health charity SANE to write 500 words on the problems of mental illness (**GIVE HIM THE TIME TO HEAL**, 24 September 2003). The episode demonstrated the central importance of judging the values and temperament of your target audience and the costs of failing to do so.[12]

Linguistic style

In any analysis of news text at the discourse analytic level, it is important to connect media audiences with the notion of linguistic style. Linguistic style is a concept that attempts to account for variations in the lexical and syntactic structures of texts. As Jucker (1992: 1) puts it, style is

a comparative concept in that it describes some relevant differences between a text or a discourse and some other texts or discourses [. . .] It generally applies to instances of real language, language that has been *produced* by speakers with their beliefs, aims and goals *in specific situations*, and *in particular physical, social and temporal environments*. (emphasis added)

Therefore stylistic variation is by no means 'free' or 'arbitrary', but rather should be regarded as a contingent part of the role that context plays in the formation of text and talk (van Dijk, 1988: 27). This, in turn, suggests that analysts need to relate stylistic variation in language to the social context and the social roles which people both symbolise and play in communication. In other words, the language that journalists use to address the audience (or reader) tells you something about the identities of both the *journalist* and the *audience* and *also* something about the assumed relationship between them. For example: the style employed may be chatty or more formal; it may be 'correct' or more colloquial; it may use specialist terms, slang or 'tabloidese' – words such as 'bonk', 'stunna' or 'rap' (meaning 'criminal charges') that you rarely see outside of newspapers. These stylistic choices suggest a relationship between the journalist and the audience, in terms of friendliness or distance, familiarity or formality, a relationship of equals or of the speaker taking more of a pedagogic role.

However, two very important points also need to be borne in mind. First 'media institutions typically do have explicit policies on at least some aspects of language use [so] when analysts look for ideological effects resulting from lexical and syntactic patterning in news discourse, it needs to be acknowledged that some textual regularities may be the outcome of explicit style rules rather than implicit assumptions about the matter in hand' (Cameron, 1996: 315–316). In other words, when Polly Toynbee of the *Guardian*, Colleen Harris of *New Nation*, or any other journalist repeatedly uses a particular term or phrase, this may be as a result of the policy of the newspaper they work for rather than the (political, ideological) assumptions of the individual concerned. Second, this does not mean that stylistic choice is empty of ideological importance. As Cameron (1996) points out, it should be acknowledged that

> style policies [...] *are ideological themselves*. Though they are framed as purely functional or aesthetic judgements, and the commonest criteria offered are 'apolitical' ones such as clarity, brevity, consistency, liveliness and vigour, [...] it turns out that these stylistic values are not timeless and neutral, but have a history and a politics. They play a role in constructing a relationship with a specific imagined audience, and also in sustaining a particular ideology of news reporting. (Ibid.; emphasis added)

A very short comparison of the style guides of *The Times* and the *Guardian* will illustrate this.[13] The *Guardian* has recently published its style guide for the first time as a book. It has been available online for some time, where they actually invite readers to comment on it. According to Ian Mayes (the newspaper's reader's editor), some comments from readers were apparently used to amend the paper's style policies, 'one of many examples of responsiveness to readers that make the stylebook participatory' (Marsh and Marshall, 2004: 8).

It should be pointed out that the majority of the entries of any style guide are made in the interests of consistency. Such entries take one of three main forms: first, they may provide the newspaper's policy on words which can be written in different ways, for instance the *Guardian* prefers 'machinegun noun; machine-gun verb; submachine gun' while *The Times* adds a hyphen for 'sub-machinegun', drops it for 'machinegun' and, presumably, does not entertain the idea that the word could be used as a verb. Second, entries provide the policy on commonly confused or mis-spelt words. For instance, *The Times* helpfully points out that journalists should write 'Magdalen College, Oxford; but Magdalene College, Cambridge'; the *Guardian* doesn't feel such an entry is required. Third, entries on consistency provide the policy when transliterating words from language that don't use the Roman alphabet – for instance, *The Times'* entry for madrassa reads: 'Islamic school. No h, two esses. Plural madrassas.' Guidance in the name of consistency, such as these entries, are interesting from a discourse analytic perspective. They are interesting, first, because of the manner of their description, demarcating *the words* to be used not the context of their use or to whom or what they refer. For instance, *The Times* states that 'the occupied territories' should be written lower case, but doesn't say what this noun phrase refers to; which territories are 'occupied territories'? Second, we need to remember that style policies policing consistency are made in the interests of looking after the brand – or, more derogatively, of 'keeping up appearances' – and are always maintained in the interests of the particular interpersonal relationship developed between paper and reader.

Of course, this doesn't mean that the brand and the relationship between paper and reader do not change. As Cameron points out in the quote above, style guides are often changed in response to social circumstances and changing discursive circumstances – that is, changes in the audience or a re-branding of the paper. For example, it is only recently that *The Times* have decided that the plural of stadium is *stadiums* and not *stadia*. This class characteristic is also indicated by the fact that the paper regards the terms 'Prince Charles' and 'Prince Philip' to be far too familiar – they state that journalists should 'avoid the familiar forms of Prince Charles and Prince Philip *at least until* they have been given their full designation of the Prince of Wales and the Duke of Edinburgh; even then, *prefer* the Prince and the Duke at subsequent mentions' (my emphases). Interestingly, this policy has been relaxed in recent years. In 2002, when I first printed off their online style guide, *The Times* stated that they should be given their full designation on first mention, then 'the Prince' or 'the Duke' on subsequent mention. What does this change tell us about the changing brand of the paper? What does it tell us about the changing class profile of the audience? These stylistic alterations reflect the changing discursive circumstances of the newspaper, being less characterised by establishment readers and less keen on being associated with such a demographic. That said, the paper also still feels it necessary to inform journalists that Sri Lanka shouldn't be called *Ceylon* unless in a historic context – and Ceylon changed its name to Sri Lanka in 1972. This is, nevertheless, a conservative paper, with journalists and readers to match.

Two more extended examples ought to reveal further differences between the identities of the *Guardian* and *The Times*. First: What do their style guides say about the use of accents on foreign words?

(*Guardian*) **accents**: use on French, German, Spanish and Irish Gaelic words (but not anglicised French words such as cafe, apart from exposé, resumé)

(*The Times*) **accents**: give French, Spanish, Portuguese, German, Italian and Ancient Greek words their proper accents and diacritical marks; omit in other languages unless you are sure of them. Accents should be used in headlines and on capital letters. With Anglicised words, no need for accents in foreign words that have taken English nationality (hotel, depot, debacle, elite, regime etc), but keep the accent when it makes a crucial difference to pronunciation – café, communiqué, fête, fiancée, mêlée, émigré, pâté, protégé; also note vis-à-vis, façade.

There are two major differences here: the use of accents on certain Anglicised words, and the number of languages which are to be cited with their proper accents. First, *The Times* expresses its conservatism through the forms of language it favours – including careful attention to the use of accents – and attempt to avoid any taint of trendiness, laxity or slipping standards. The *Guardian*, however, which likes to represent itself as politically progressive, will be more inclined to take a more relaxed view on these matters. To avoid 'fogeyishness' and take a more 'liberal' line on how language is used, they adopt a more 'democratic' outlook rather than an elitist (élitist?) display of knowledge that could appear pretentious or pompous.

Second, the number of languages given accents in *The Times* may have to do with showing off, since the accenting of words still functions as a sign of education, culture, sophistication and style to the

British: accenting more words demonstrates knowledge of languages and implies that your readers are also so knowledgeable. Again, interestingly the *Guardian*'s advice on accents has changed slightly in recent years. Reading from my copy of their online style guide from 2002, their entry for accents reads:

> include all accents on French words (but not anglicised French words such as cafe; exception: exposé to avoid confusion with expose), and umlauts on German words. Do not use accents on other languages.

Thus, in two years the *Guardian* have chosen to also include all accents on Spanish and Irish Gaelic words. This decision has had a knock-on effect and required a lengthy entry explaining the accents to use on Spanish surnames, forenames,[14] place names and sports teams (ibid.: 145–146). The reasons for this are unclear, other than the aim to make the language that the paper uses 'contemporary'. Perhaps Spanish is now considered a more contemporary language to the readership.

A final example – the respective style guide entries on swearing – is particularly instructive of the political views of these papers:

> (*Guardian*) **swearwords**: We are more liberal than any other newspaper, using words such as cunt and fuck that most of our competitors would not use, even in direct quotes. The editor's guidelines are straightforward: First, remember the reader, and respect demands that we should not casually use words that are likely to offend. Second, use such words only when absolutely necessary to the facts of a piece, or to portray a character in an article; there is almost never a case in which we need to use a swearword outside direct quotes. Third, the stronger the swearword, the harder we ought to think about using it. Finally, never use asterisks, which are just a copout

The Times, on the other hand, frames the issue differently:

> **Obscenities**: "four-letter words" and profanities should be avoided because they upset many readers. However, in direct quotes and where they are essential to the story, style obscenities thus with asterisks; f***, c*** etc. Always refer their use to the Editor or editor of the day for final ruling

It is interesting, first, that *The Times* labels such words as 'obscenities': this is clearly more judgemental than 'swearwords' and flags up how the paper should approach and treat them – they are obscene; they should be censored. 'Obscenities' can only be used in *The Times* when they are in *direct* quotations that are *essential* to the story; and then they can only be alluded to through the use of asterisks. However, in both papers' entries we again see the reader being used to justify the choice of the newspaper. It is in the interests of the reader that such decisions are made and, more specifically, in the interests of preserving the brand identity of the newspaper that attracted these readers in the first place. In the preface to the *Guardian* style guide, Ian Mayes states many of the entries – for example those that set out the rules for references to asylum seekers or mental illness – 'are descriptive of the *Guardian* ethos' (p. 9). More precisely, the authors of the guide write: 'house style exists to help us communicate with readers' (p. 13); it reflects 'the paper's values and the point of view of the people that we are writing about' (Marsh and Marshall, 2004).

Intertextuality

The concept of intertextuality is founded on the notion that texts cannot be viewed or studied in isolation since texts are not produced or consumed in isolation: all texts exist, and therefore must be understood, in relation to other texts. Intertextuality is central to the model of CDA proposed by Fairclough. In the words of Phillips and Jørgensen (2002: 70), Fairclough's model of CDA 'is based on, and promotes, the principle that texts can never be understood or analysed in isolation – they can only be understood in relation to webs of other texts and in relation to the social context'. This may be understood across two inter-related axes: in terms of internal and external intertextualities. Both these characteristics are of significant importance to the study of journalism.

Taking external intertextuality first: texts are only fully intelligible (or rather: their detailed, more complete meaning is only revealed) when contextualised and 'read' in relation to other texts and other social practices. In the words of Blommaert (1999: 5): 'Every text incorporates, reformulates, reinterprets or re-reads previous texts, every act of communication is grounded in semantic and pragmatic histories which are not simple and linear, but complex, multi-layered and fragmented.' A journalistic example of this is the running story. Franklin *et al.* (2005: 327) define a running story as news that generates 'further developments or fresh revelations, media coverage over a period of days, months or even years'. When we read the latest instalment of a running story, we do so in the knowledge that this *is* the latest instalment – in other words, we are aware that the text is a link in a chain. The existence of this textual chain is revealed in the use of discourse markers such 'another', 'further', 'additional' and modifiers such as 'new'. For example, in the headline **Palestinians and Israelis take new step on peace path** (*Daily Telegraph*, 18 March 2005), the use of the modifier 'new' suggests that steps have been taken on this 'peace path' before.

In recent years, the archetypal running story has been the invasion and subsequent occupation of Iraq. Despite the sometimes fervent attempts of the Bush and Blair governments to keep it off the front pages, the story has just kept rolling on. At the time of writing, the latest instalment of this story read:

> The US ambassador to Iraq left Baghdad for a new post in Washington yesterday, enhancing the mood of instability in a nation still struggling to put together a credible government. (**More instability for Iraq as US ambassador departs**, ibid.)

Two features of this lead indicate that this report is the latest in a string of reports on this subject. First, take the way that the noun *instability* is modified: the headline suggests 'More instability' while the lead states that the US ambassador's move has 'enhanced' the mood of instability. These are both variations on the same scalar implicature, which assume a level of instability from which an increase is possible. Second, and in a similar way, modifying the verb 'struggling' with the adverb '*still*' changes the aspect of the verb phrase from the present tense to the continuous present tense. Hence, this is the latest instalment of an ongoing process.

Finally, external intertextuality can also be signalled through the use of 'wh- questions'. For example, the headline **Jacko Boy: Why I Lied** (*Daily Mirror*, 16 March 2005) necessarily presumes that he *did* lie – as reported in the instalment of the story of the Michael Jackson molestation trial included in the paper the previous day.

Internal intertextuality: quotation and reported speech

As Leitch (1983) noted, 'prior texts reside in present texts' – indeed all texts consist of, or are composed from, fragments or elements of previous texts. This is particularly the case with news reporting, which must necessarily reproduce the actions and opinions of others. Thus, a news report may contain elements of a press release, or a quote from a source either involved in the reported action/event (information) or commenting on it (evaluation), or background information taken from the paper's cuttings archive, or all three of these text forms (see Fairclough, 2003). Of course, it is not enough to simply state that 'prior texts reside in news reports' without examining *how* this occurs. Taking just one of these prior text forms suggested above – reported speech – it quickly becomes clear that the way the speech of others is used is a complicated aspect of news reporting.

Reported speech is a central building block of news reporting. Whether publishing the pronouncement of some politician, a legal sentence given by a judge or the findings of some study, a large amount of the daily news in any paper is written in response to such speech events. The prior text of a source's opinion can be incorporated into the present text in a variety of ways (ibid.: 49–50); I have chosen five that I feel are most relevant to the study of news journalism.

First, reported speech may be included through *direct quotation*. In such as case, the exact words used are included in quotation marks, often with a reporting clause. Such reported speech appears so often in reporting that we can select any newspaper at random for examples. For instance, a report for the *Sheffield Star*, explaining why the city of Doncaster has a special place in the hearts of the band Human League, quotes singer Susan Sulley in the following way: 'Susan said: "We did two shows in England when we first joined, that were already booked, at Rotters in Doncaster and Liverpool. I was 17"' (**No place like Dome for Human League**, 11 October 2004). Such examples of reported speech are usually straightforward, since they (apparently) faithfully record what was actually said or written. However, as suggested above, the readers' interpretation of the quotation and the source responsible is inevitably framed by the reporting clause that the reporter chooses to employ. There is a world of difference between introducing a quotation with 'John said . . .' or 'John claimed . . .' or 'John revealed . . .' or 'John admitted . . .' or the wide variety of alternative verbal processes.

Second, reported speech may be included in news reporting through *strategic quotation*. Conventionally known as 'scare quotes', the reported speech, writing or thoughts of others are often placed in quotation marks in order to indicate their contentious nature. For example: **Jury hears father's 999 call admitting 'murder' of son** (*Independent*, 8 March 2005). The word 'murder' is taken from a tape recording of a call to an emergency services operator, in which a man described how he has just killed his son; it is therefore an example of reported speech and not the paper simply editorialising. The direct quotation of this man's call to the emergency services reads: 'I have just murdered my son. I have killed him with a pillow over the face. He is 10.' The report continues by stating that now the incident has come to trial, 'The former SAS soldier [again, note the referential strategy] admits manslaughter on the grounds of diminished responsibility but denies murdering [his son].' The fact that he killed his son is uncontested in this case; what is at issue is whether he *murdered* him; and because the trial of this man for murder was still active, the newspaper is required, under the Contempt of Court Act (1981), to strategically quote the word 'murder'.

Third, reported speech can be included in news reporting via *indirect quotation*. Here the reporter provides a summary of 'the content of what was said or written, not the actual words used' (Fairclough, 2003: 49). Examples of this type of reported speech are legion in the press. Taking a single edition of the *News of the World* (16 January 2005; all my emphasis) we find: 'Tory leaders are *pledging* to slash public spending by £35 billion' (**£35bn Slash and Burn**); 'Prince Harry was plunged into a new scandal last night after *it was claimed* he laughed at a sick joke about having sex with the Queen' (**Who'd want to bed Queen?**); 'Jackie, who *claims* to be 71 but is thought to be at least 10 years older, immediately *savaged* racing tipster John' (**Granbo: Motormouth Jackie takes no prisoners!**); and many more. In each of these examples, it is the verb chosen and the alternatives that were passed over that is of significance. In the first example the reporters could as easily have used 'admit' instead of 'claim' or 'pledge' (though in this case the tense would also have to be changed from present to future) but they did not and during analysis we should ask *why*. The verbal process chosen to characterise reported speech frames reader understandings of the reported event and, in some cases, this may be ideological. During the 1997 UNSCOM inspection stand-off, the verbal actions of Iraqi actors were represented as 'threats', whilst 'the West' and 'Western' actors 'warned' or simply 'said'. In the following excerpts, I have italicised the relevant verbal processes:

A senior Pentagon official last night gave a *warning* that any Iraqi attempt to shoot down US reconnaissance aircraft would be considered an act of war and be met with a military response. As Iraq renewed its *threats*, America *urged* the United Nations to implement tougher sanctions against Iraq. (*The Times*, 8 November 1997)

[. . .] a senior Iraq official *threatened* to shoot down US spy planes if they resumed flights over his country. A senior Pentagon official *said* yesterday that any Iraqi attempt to shoot down a UN surveillance plane would be considered an act of war (*Guardian*, 8 November 1997)

In both these examples, and in many others during this period, American verbal processes, 'which could be construed as "threats" or at the very least "threaten*ing*" are de-emphasised through the lexical choices of the journalists. In contrast, the actions of Iraq and Iraqi actors *are* labelled as "threats"' (Richardson, 2004: 165).

Fourth, reported speech can be included in news reporting via *transformed indirect quotation*. Like with simple indirect quotation, *transformed* indirect quotation dispenses with quotation marks, but it also drops reporting clauses like 'said', 'accused', 'alleged' and so on and replaces them with transitive action (e.g. 'discovered', 'revealed') or mental state verbs (e.g. 'believes'). For example, an article summarising the findings of a report into the NHS's cancer treatment states: 'A survey of 4,300 cancer patients by the National Audit Office *found* widespread improvement in services provided by the NHS since 2000' (**One in five cancer patients faces delay**, *The Times*, 25 February 2005; my emphasis). The use of this verb transforms the survey's reported speech in a significant way: it presents the survey as a social actor *discovering* a state of affairs rather than as a document that asserts the National Audit Office's (NAO) *opinion* on the state of the NHS. On occasion, the reported speech is transformed to fit with the agenda of the newspaper. Take, for example, the reporting of a meeting between President Bush and President Putin (Table 4.3).

The *Express* reconfigures the verbal process ('said') into a mental process ('wants') and in doing so enables at least two other important

Table 4.3 Reported speech

Direct quotation	Transformed indirect quotation
Putin loses his smile after lecture from Bush on democracy, *Independent*, 25 February 2005	**Putin gets chilly hello from Bush**, *Daily Express*, 25 February 2005
'Mr Bush said: "Yet democracies have certain things in common; they have a rule of law, and protection of minorities, a free press and a viable political opposition."'	'Mr Bush wants greater commitment from Russia to the rule of law and freedom of the press as well as support for democracy across the ex-Soviet states.'

transformations. First, the collocation of 'democracies' and 'a viable political opposition' in the direct quote is reconstructed into a desire for 'support for democracy across the ex-Soviet states' despite this not being explicitly mentioned. Second, the 'protection of minorities' in the *Independent's* direct quote is deleted in the *Express'* version. This absence is significant; the indirect version contains reference to 'the rule of law and freedom of the press' so why not the third clause as well? The reason, I believe, lies in the editorial priorities of the *Express* at this time: virulent opposition to immigration and against refugees and asylum seekers in particular.

Fifth, reported speech can be included through *ostensible* direct quotation. In ostensible direct quotation, the structure of the clause entails direct speech but is conceptually different from direct quotation, in as much as *it is made up*. Ostensible direct quotation is also different from simply being inaccurate direct quotations, though in practice the line is blurry. Why would a newspaper invent a quotation? Perhaps an invented quote sounded better than the real thing. Take this news report printed in *The Times*, for example: **Yes, I was a 20-franc tart. No, you can't be a Labour MP** (25 February 2005). The headline suggests an exchange between two people; but the exchange never took place in this exact form or using these exact words. The woman involved in the story – Christine Wheatley – did affirm that she had worked as a prostitute (described as an 'admission' by the paper), but not using these words. In the first third of the article she states: 'Yes, I worked as a tart. I'm not ashamed'; and it is not until the lower third that she adds that sex with her clients 'was usually only three minutes. I used to charge about 20 Fr.' The paper combines these two facts, and adds the entirely imagined response of the Labour Party (though she was deselected) in order to add impact.

The content of ostensible quotation is often such that we are intended to 'see through' the claim that the purported source actually came out with the quotation: the view is too direct, extreme or outlandish to have come from the source involved. This form of reported speech is frequently seen not only in tabloid reporting but also in satirical publications (such as *Private Eye*), where the disjunction between the reported speech and the identity of the speaker is meant to be humorous. Take the following headline, for example, taken from the *Daily Mail*: **There'll be no wedding feast, Charles. You're having a buffet** (25 February 2005). This headline ostensibly records the words of the Queen, talking to her son Prince Charles about the eating arrangements at his wedding to Camilla Parker-Bowles. Lower down, the report claims that 'the Queen has laid down the law over Prince Charles' wedding plans', except there is no evidence from the report that the Queen said what is claimed in the headline, nor any evidence that it was the Queen that made the decision.

In sum, reported speech is an intertextual issue for analysts, because it is evidence of a journalist taking information, opinion and so on from a prior text and embedding it in another. As Fairclough (2003: 51) points out, 'in the case of reported speech, writing or thought, there are two inter-connected issues to address'. First, we need to consider 'the relationship between the [quote] and the original (the event that is reported)' (ibid.). In whatever form it takes (direct, indirect, transformed, etc.), a quote may be more or less accurate to the original speech event it professes to report. In analysis it is useful to imagine a progressive line of accuracy with direct quotation at one end, moving through indirect speech and with ostensible direct quotation at the other: the further away from direct quotation that reported speech moves, the greater the interpretative influence of the reporter is and hence the greater the potential for distortion or misrepresentation. Second, we need to consider 'the relationship between the [quote] and the rest of the text in which it occurs' (ibid.). An awareness of this relationship is particularly important given the ability of powerful individuals and groups to shape reporting agendas and the partisan nature of British newspapers.

Using texts: press agency copy

Finally for this chapter, we need to bear in mind that some prior texts arrive at newsrooms as fully formed news reports. Press agencies such as Reuters, the Press Association (PA), Agence France Presse (AFP) and others sell 'copy' to subscribing newspapers, broadcasters and other interested parties. News agency reports are sometimes included in the newspaper in a form so close to the original that the news agency responsible is 'bylined' at the top of the article. Even in such circumstances, news agency reports are rarely included verbatim, but are edited in accordance with the specific requirements of the newspaper, including stylistic, political and simple 'spatial' requirements (van Dijk, 1988). On occasion, two different newspapers print versions of the same news agency report. Recognising and recording this when it occurs offers an opportunity to analyse how newspapers with different audiences, identities, political commitments and hence editorial policies mediate the information they receive.

Table 4.4 compares an instance where two newspapers printed a news report about the UNSCOM weapons inspection programme in Iraq, based on the same *Associated Press* (*AP*) wire copy. Both articles were printed on the same day, 6 October 1997, in the 'liberal' British broadsheet newspapers the *Guardian* and the *Independent*. The articles are transcribed chronologically, with matching or corresponding paragraphs numbered and positioned next to each other for ease of reference. The following rules of transcription apply:

- text with no highlight: identical text in both articles
- text highlighted in grey shading : stylistic differences (lexis or syntax) in paragraphs of identical or comparable textual position
- text in *italics*: textual elements not present in the opposite text.

Table 4.4 Newspaper utilisation of an AP press release

Row	*Independent*, 6 October 1997	*Guardian*, 6 October 1997
1	**UN anger as armed gang launches grenade attack on oil-for-food HQ in Baghdad**	**Gunmen attack Baghdad's UN oil-for-food office**
2	Four gunmen hurled grenades and fired bullets at an office of the UN oil-for-food agency in *the capital* Baghdad, *destroying and* damaging at least three vehicles in the compound, officials said.	Four *unidentified* gunmen hurled grenades and fired bullets at an office of the United Nations oil-for-food programme in Baghdad, damaging at least three vehicles in the compound, officials said *yesterday*.
3	No one was injured except one of the attackers and taken into custody by the Iraqi army, said a UN statement *sent to Cairo*. The remaining three gunmen fled, *it said*.	No one was injured except one of the attackers, who was taken into custody by the Iraqi army, a UN statement said. The other gunmen fled.
4	The attack was on Saturday night at the World Health Organisation's headquarters in Baghdad, which houses an office for UN officials monitoring the oil-for-food programme. *According to preliminary reports the four men lobbed grenades and also opened fire at the WHO building.*	The attack happened on Saturday night at the World Health Organisation's headquarters in Baghdad. It has an office for UN officials responsible for distributing medicines in northern Iraq under the oil-for-food programme.

Table 4.4 Newspaper utilisation of an AP press release (*continued*)

Row	*Independent*, 6 October 1997	*Guardian*, 6 October 1997
5	Eric Falt, spokesman for the oil-for-food programme, told the Associated Press in Dubai that the attack came after office hours and only guards were present in the building.	Eric Falt, spokesman for the oil-for-food programme, said in Dubai that the assailants threw three grenades and fired at the building.
6	*The UN's humanitarian co-ordinator in Baghdad, Denis Halliday, condemned the attack, the first ever at a UN building in Iraq, the statement said. 'It is the Iraqi government's responsibility to protect UN personnel and property against any harm and Mr Halliday has asked for an urgent meeting at the highest levels with the Iraqi leaders in order to express his concern', said the statement.*	
7	*No one claimed responsibility for the attack.*	
8	Iraq has been under UN sanctions banning the sale of oil, *its economic mainstay*, since its 1990 invasion of Kuwait. *But a special* UN programme, *put in place in December 1996*, allows Iraq to sell $1 billion of crude every 90 days to buy *needed* food and medicine under UN supervision.	Iraq has been banned from selling oil, under sanctions since its 1990 invasion of Kuwait. A UN programme allows Iraq to sell $1 billion of crude every 90 days to buy food and medicine under UN supervision.
9	*The WHO building is located in the al-Wahda district, where an Iranian opposition group in exile is based.*	

At the first glance of Table 4.4, the two articles wired from *AP*, and subsequently printed in the newspapers, appear remarkably similar. The ordering of the paragraphs in both articles, for example, is for the most part identical, following the standard schematic structure of *lead*, *episode* and *event*, with the event being subdivided into *setting*, *actors*, *action* (physical and verbal) and *background* (see Bell, 1991; van Dijk, 1988). In addition, the ordering of clauses within the paragraphs are identical: differences between the two newspapers' reports only exist in clauses which have been either added or deleted, or in clauses which have been altered to conform to stylistic or textual requirements. These similarities should not be that surprising given that both articles are bylined to *AP*; it is in the *differences* between the two reports that our real interest should lie.

The differences in the phrasing of the two reports (shaded sections) provide interesting evidence regarding the stylistic and political preferences of the newspapers. On occasion these differences appear at first glance to be quite arbitrary. For example, the *Independent* refers to the 'UN oil-for-food *agency*' in row 2 but it's referred to as a 'programme' throughout the rest of the article; row 2 of the *Guardian*'s report also refers to the 'UN oil-for-food *programme*'. Similarly in its headline, the *Independent* refers to an 'oil-for-food *HQ*' as opposed to the *Guardian*'s contrasting 'oil-for-food *office*'. Lower down in the article the *Independent* switched back to referring to an 'office' (see rows 2 and 4) like the *Guardian* article. These changes only occurred in single clauses, suggesting that the newspaper's style guide did not dictate the alterations. That these anomalies in the *Independent* report occurred in the article's leader (headline and first paragraph) suggests that the *Independent* wanted to open their article by foregrounding the 'importance' and 'authority' of UN activities in Baghdad and of the building which was attacked: an 'agency' not a 'programme'; a 'HQ' not an 'office'. These choices increase the *intensity* of the reported actions in the *Independent*'s report, which in turn increases the rhetorical weight behind their reading of events in the headline: that the UN are 'angry'. This scale is also indicated in row 8, where the *Independent* refers to 'a *special* UN programme' whilst the *Guardian* simply refers to 'a UN programme'.

Other stylistic differences are the result of a number of textual features. First, there are syntactic variations, for example between active, passive and nominalised constructions. In row 3 the *Independent* opts for the inverted construction 'said a UN statement' in order to include the qualifying prepositional phrase 'sent to Cairo'. The *Guardian* omits this prepositional phrase and uses the active construction 'a UN statement said'. Second, and related to this, these differences in transitivity appear to conceal elements of the event, or the background to the event being reported. In row 9 for example, the *Independent* states that the bombed UN office housed 'UN officials *monitoring* the oil-for-food programme', whilst in the corresponding *Guardian* account, the same office houses 'UN officials *responsible for distributing medicine in northern Iraq under* the oil-for-food programme'. Similarly, in row 5 the *Independent* states that Eric Falt '*told the Associated Press* in Dubai' whilst the *Guardian* deletes the agency's role stating that Eric Falt '*said* in Dubai'. Third, differences exist for reasons of economy: in row 3, the *Independent* writes 'The *remaining three* gunmen' whilst the *Guardian* writes 'The *other* gunmen'. And fourth, differences exist due to grammatical error: in row 3 the *Independent* wrote 'and taken into custody' and the *Guardian* corrected this to 'who was taken into custody'; in row 4, the *Independent* wrote 'The attack *was* on Saturday night' whilst the *Guardian* corrected this to 'The attack *happened* on Saturday night'.

The fifth and largest form of stylistic difference between the articles occurs in row 5, where the two newspapers credit 'Eric Falt, spokesman for the oil-for-food programme' with wildly divergent quotes. Both are examples of indirect quotation, but the prior speech attributed to Falt is so different in the two papers that it is unclear whether they should be 'shaded' or 'italicised' in the transcription. The *Independent* indirectly quotes him saying, 'the attack came after hours and only guards were present in the building', whilst the *Guardian* indirectly quotes 'the assailants threw three grenades and fired at the building'. Here, Falt's words are being used by the two newspapers to perform slightly different functions in their reports. Essentially in both cases the source is being used to provide more information on the event being reported (which is why they are still shaded, indicating stylistic differences rather than absences): the *Guardian* uses Mr Falt to provide more information on the *action*, specifically the form that the attack took; the *Independent,* which had already provided further information on the form of the attack in the previous paragraph (row 4), opts to use Mr Falt to provide more information on the *setting*, specifically the time of the attack. This suggests that a hierarchy of action exists in these articles, whereby the form of violence (in this case a 'grenade attack') was thought more worthy of expansion than the context: that is, the 'what' of this event was considered more newsworthy than the 'where' and 'when'.

The italicised sections of the transcript indicate material missing from the report in the opposite column. Such material is included (or omitted) for a number of reasons. First, it is included in order to provide additional contextualisation, such as in row 2, where the *Independent* writes 'in *the capital* Baghdad' whilst the *Guardian* writes 'in Baghdad'. Here the *Guardian* assumes that their readers hold a level of knowledge that the original report from *AP* does not;

editing out the modifier 'the capital' also saves space. Second, as suggested above, the *Independent* uses material to further increase the 'scale' of the reported actions. In row 2, for example, the *Independent* describes the result of the attack as '*destroying and* damaging [. . .] vehicles' whilst the *Guardian* describes the grenades 'damaging [. . .] vehicles'; and in row 8 the *Independent* describes oil as Iraq's '*economic mainstay*' that is sold in order 'to buy *needed* food'. These additions support the 'amplification' of the reported action, present across the *Independent* article.

Row 6 represents the largest section of text printed by only one of the newspapers – in this case included by the *Independent*. It is the inclusion of this paragraph that provides the majority of support for the implicit claim, made in the *Independent*'s headline, that the UN is *angry*. The paragraph suggests that 'Denis Halliday *condemned* the attack', without which the direct quote that followed would appear far less confrontational. His statement actually '*asks for an urgent meeting* at the highest levels with the Iraqi leaders *in order to express* [. . .] *concern*'. The *Guardian*'s headline, on the other hand, fore-grounds the event itself – 'Gunmen attack Baghdad's UN oil-for-food office' – as opposed to the (UN) reaction to and evaluation of the event; hence the response of Denis Halliday is superfluous.

On one interesting occasion, the *Guardian* states in row 2 that the gunmen are '*unidentified*', enabling their article to dispense with the statement '*No one claimed responsibility for the attack*', included in row 7 of the *Independent*'s report. At first this transformation appears to follow a simplification–generalisation rule (see van Dijk, 1988: 32), but it is in fact a little more complicated. These clauses are both directed at fulfilling the 'who' criterion of journalism – 'who was involved in the action?' – a question which was, at that point, unknown. In the *Guardian*, the burden of proof appears to rest with the *AP* journalist and the newspaper that were unable to *identify* the gunmen; in the *Independent*, the burden of proof appears to rest with the gunmen themselves, who have not identified themselves by *claiming responsibility* for the attack. What the *Independent* version implies therefore is that the gunmen *ought* to have claimed respons-ibility. In addition, by suggesting that the gunmen have not 'claimed responsibility', the possibility that the *Independent* actually 'knows' who was responsible is not ruled out. This enables the newspaper to 'point the finger' at possibly guilty parties, for example in row 9, where they claim: 'The WHO building is located in the al-Wahda district, where an Iranian opposition group in exile is based.' The inclusion of this material implies its pertinence to the event being discussed, which, when combined with the 'vacuum of agency' left by the gunmen not claiming responsibility, acts to implicate the unnamed 'Iranians'. This implication is unavailable to the *Guardian*, since they admit that they, like everybody else involved, have not or cannot identify the gunmen.

In summary: as stated at the onset of the analysis above, due to the identical source material and the comparable intended audiences of the two newspapers (in terms of educational, political and class characteristics), the articles appear remarkably similar. Second, the additions to the *Independent* article – particularly the Halliday paragraph – reframe the report to include the reaction of the UN to the event to a much greater extent than in the *Guardian* article. Ignoring more prosaic concerns such as space, this appears to have been the primary reason for such differences in both the reports' headlines and the 'angle' on the event presented by the two newspapers.

Summary

In this chapter, I have introduced some of the discursive practices of newspaper journalism. That is, the processes that journalists use to construct news texts for an identified (or imagined) target audience. Such practices can be conceptualised as a series of 'levels of analysis', from a broad macro-analysis of economic factors, through organisational and professional considerations, and down to the way that news-texts are assembled using fragments of prior texts, such as press releases and press agency reports. Any consideration of discursive practices, therefore, needs to consider the relationship between each level of analysis and the *production* and *consumption* of news. Second, and as important, analysis of the discursive practices of newspapers needs to consider the way that production and consumption of journalism are fundamentally inter-related. News is produced with an assumed audience in mind – their class, their education attainment, their values and preferences and so on. In turn, news is read (consumed) with the producer in mind – the 'brand' of the paper, its politically partisan commitments, its (news) values and so on. The news-text needs to be viewed in the context of this dialectical process of production and consumption.

However, this picture of news discourse – as a dialectic relationship between producer and consumer – is only partial. Newspapers do not exist in a social vacuum, but also, as Gerbner (1958: 488) put it, 'reflect physical and social qualities of communicating agencies (publishers) and their relationships to other systems'. With this in mind, our discussion now turns to an examination of the social practices of newspapers, or the relation of news discourse to other social institutions and wider social factors.

Social Practices: Journalism and the Material World

Introduction

This chapter expands and discusses the final third of the proposed model of CDA: social practices. Social practices cover the structures, the institutions and the values that, while residing outside of the newsroom, permeate and structure the activities and outputs of journalism. In a little more detail, when analysing the social practices of discourse, we need to consider: economic practices, such as the mode and relations of production, the class composition of the audience and their relative value to other agencies such as advertisers; political practices, such as the structuring influences of political and legal institutions; and ideological practices, such as the role of journalism in spreading and supporting social values and the relationship of such social values to wider structured social inequalities. Social practices surround and shape the work of journalists, meaning that an analysis of the social practices of newspaper discourse requires the analyst to look outside the text and examine the relationships between journalism and the social formation as a whole.

The study of the social practices of news discourse assumes a dialectical relationship between society and journalism. In other words, a two-way relationship between the social world and journalism, in which both affect each other: the world acting on journalists and journalists acting on the world. Society influences the work of journalists in a great variety of ways, from the constitutive effects of ideology, social structures, social power, other agencies and institutions to the values and preferences of the target audience.

However this constitutive influence does not go unchecked by journalism as a profession or by journalists as workers: there may be a certain resistance to such structuring structures on the part of journalists – like with all of us. While operating within structurally determined limits, journalists – both individually and institutionally – still have the ability to act as autonomous human agents. Hence, while their reporting practices are not completely open, nor are they completely controlled by social circumstance – and, as explained in the introduction, it is this degree of choice which enables critique.

At the other end of the discourse process suggested by CDA, journalists act upon the world, producing and reproducing social realities through either maintaining or transforming social beliefs. Here, again, we see that this discursive power does not go unchecked. Clearly 'society', in whatever way we may choose to define it, does not suddenly get reshaped in response to every journalistic text; there is resistance (or at the very least inertia) at the individual, the institutional, the political and the structural levels when faced with a call for social change. CDA is particularly interested in examining the role that *discourse* plays in producing, reproducing or resisting social inequalities. In the case of this book, I am most interested in examining the way *journalism* may have an effect on resisting or reinforcing relationships of dominance, discrimination and exploitation and the cases chosen for this chapter reflect this. My analysis of the economic practices of journalism focuses on newspaper campaigns and appeals, examining the way local and regional newspapers use populist, sensationalist but politically timid subjects to market themselves and hence increase profit. The discussion of political practices examines the influence that governmental forces and sources have on the content of the news. Finally, I look at the representation of class in newspaper discourse, and argue that certain key ideological themes, which characterise the representation of both the middle and working classes, help justify and naturalise the exploitation and inequality inherent in a capitalist mode of production. Such an approach should *not* suggest that these three levels of socio-discursive analysis are discrete and independent. Just as a full CDA requires us to examine discourse in terms of its textual, discursive and social characteristics, so too a focused socio-discursive analysis requires us to acknowledge and foreground the interaction and inter-relation between economic, political and ideological practices. It is this requirement that guides the remainder of this chapter.

Economic practices and journalistic discourse: newspaper campaigns

Newspaper campaigns are started explicitly in order to elicit a response from either the public or people in power; in other words, they are always aimed at *changing things* in one form or another. Newspaper campaigns are therefore particularly instructive of the political position of newspapers in a social formation – that is, the relationship between a newspaper and its readership, and the relationships between a newspaper and the rest of society. Campaigns demonstrate that newspaper discourse is a medium of power, and with this in mind, we should ask what kinds of 'things' they are directed towards changing, what kinds of issues they bring to the foreground and, specifically, their relation to wider iniquitous social relations. Where such relations are backgrounded, inarticulated or legitimated, newspaper discourse acts in ideological ways.

As stated in Chapter 2, ideology may be conceived of as a material practice. Ideologies are composed of matrices of beliefs, attitudes and practices that constitute ways of looking at the world and ways of acting in the world, that accept and naturalise the contradictions at the heart of capitalist society. In other words, ideologies help 'group members' act as if they share general aims, values, positions and resources. Every year in the UK, hundreds of local and regional newspapers run editorial campaigns and editorial appeals. When these campaigns connect with the concerns of the local newspaper buying public, they 'generate considerable reader interest' (Temple, 2004: 8). After all, the strength of a local or regional newspaper lies

> [. . .] in the service that it gives to its own region, a service which cannot be offered by newspapers published elsewhere. While a provincial must aim at being a complete newspaper it must provide its readers with news of their local and district affairs, in short, become their newspaper. (*Birmingham Post*, Centenary Edition (7.12.57), cited in Ross, 1998: 231)

Newspaper campaigns, therefore, provide an opportunity to create 'readership loyalty and identification by positioning the paper as an effective change agent' (Aldridge, 2002). In the words of the editor of the Ipswich *Evening Star*, 'We are community commandos fighting for the people of Ipswich' (Aldridge, 2003: 501). Second, and consequent to the above point, campaigns should be viewed as a method used by editors to attempt to improve the profitability of their newspapers. The circulations of local evening newspapers are characterised by a steady year-on-year decline. Of course, this is also true of the national press, but local newspapers find themselves in the inimitable position of having to appeal to a much more diverse audience than the nationals. While the audiences of the nationals are differentiated by class and by political commitment, local newspapers are only constrained by the geography of their distribution areas, reaching across boundaries of class, education and political belief. Campaigns represent one way of cementing this diverse audience demography, foregrounding the 'localness' that the readers have in common and obscuring any other social category. In addition, campaigns can provide cheap and controllable local stories. They help 'to fill space at a time when 'rationalisation' means fewer reporters to process a regular volume of [. . .] news' characteristic of a traditional 'courts and council' local press agenda (Temple, 2004: 8).[1] In short, launching a newspaper campaign offers a solution to both the operating and marketing problems of local evening newspapers (Aldridge, 2003). From a discourse analytic perspective, therefore, campaigns should be viewed as a reaction to the prevailing (capitalist) social practices and the discursive practices of the newspaper industry: newspapers, as products, are created and marketed in the light of determining economic forces.

For the purposes of this study, I turned to the British newspaper website Hold the Front Page (*HtFP*). *HtFP* is a useful resource for the study of journalism in the UK, providing an updated summary of the officially declared editorial campaigns currently running across the country.[2] Due to the number of campaigns, I limited my sample to a 12-month period (June 2004–May 2005) in order to keep it of a manageable size.[3] In the light of my above point about determining economic forces, it is interesting to first look at the campaign activities of these newspapers in relation to their circulation figures. Recurrently, the newspapers with the highest circulation losses (for the period July–December 2004, see ABC) also tended to be the newspapers that were most campaign active. Thus, the Bristol *Western Daily Press* dropped 4.9 per cent of its circulation and ran two campaigns; the *Nottingham Evening Post* dropped 5.3 per cent of circulation and ran three campaigns; the *Bath Chronicle* (−7.2%) ran two campaigns; as did the *Cambridge Evening News* (−4.0%), the *Liverpool Echo* (−4.5%), the *Oldham Evening Post* (−6.1%) and many others.

However, 'across *all* sectors except the expansive paid weekly papers' (where there has recently been some marginal increase), local newspaper 'circulations continue their steady decline' (Franklin, 2005: 140; emphasis added). In short, pick out any paid-for local newspaper and in all likelihood its circulation will be in decline.[4] Therefore, solely studying circulations does not provide a wholly reliable method of predicting how 'campaign active' a local or regional newspaper will be. For instance, the Sussex evening paper *The Argus* showed a 9.7 per cent circulation drop July–December 2004 (down to 38,361 copies) yet did not launch any campaigns. Looking at local and regional newspapers across the UK, campaign activity is exaggerated in certain regions, completely absent in others, and particularly exaggerated in certain newspaper groups. The East Midlands and the North East were the two areas of the UK that saw the most newspaper campaigns in the 12 months to May 2005. Tables 5.1 and 5.2 summarise the campaign activities of Evening newspapers in these regions.

Table 5.1 Evening newspapers in the East Midlands

Newspaper	Owner	Circulation	Circulation change (%)	No. of campaigns
Leicester Mercury	Northcliffe	84,419	−7.5	2
Nottingham Evening Post	Northcliffe	72,269	−5.3	3
Derby Evening Telegraph	Northcliffe	50,133	−2.4	2
Kettering Evening Telegraph	Johnston Press	27,536	−6.7	1
Lincolnshire Echo	Northcliffe	25,169	−4.5	2
Northampton Chronicle and Echo	Johnston Press	24,434	−5.5	0

Sources: Newspaper Society; HtFP; ABC; Northcliffe Newspaper Group

Table 5.2 Evening newspapers in the North East

Newspaper	Owner	Circulation	Circulation change (%)	No. of campaigns
Newcastle Evening Chronicle	Trinity Mirror	89,074	−1.5	2
Teesside Evening Gazette	Trinity Mirror	58,446	+0.5	3
Sunderland Echo	Johnston Press	47,184	−2.8	1
Shields Gazette	Johnston Press	20,967	−2.3	0
Hartlepool Mail	Johnston Press	20,719	+0.9	0

Sources: Newspaper Society; HtFP; ABC; Northcliffe Newspaper Group

Tables 5.1 and 5.2 demonstrate that campaigning is at least partially dependent on ownership. Newspapers owned by the North-cliffe Newspaper Group tend to be extremely campaign active, those owned by Trinity Mirror are less so while those owned by Johnston tend to ignore campaigns and appeals entirely. Local newspapers always have at least one eye on the editorial content of neighbouring papers. This is especially the case when newspaper distribution areas overlap – as is the case with all four Northcliffe newspapers in Table 5.1,[5] while the *Newcastle Evening Chronicle* is in competition to a greater or lesser extent with all the remaining newspapers in Table 5.2. Given that one of the aims of campaign activities is to demonstrate the dedication of a local newspaper to its readers – to suggest that the paper is fighting in their corner – it is necessary to keep up with the campaign activities of other papers in the region in the interests of staying competitive. In accordance with the general irrationality of a capitalist system, these campaigns are used to mark a paper out against its regional rivals, *irrespective* of the *ownership* of these papers. Therefore, even local newspapers that are doing comparatively well, like the *Teeside Evening Gazette*, are compelled to run campaigns to keep up with other campaigning newspapers in the region, despite this competitor (the *Newcastle Evening Chronicle*) also being owned by Trinity Mirror.

'Don't let them get away with it'

Given that campaigns provide the opportunity for newspapers to present themselves as 'community commandos', we need to question how the community is conceptualised and the kinds of fights that local newspapers take on. Table 5.3 lists the *HtFP* 12-month sample of newspaper campaigns by issue focus. In presenting the data, I have made a distinction between a newspaper *appeal* (a direct and straightforward request for money) and a newspaper *campaign* (activities in which money may be part but not the sole target of success).

While the campaign issues pursued by the regional press in this list may seem diverse, the vast majority accord with Johnson's (1996) suggestions for a successful campaign: they are defined in such a way that it is possible to get a positive result; possible to get a positive response from the readers; and possible 'to maximise sales and sponsorship opportunities' (ibid., cited in Aldridge 2003: 500). In keeping with previous research (Temple, 2004), 'health' was the most frequently observed campaign issue. Three quarters of

Table 5.3 Issue focus of appeals and campaigns, June 2004–May 2005

	Campaigns	Appeals	Total
Health	8	23	31
Crime reduction	18	0	18
Local Heroes/commemorative	10	5	15
Local amenities/services	6	4	10
Road safety/transport issues	9	0	9
'Local Pride'	7	1	8
Jobs/Pensions	5	0	5
Schools/education	4	1	5
International campaigns	0	3	3
Smoking bans	3	0	3
Asylum/race	2	0	2
Animal welfare	0	2	2
Total	72	39	111

these campaigns were in fact *appeals* for donations from the readership aimed at meeting a certain target; cancer charities were particularly popular beneficiaries of such charity, with some newspapers raising very large amounts of money in very short periods of time. For instance:

- the *Eastern Daily Press* (Norwich) announced that its Breast Cancer Appeal hit its £200,000 target in under a year;
- the *Somerset County Gazette* raised £485,000 needed to expand the county's cancer services in less than a year, proudly announcing this as the most successful campaign in the newspaper's history;
- *Swindon Evening Advertiser* upped the target of its cancer appeal to £1 million after it reached the original target (£600,000) a year ahead of schedule;
- 10 other newspapers also ran cancer appeals during this time period.

Such charity appeals tick all three requirements for a successful local press campaign: an objective and realisable target; a cause that few could argue against (who *doesn't* want decent cancer care?); and an issue that provides a sponsorship opportunity for the growing number of private hospitals to advertise their 'health care plans' (for instance, the Westfield Health company sponsors the *Healthy Living* feature pages in *The Sheffield Star*). Indeed, appeals of this nature actually provide the ideological rationalisation for the *existence* of private health care companies, since they repeatedly and insistently index the failure of the NHS to provide an adequate level of care.

Following tradition, the vast majority of newspaper campaigns during this period were 'responsive rather than proactive' (local editor, quoted in Aldridge, 2003: 500), responding to the material realities of the newspaper's distribution area. Thus, there may be an identifiable need for better cancer treatment in a local hospital, or a need for jobs in the region, or readers may have written in to the paper complaining about plans to scrap the local regiment. Newspapers aim at developing a relationship between themselves and their readers, in which the readers recognise themselves, their needs and their values in the paper's outputs and activities. Therefore, newspapers choose to launch campaigns that strive to alleviate the identified problem or preoccupation of their readers, since reader–paper identification of this kind encourages brand loyalty and hence will buoy up flagging sales. That said, this does not mean that the preoccupations that some campaigns aimed to address were not misguided or imagined. Take the frequent campaigns aimed at alleviating crime, for instance, which remain as popular as ever despite the fact that the actions of a newspaper, however impassioned, could *never* actually *reduce* crime. Crime reduction campaigns revolve perpetually around a central constellation of provocative subjects – vulnerability, social disorder, outsiders, youth and sex – and certain associated criminal activities. Looking at the sample: the *Newcastle Evening Chronicle* ran a 'War on Drugs' campaign, which was launched using a photo of a 21-year-old who died of a heroin overdose (social disorder; outsiders; youth); the *Maidenhead Advertiser* ran an anti-graffiti campaign called 'Bag a Tagger' against the 'yobs [. . .] defacing our town', as did both the *Driffield Times* and the *Oldham Evening Chronicle* (social disorder; youth); the *Leicester Mercury* campaigned to 'Ban the Cyberfith' to protect children from pornographic websites (vulnerability; youth; sex); while the *Sutton Coldfield Observer* ran a 'Safe Text' campaign, intended to 'alert parents and children to the dangers of text pests – following the conviction of a local paedophile who "groomed" a young girl for sex by bombarding her with texts'[6] (vulnerability; outsiders; youth; sex). The more that this central constellation of populist subjects can be combined in a selected issue, the easier it becomes for a newspaper to construct a campaign around it and the more likely this campaign will resonate with the readership.

Clearly, simply recording the issue focus of a campaign only tells you so much since, as suggested above, there are a number of different angles that a newspaper can take on a particular issue. With the above points in mind, it is possible to identify three ideological themes that guide the construction of newspaper campaigns.

Sensationalisation

A desire to connect with the concerns of the readers, and to do so in as direct and immediate a way as possible, almost inevitably pushes local newspapers to sensationalise a campaign issue. The usual approach relies on adopting more rhetorically tailored language to represent the identified problem. For instance, the name of the campaign may use alliteration ('Bully Busters', *Liverpool Echo*; 'Save our Sausages', *Lincolnshire Echo*), a newspaper may describe their activities using metaphors of war ('fight', 'crusade'), or pepper their justification for the campaign with scores of negativised or otherwise judgemental adjectives.[7] On occasion, however, newspapers adopt a sensationalist angle to an issue itself, with more objectionable results. For instance, at the start of 2005, the *Birmingham Post* (Trinity Mirror; −9.5% circulation) launched a campaign calling for funded fertility treatment for all. In explaining this campaign, 'the newspaper reported that one in six Midlands couples have fertility problems, but only 30 per cent of those who require fertility treatment have NHS funding' (*HtFP*, 25 January 2005).[8] The campaign, therefore, responds to a material need for better health service in the newspaper's distribution area and was purposefully aimed at attracting the interest of a younger readership group (traditionally under-represented in local newspaper readership). However the angle they took on this important issue was appalling: readers were offered the chance *to win* fertility treatment. A private health clinic (Midland Fertility Services) would choose 'the winners [. . .] based on current NHS criteria' (ibid.) and the paper would pay the bill for their treatment. Implicitly acknowledging the questionable nature of such a campaign, the *Post's* editor, Fiona Alexander, attempted to justify it by saying 'our duty as a newspaper [is] to inform and to educate, even if the subject is unbelievably still considered taboo in some circles'. Of course, her response is a highly strategic way of defining and hence countering any possible objections: it was not 'the subject' of infertility that is 'taboo' (a word that connotes 'fogeyishness'); rather, the approach that the newspaper chose to take on this important issue was unprincipled. The campaign was not only exploitative – literally using the anguish experienced by some childless couples to sell more newspapers – but also by directing money into the private health system, it contributed to the continuation of a system that privileges the needs of those who are able to pay.

Perhaps more seriously, since 2002 the *News Shopper* (Newsquest-Garnett, free weekly) has been running a campaign against anti-social behaviour called 'Shop A Yob'. The campaign has been highly successful, winning the paper the 2002 Newspaper Society Free Weekly Community Award and, the paper claims, receiving widespread support from all sectors of the community. Other newspapers that have ran 'Shop A Yob' campaigns include the *Hemel Hempstead Gazette*, the *Oxford Mail*, the *Manchester Evening News*, the *Liverpool Echo*, the national tabloid *The Sun* and many others, so in this respect the campaign is unremarkable. What marks the *News Shopper's* campaign out is what it calls 'its latest weapon in the war against vandals and mindless thugs – Shop A Yob *Bingo*' (*HtFP*, 26 May 2004).[9] Explaining the rules of this game:

> Together with London Central Buses, the paper is running four pages of CCTV images of more than 80 yobs who have caused thousands of pounds of damage to buses. Readers who can identify three yobbos in a row, or get four corners on any page, could win themselves a digital camera. (Ibid.)

Across the three-year campaign, the newspaper has referred repeatedly to 'yobs', 'scum', 'thoughtless scumbags', 'hooligans and miscreants', 'yobs and vandals', 'lowlife', 'the scum of our society' and other terms of abuse intended to mark out and represent the guilty as being so different to 'Us', so far removed that the only response possible is a form of post-modern vigilantism. So, what kind of person qualifies to be given such labels? Who receives such vilification? Looking at the newspaper's campaign website on one day,[10] 18 of the 23 mug shots are of Black men; 4 are of White men; and 1 is of a White woman. And this depiction of 'the scum of our society' is reflected in the campaign as a whole. Take this front page from the *News Shopper* (Figure 5.1).

This front page demonstrates the racialisation of criminality implicit in the campaign: every face is Black; every 'scumbag', 'yob' and 'lowlife' that the newspaper presents to its readership in this edition is Black. It is not unthinkable that the readership associate the newspaper's relentless and hyperbolic depictions of 'marauding criminals' with the Blackness of the faces on display, further supporting a prevalent populist association between Britain's Black populations and crime, disorder and anti-social behaviour.

Figure 5.1 'Shop A Yob' front page

Sentimentality

The second ideological current running through these campaigns is sentimentality – a tendency to represent an issue from an emotional perspective or to foreground emotional campaign issues. Taking each of these manifestations, sentimentality can first be instilled into local newspaper campaigning through choosing an emotional exemplar for a wider issue. Almost universally, this occurs through using children's illnesses either through selecting a children's charity or by focusing on alleviating the suffering of a particular child. For instance, the *Manchester Evening News* ran a number of fundraising initiatives in support of *Kirsty's Appeal* – a fund named after Kirsty Howard, which aims to raise £5 million to safeguard the Francis House children's hospice charity. Similarly, in three weeks the *Western Morning News* raised £25,000 for their *Sarah's Appeal* – a fund named after four-year-old Sarah Laslett, to 'ensure that pioneering treatment for a rare form of epilepsy in children can continue for another year [...] at Great Ormond Street Hospital'.[11] More structurally focused, the *Glasgow Evening Times* ran a successful campaign to save the Queen Mother's maternity unit and to maintain the unit's links with the Royal Hospital for Sick Children. A total of 156,000 petition signatures were collected, leading to the Scottish Executive reversing their plans to close the unit. Focusing purely on individual anguish, the *Chester Chronicle* asked their readers to donate money to fund a holiday for a 6-year-old boy with an inoperable brain tumour, and raised £11,000 in three weeks. All these campaigns use the illness of a particular child to raise money to help alleviate or treat the wider group of people who also suffer from the illness.

Second, sentimentality can be instilled into local newspaper campaigning through choosing a campaign topic that is, by its nature, determined by emotion. Such sentimental campaigns may lead on unquantifiable issues such as 'local pride', imply that 'things were better in the past' or explicitly argue that '*Our whatever*' is being ignored, downplayed or downgraded in an unacceptable way. For instance, the *Walsall Advertiser's* rather flamboyantly titled 'Brave New Walsall' campaign aims to 'improve the image of the borough and create a feel-good factor amongst locals'.[12] Explaining the campaign, the paper's news editor stated 'I wanted the paper to [...] raise the aspirations of local people so they would feel good about Walsall' (ibid.). During the period under analysis, the great majority of such sentimental campaign topics centred on the activities of soldiers past and present. In these papers' terms, every British soldier is a 'hero'. This eulogising is then rhetorically used as a campaign tool to ensure that either dead soldiers are properly commemorated, living soldiers receive their due recognition or local regiments continue to exist in order to bring future (*local*) glories. For instance, *The Northern Echo* ran a 'Forgotten Hero' appeal to raise £40,000 to create a statue commemorating the bravery of a Second World War soldier (strangely, a Canadian air gunner). In a similar vein, *The News* (Portsmouth) ran a campaign called 'Last Chance for Justice' calling for veterans of the Arctic Campaign of the Second World War to be awarded with a medal while *The Burton Mail* campaigned for a posthumous bravery medal for Corporal Russell Aston, a local soldier killed in Iraq.

In contrast to the first form of sentimentalised campaigning, in which the victimhood of children is rhetorically mobilised to provoke readers into making charitable donations, this second form emphasises the concerns and anxieties of older people. However, aside from this difference of focus, these campaigns share certain fundamental similarities. Most significant *'is that they could have been anywhere'* (Aldridge, 2003: 503; original emphasis). The claimed localness of the campaign dissolves when you realise that papers from Strathclyde to Somerset (and most places in between) are using cancer to sell papers or campaigning to commemorate their war dead. As Aldridge puts it, the recurring 'appeal to universal values' such as the health of children or adults' fear that their contributions and sacrifices are being made light of, 'generates a blandly consensual discourse of sentimentalised "insiders", with the demand that we identify with them' (ibid.).

Symptoms not causes

Finally for this section, the campaigns and appeals of local and regional newspapers focus almost universally on the *symptoms* rather than the *causes* of social inequalities. For instance, all the 'health' campaigns cited above aim to raise a certain quantity of money to buy needed equipment or to meet some other shortfall in the provision of health care in a newspaper's distribution area; none of them aspire to overturn the system of taxation and public spending that creates such a dearth of funding. Nor is such timidity limited to health campaigns. For instance, readers of the *Hampstead and Highgate Express* 'rallied round a budding actress by raising more than £1,500 in just a few hours to pay for her tuition at a top drama school' (*HtFP*, 13 September 2004).[13] The editor, Geoff Martin, added 'It's very heartening when readers respond so generously to an appeal' (ibid.) – and the result would indeed be heartening were it not so hollow. The borough in which this newspaper is distributed is amongst the richest in the country: 69.8 per cent of the residents work in managerial or professional occupations (compared to a national average of

40.5%) and the average weekly wage is £652.60 (again, compared to a national average of £475.80).[14] Assuming that only people in full-time employment contributed to the cause (97,000 in the borough), this means they gave an average of 1.55 *pence* to fund a single student for a single year of education. The idea that the *noblesse oblige* of a rich and successful (and under-taxed) population is held up as a shining example of a successful campaign is particularly disheartening.

To summarise: none of these papers consider the wider social or political implications of their preoccupation with campaigns that yield objectively attainable results; their provincial gaze necessarily means that they do not mention (let alone examine) the fact that not all areas of the country will be rich enough for the local residents to subsidise their own health care through direct charitable dona-tions; nor do they acknowledge the corollary of their campaigns: that *national* social services, in which a standard level of care is meant to exist for all members of the UK regardless of where they live, are gradually being degraded.

Political practices and journalistic discourse: reporting Algeria

The quality of newspaper reporting is directly related to the quality of journalists' access to the story. If journalists cannot access a story – to investigate, to speak to sources, to take photographs and so on – then the quality of the reporting invariably suffers. While this may seem to be a platitudinous observation, governmental, military or other powerful institutions can exploit this requirement of journalism in order to control the content of the eventual journalistic product. That is, social and political actors outside the newsroom (social practices) can shape the content of reporting (text) via controlling the manner in which journalists produce the news (discursive practices). As Ian Black of the *Guardian* has put it, 'Algeria is good recent example [...] it's been very difficult for journalists to get in except at times of the choosing of the regime. When journalists have been allowed in they haven't been allowed free access.'[15]

As part of a wider project on the representation of Muslims, I have analysed the way that British broadsheet newspapers reported Algeria (October 1997–February 1998). During this time, 'Algeria was marked by a strikingly consistent topical focus – death, 'terrorism' and 'Islam' – and equally striking shifts in the apportioning of blame for these deaths' (Richardson, 2004: 192). Over the course of four months, the sampled broadsheet newspapers (with the exception of the *Financial Times*) made frequent changes in identifying the groups they felt were responsible for killing civilians: first Muslim terrorists, then the Junta, then back to terrorists, then reverting to the Junta. These shifts in argumentation and explanation were directly attributable to the management of information and journalist access by the Algerian Junta. This I will now attempt to demonstrate (for an expanded discussion, ibid.: 191–225).

In the first half of October 1997, journalists blamed 'Muslim terrorists' for killing civilians. For example:

> Islamic extremists have cut the head off a baby and killed 83 other people [. . .] in five separate attacks in Algeria. [. . .] No group has claimed responsibility for the outrages. (**Baby is beheaded in Algerian slaughter**, *AP, Telegraph*, 1 October)

Here, even though 'No group has claimed responsibility', 'Islamic extremists' are blamed for the massacres. This pattern developed further in the second week of the month, in all broadsheet except the *Financial Times*: whilst the other newspapers were confidently blaming 'Muslims' for the deaths of civilians, the *Financial Times* presented a considerably more measured account. For instance, in its first report of October the *Financial Times* quotes Lionel Jospin: 'We are confronted with a fanatical and violent opposition fighting against a regime which [. . .] has recourse itself to violence and the power of the state: so we have to be careful [in the allocation of blame]' (**Another 67 die in Algiers**, *AFP* (Algiers), 1 October 1997).

The presentation of the Algerian conflict changed in the second half of October, when, due to the immanent municipal elections, the Algerian authorities started to admit British journalists to Algeria. The *Guardian* published the first report bylined to a staff journalist writing from Algeria, and *immediately* the presentation of events offered by the Algerian authorities started to be questioned. Two days later, in another *Guardian* report, David Hirst wrote:

> The rest of the world is beginning to ask the same sinister question that Algerians have been asking themselves for years: *who* is behind these atrocities? Is it simply, according to the regime, religious

fanatics, bandits or psychopaths? Or do they enjoy the complicity of others – perhaps of some die-hard faction of the regime itself . . . (**'This is where they shot my wife. Here they killed my daughter with an axe'**, *Guardian*, 20 October 1997)

Similarly, in a report for the *Independent*, Robert Fisk quotes an Army source, who adds more evidence of the Army's suspected involvement in the reported massacres of civilians:

[. . .] he had found a false beard amid the clothing of soldiers who had returned from a raid on a village where 28 civilians were later found beheaded; the soldier suspects that his comrades had dressed up as Muslim rebels to carry out the atrocity. (**Lost souls of the Algerian night: now their torturers tell the truth**, 30 October 1997)

Thus, 'massacres' of civilians dominated the reporting of Algeria during the first half of October; these murders were blamed on 'Muslim terror groups' despite the lack of evidence supporting such confident allocation of blame. The Algerian Junta was, for the most part, completely absent from the reported action. This version of events changed with the entry of five broadsheet journalists into Algeria to report the forthcoming municipal elections. Not only did the confidence in blaming 'Islamist extremists' falter, but reports became dominated by suspicions of Algerian Army involvement in the 'massacres' and the involvement of the Algerian police in the torture and murder of civilians.

Following the Algerian municipal elections, the reporting of the Algerian conflict moved into a decline, with British journalists' access and movements being more and more restricted. Initially, reports continued the themes developed during the previous month. But steadily, newspapers increasingly relied on the copy provided by press agencies and on rephrasing articles printed in French language Algerian newspapers. This is an important observation to make, given that all the material on the civil war printed in Algerian papers is sourced with Algerian Security services (Slisli, 2000). In rephrasing or reprinting such reports, British newspapers were therefore reliant on information provided by the Junta. Unfortunately, British broadsheets did not make such a connection, and after the second week of November, the reporting of Algeria reverted back to disseminating the Algerian Junta's version of events, as printed in Algerian dailies and wired from press agency sources. One Algerian news story that was frequently printed in British broadsheets during this period referred to civilians being killed at 'fake roadblocks'. To label such incidents 'fake roadblocks' is interesting, given that this referential strategy automatically connotes that such roadblocks were illegitimate. For example:

> Ninety-seven Algerians have been killed in massacres at *fake road-blocks*, in a bomb attack and in raids on remote villages since the weekend *the Algerian press reported* yesterday. [. . .] No one has claimed responsibility for the killings, which have yet to be confirmed. (**97 killed in Algerian massacres**, *Daily Telegraph*, 31 December 1997; emphases added)

Here the journalist feels able to argue that the roadblocks were 'fake', even though 'No one has claimed responsibility for the killings *which have yet to be confirmed.*' How she could support the claim that they were 'fake' on the basis of the information she reports – especially given the allegations against the Junta printed even a week before – is unclear.

In addition, the role of actors and interests outside of Algeria were almost completely absent from reporting. Of the sampled broadsheets, only Roula Khalaf in the *Financial Times* reported the conflict in a way that showed how the business of oil continued unabated in Algeria, despite civilian massacres. In one article she shows that when the violence reaches new highs, certain traders *buy* Algerian shares. Some companies *specifically* target the depreciated prices caused by the massacres of Algerian civilians. She quotes a trader who explicitly states: 'The hedge funds buy Algeria because it's high yield paper. *If there were no massacres, the spread would narrow and they would stop buying*' (**Opportunities in Algeria for cynical traders**, *Financial Times*, 22 December 1997; emphasis added). It is therefore in the interests of (certain) capitalists that the civil war continues in Algeria.

To summarise: although the dubious status of the Junta's version was questioned in articles printed at the start of this mid-period in reporting Algeria, by December only the *Financial Times* had maintained a critical reading of the reported events. The remaining broadsheets, relying predominantly on press agency and Algerian newspaper reports, had returned to covering (numbers of) civilian deaths from a position that implied 'extremist' involvement (*'fake* roadblocks') and backgrounded or removed the active role of the Algerian Junta (*'newspapers* said').

'Blaming the terrorist' took a step up in the first week of January:

After prayers, the slaughter. As Islamist militants carry out their biggest massacre, Algeria's army looks increasingly unable to cope, David Hirst reports [. . .] An upsurge in terrorist violence in Ramadan has become a tradition. (*Guardian*, 5 January 1998)

Here a *Guardian* sub-editor placed the obviously juxtaposed imagery of the sacred ('prayers') and profane ('slaughter') conspicuously in the headline, and David Hirst suggested that Ramadan usually brings an '*upsurge* of terrorist violence'. Remember, this is the same David Hirst who only two months previously (20 October 1997 report, quoted above) suggested that the Algerian army were involved in the killings.

Similarly with the editorials printed during the first week of Ramadan:

Each year, terrorists have chosen the period of fasting to intensify their "holy war" against the regime. [. . .] The Western world breathed a sigh of relief when the FIS bid for power was scotched. Six years on it is faced with a country a short distance across the Mediterranean whose instability threatens an exodus of refugees to Europe. (**Holy Terror**, *Telegraph*, 5 January 1998)

These articles, better than any others printed at this time, illustrate the explanation of the Algerian massacres that the newspapers (as opposed to journalists or the cited sources) felt most accurate. The reference to 'an exodus of refugees' is an important one – a few days later the EU announced its intention to send a diplomatic mission to Algeria to investigate the mass killings. In the *Telegraph* editorial that criticised the planned mission, the paper managed to completely reverse its argumentative position of January 5 (which was *itself* a reversal):

The EU will not address the heart of the problem, which is *the theft of the 1992 elections* by the generals and their subsequent refusal to enter into serious dialogue with *moderate members of the Islamic Salvation Front* (FIS). [emphasis added]

Extraordinarily, lower down, the editorial even argued:

The West's acquiescence in the curtailing of the electoral process six years ago has been cowardly and inconsistent with democratic principle. (**Terror in Algeria**, 9 January 1998)

The 'cowardly and inconsistent' acceptance of the dictatorial anti-FIS regime and their 'theft' of the elections was not something that the *Telegraph* was overly concerned with only four days prior to printing this editorial. The about-face is truly extraordinary but, again, explicable in relation to wider socio-political forces (in this case the involvement of the EU and the *Telegraph's* antipathy to anything the EU does).

Backgrounded in reports of how the EU now plans to 'save Algeria from itself' were other *far less noble* reasons why Britain and the EU may have a vested interest in intervening: Muslim terrorism and Muslim refugees. At this time, the EU guidelines on asylum 'took a "restrictive approach" by recognising as refugees only people who feared persecution at the hands of a state' (*Reuters*, *The Times*, 21 January 1998). Therefore, all the 24-hour visit by the EU would have to do in order to stem asylum would be to confirm that 'terrorists' and not the Junta were committing the murders. Sure enough, following their whistle-stop tour, various reports were printed declaring the EU's belief in the complete innocence of the Junta:

> "My personal feeling is that there is no involvement on the part of the government vis-à-vis what is happening; no responsibility at all", Manuel Marin, responsible for EU relations with the southern Mediterranean and Middle East said in Brussels. (**EU official rules out Algiers link to killings**, *Sunday Times*, 17 January 1998)

These conclusions were to a certain degree understandable. As with journalists, the Junta restricted the movement and access of the EU delegates. The EU delegation were stopped from visiting any of the massacre sites, and also stopped from speaking to either members of the opposition or the Algerian public. In addition, several opposition leaders were arrested on non-existent charges and the Algerian press were *harassed* during the visit (**Leader of banned activists arrested**, *The Times*, 15 January 1998), with several massacres of civilians going unreported by even the larger newspapers because they didn't want to give the impression that the state was incapable of protecting its citizens (**Press holed up in no man's land**, *Guardian*, 23 January 1998). With such suppression of material contesting the Junta's version of events, the EU delegation found itself quite able to reject the 'allegations of direct government complicity' (**EU uses rights as weapons against Algeria**, *IoS*, 25 January 1998).

Contrary to the EU's assessment, evidence was in fact mounting against the Algerian Junta. Many of the reports wired from Ian Black (*Guardian*), who had been allowed into Algiers to cover the EU visit, contained accusations of military complicity in civilian massacres identical in style and content to those printed at the end of October 1997. Even the *Telegraph's* Defence Correspondent, Tim Butcher, started to seriously doubt the official version of the massacres after he was allowed into Algiers to cover the visit of the EU delegation. After talking to 'half a dozen' survivors of a massacre at Sidi Hamed, on the outskirts of Algiers, Butcher wrote:

> [...] It appears that a group of men dressed in army uniforms knocked on some of the doors and told the villagers to be quiet. Others in baggy clothes, described as "Afghan-style Mudjahideen" then surrounded the hamlet. There was an army outpost about 300 yards away but the survivors said that the soldiers did not emerge until the attack was complete. (**EU unable to end the nightmare of Algeria**, *Telegraph*, 21 January 1998)

While the headline appears to be that of a different story (again demonstrating the anti-European politics of the paper), the contents of the report clearly insinuate the involvement of the Algerian Army.

The reporting of Algeria demonstrates that during the periods in which broadsheets relied upon press agency copy or the reports of newspapers based in Algeria, 'Muslims' were blamed for the violence. This is because information is 'first produced by the security services in Algeria, passed through the Algeria press and the *AFP*, then reproduced in the Western media' (Slisli, 2000: 53). The Algerian Ministry of Internal Affairs, the only source in Algeria which is allowed to divulge 'security information', operates as a propaganda arm of the Junta and 'on the basis of western stereotypes, [directs] a deliberate campaign of misinformation' (ibid.: 49).

Broadsheet journalists were only allowed to enter Algeria at such time as an opportunity arose to promote the Junta's preferred image of a 'fledgling democracy' – during the municipal elections and later during the visit of the EU delegation. That the journalists generally did *not* represent Algeria in such a way is testament to the availability of evidence in Algeria that contradicts the explanation of the Junta. However, this case study should not be viewed as a success story for press diligence. We should remember that both following and *during* the periods in which staff journalists were in Algeria, broadsheet newspapers also reverted to the simplicity and clarity of blaming 'Muslims' for murdering other Muslim Algerians. The Algerian Government is a powerful and organised source, effectively ensuring that their stereotypes and misinformation are reproduced as 'fact'. This, combined with the fear of European governments that any meaningful intervention may result in a 'flood of *Muslim* refugees', has since contributed to the deaths of more civilians and ensured that the civil war is still not resolved.

Ideological practices and journalistic discourse

Ideological practices justify, smooth over and (in final analysis) naturalise the contradictions and exploitation of capitalist societies. Ideological practices work through signs – that is, through the circulation of ideas, representations and portrayals of social reality. As stated in Chapter 2, a Marxist perspective on the ideological functions of language in use maintains that in every social formation it is the ideas of the ruling class that are dominant (Marx and Engels, 1974). This doesn't mean that everything that is thought, written or represented is *literally* and *directly* the product of the ruling class. Rather, it means that 'the ruling ideas are by and large *compatible* with or at least do not openly confront the ideas or (an important distinction) *interests* of the ruling class' (Wayne, 2003: 135). Murdock (2000) argues that journalism mediates ruling class ideology through its content. Some may ask: Does this provide us with a reasonable and practical starting point for the analysis of journalism? As Wayne (2003: 136) has argued:

> If it were not a reasonable starting point then one would expect to see the mainstream news media calling capitalism into question on a regular basis; one would expect to find them attacking the profit motive routinely, pointing out the irrationality of capitalism's priorities, highlighting its wastefulness, attacking *wealthy* minorities that control vast resources rather than the poor and the vulnerable (such as asylum seekers), and linking the various tragedies, discontents and crises which they find in the world back to capitalist relations of production. No one could seriously suggest that this is in fact what the mainstream media do (even its liberal wing) and so Marx and Engels' proposition of a link between ruling ideas and the ruling class does indeed seem to me to be a reasonable proposition from which to start.

In order to explore this proposed link between ruling ideas and the ruling class, the remainder of this chapter will examine aspects of the representation of the capitalist system. Compared to examinations into the reporting of 'race' and racism, sex and sexism, homosexuality, or other marginalised social groups, there are very few studies of the representation of class and capitalism. Seemingly, 'within the hierarchies of oppression, class has sunk to the bottom because it is not sexy enough for the intelligentsia (unlike feminism, "race" studies, and lesbian and gay studies, all of which have attracted at times the intellectual eroticism of studying "the other")' (Munt, 2000: 7). Less flippantly, Munt (2000: 8) points out 'There is plenty of empirical data to support the view that inequalities in society are structural; the fact that this view is not recent may support the idea that class studies are not popular because there "realities" are ostensibly intransigent, i.e. there is nothing new to be said.' On the surface, this also provides us with an explanation for some of the lacunae of journalism listed above by Wayne (2003): class injustice isn't newsworthy because it's 'not new'. In actual fact, there *is* a great deal of class 'in' the news; it just isn't explicitly indexed *as* 'class' and is rarely examined in these terms. As Ehrenreich (1989: 3), commenting on academic studies of class, put it, 'We are told, periodically, that 'Americans' are becoming more self-involved, materialistic, spineless, or whatever, when actually only a subgroup of Americans is meant: people who are more likely to be white-collar professionals – lawyers, middle managers or social workers, for example – than machinists or sales clerks.' This argument is also true of journalism: reporting practices construct the (white, male) middle class 'as a social norm [. . .] from which every other group or class is ultimately a kind of deviation' (ibid.). The discussion below starts with a brief examination of capitalism generally, before moving on to discuss the representation of the working class and the middle class. In keeping with the class profile of the papers under analysis, the representation of the working class focuses on tabloid reporting (i.e., newspapers representing the working class *to* the working class) while the representation of the middle class examines broadsheet reporting.

Capitalism

There is little that divides the British public along class lines as straightforwardly as newspaper readership (Worcester, 1998), and the class-specific nature of newspaper readerships is reflected in coverage. That said, very little journalism actually *discusses* capitalism – in other words, what it is, how it works, the arguments for and against its perpetuation and so on. This in itself is evidence of a discourse of naturalisation, since any discussion or critique of capitalism (as a concept, as a system, as a material reality) is, almost universally, off the agenda. Such acceptance is mirrored in other social fields. For instance, on the eve of the 2005 General Election, an editorial in the *Financial Times* (**Why it is not yet time for change**, 3 May 2005) claimed that there now exists a 'cross-party consensus' about 'things that matter':

> The economy and business are at the epicentre of this new align-
> ment. It shows Britain has moved well beyond the old left-right
> disagreements about the economy, profit and the role of the
> market. [. . .] In other words, Britain no longer has a 'business
> party' and an 'anti-business party'. Try as some might to point
> up the ideological distance between the parties, in fact the gap
> between Michael Howard's Conservatives and Tony Blair's Labour
> party is smaller than the one at the last US presidential election
> between Republicans and Democrats.

The *Financial Times* worries little about this consensus (it is after all a business newspaper), and does not mention (let alone question) the alienating influence this naturalisation of capitalism by all main-stream political parties is having on working-class voters. While the similarities between the two main parties' views on 'the economy, profit and the role of the market' are unquestionable, this excerpt is nevertheless ideological since it commits a *fallacy of composition*. The fallacy of composition is committed when a conclusion is drawn about a *whole* based on the features of one or some of its constituents when, in fact, there is no justification for the inference. Here, the paper argues that because 'Britain no longer has a "business party" and an "anti-business party"', 'Britain [as a whole] has moved well beyond the old left-right disagreements'. This is untrue: the injuries suffered because of profit motivation are as real as ever – indeed, the ever-widening gap between rich and poor (see Chapter 4) and the creeping marketisation of the public services demonstrate that these injuries of class are increasing. Politicians rarely acknowledge such material deprivation because, due primarily to their high salaries and the company they keep, they are insulated from it. The same can also be said of many journalists, particularly those who work for the national press. As Cunningham (2004: 31) puts it, the oft-proclaimed role that journalism is meant to play in 'comforting the afflicted and afflicting the comfortable' is adulterated by the fact that most journalists '*are* the comfortable'. The increasing 'class divide between journalists and a large swathe of the populace' means that 'coverage of economic issues has steadily skewed away from stories of poverty and toward stories concerning wealth. Thus, the poor have become increasingly invisible' (ibid.: 32). It is towards the reporting of the poor that we now turn.

The injuries of class: the working class in tabloid reporting

When examining the ideological practices of newspaper discourse it is initially useful to consider the reporting of the working class – that is, their representation as a class and the representation of their material conditions. Ehrenreich (1995: 40–41) defines the working class as 'all those people who are not professionals, managers or entrepreneurs; who work for wages rather than salaries; and who spend their working hours variously lifting, bending, driving, monitoring, typing, keyboarding, cleaning, providing physical care for others, loading, unloading, cooking, serving, etc'.[16] On this basis, she argues that the American working class constitutes 60–70 per cent of the population, but that 'they nowhere appear in the media in anything like this proportion' (Wayne, 2003: 16). As explained in Chapter 4, access to the news is a power resource *in itself*, and 'members of the public' – that is, people without the status conferred by title or bureaucratic responsibilities – are consistently under-represented in newspapers.

Of course, acknowledging this under-representation is only a starting point for analysis since under-representation is not total exclusion. Moon and Rolison (1998: 129) argue that the institutionalisation of class inequalities is made manifest in two strategies used to represent the working class: invisibility and hypervisibility. These strategies function to either make the working class '*invisible*, and thus unworthy of recognition (e.g. "non-persons" such as janitors and maids), or *hypervisible* and marked as symbols of ridicule (e.g. "rednecks", poor "White trash"), disdain (e.g. welfare recipients) and/or fear (e.g. "the underclass", gangs)'. Echoing racist discourse (which constructs 'the Black other' as both fascinating and threatening, attractive and repellent), the discourses of 'invisibility and hypervisibility are simply inverted strategies of the same type, in that they objectify dominated class subjects. In other words, they are strategies that allow the treatment of certain class subjects as "persons of no consequence"' (ibid., citing Folb, 1994).

Taking the invisibility of the working class first, this manifests itself in two principle ways. First, as mentioned above, non-official, non-bureaucratic sources are very rarely referred to (and even less frequently quoted) in the news, resulting in their systematic under-representation. Second, the material realities of the working class and, specifically, their relation to the mode of production are carefully and habitually disavowed. For instance, shortly after the re-election of Blair's New Labour Government, *The Sun* (13 May 2005) printed an article headlined **I will defy ALL Europe: Blair vow on maximum 48-hr week**. The story reported a press conference given by Blair in which he declared his intention 'to fight socialist job protection rules' since 'The idea that job protection and a closed economy is the best way to guarantee businesses surviving is outdated.'[17] This declaration is rhetorically labelled a 'vow' rather than a 'threat' or other negative speech acts. His point, in a nutshell, is that the best way to protect jobs is not through job protection laws, but by defending the interests and profitability of businesses. Not a single source was quoted to oppose or counteract his standpoint, a clear indication of the pro-business bias of this paper. The introduction set the scene for the remainder of the report:

> TONY BLAIR last night vowed to lead an EU-wide fight against moves to stop people working as long as they like. He believes enough new member states will support him to block a 48-hour limit on the working week.

It is clearly highly strategic to Blair's standpoint that the EU work time directive is described as 'moves to stop people working as long as they like'. Both this description and the reported account of Blair's press conference are based on a string of highly ideological presuppositions that serve to conceal the material realities of the wage relation. To better reveal these, I have transformed the nominalisation (the 'moves to stop people working as long as they like') back into a clause with a subject, verb and object:

Subject	Verb phrase	Object	Prepositional phrase
[*The EU*	*wants*] to stop	people working	as long as they like

Most obviously, the *verb phrase* of the clause presupposes 'people *do* work as long as they like'. Through the use of the change of state verb ('stop'), the clause presupposes an existing reality that an actor (the EU) wants to bring to an end. Second, the *object* of the clause presupposes that 'people choose how long they *want* to work' as opposed to having to work long hours out of necessity. This is achieved through the use of the prepositional phrase 'as long *as they like*' in favour of alternatives such as 'as long *as they have to*', 'as long *as they must*' or even the more specific and faithfully accurate 'more than 48-hours a week'. In more detail, this prepositional phrase also implies 'people want to work *longer* hours than the EU wants to allow'. This is achieved through substituting the actual EU proposal of 'a 48-hour limit on the working week' (provided in the second sentence of the report) with 'as long *as they like*'. What this does is imply an *equivalence* between these two prepositional phrases, an equivalence which can be expressed as a clause: 'people would like to work more than 48-hours a week'. This implication further sediments the idea that 'people like work' – in other words, work may be alienating or tedious but it is something that 'people' enjoy doing.

The introduction to this report therefore typifies three key values of a bourgeois representation of workers: that of freedom, choice and homogeneity. Taking these in reverse order, it suggests that the undifferentiated term '*people*' can be used to describe workers with radically different social relations to production. In other words, the working hours and conditions of 'people' such as lawyers or lecturers can be grouped together with 'people' such as builders or barmaids. This elision of class is highly ideological. Further, the introduction implies these 'people' are *free* to *choose* to work or not, and for as long as they want. In actual fact, as discussed earlier in this chapter, the vast majority of workers have *no* control over the length of their working day and have *no* choice about whether to go to work or not – if they want to eat, clothe themselves and pay their bills, they are compelled to work. Indeed, if the reporter was *honest* and simply wrote 'The EU wants to stop people working more than 48-hours a week', the proposal would no doubt appear a great deal more attractive to the predominantly working class readership of *The Sun*, thereby undermining the rhetorical point of the article: that Blair's 'fight' to remove employment rights and deepen exploitation will protect the interests of workers.

Moon and Rolison (1998: 129) argue that, when they are not absent or excluded, the working class may be rendered *hypervisible* through foregrounding an assemblage of 'social defects'. In contrast to the 'good', deserving poor 'who are industrious and know their place', the 'bad' working class tend to be 'discursively associated with "waste"' and fecklessness (Munt, 2000: 8). The 'good' working class – where they appear in the news – tend to be depicted through 'such archetypes as the honest factory hand or "our Mam", symbol of hearth and home'; the hypervisible 'bad' working class, on the other hand, are 'lads and tarts, yobs and slags', 'the profligate spender', 'fat, cigarette-smoking, beer-drinking men who have become a drain on the social body' (ibid.). Over the course of one month, for instance, the front-page stories of *The Sun* howled about **YOB RULE** (17 May 2005), teenage pregnancies (**KID SISTERS: And guess what . . . YOU'RE paying their £31k-a-year benefit**, 23 May 2005; **I'M THE DADDY: Boy who got Jemma pregnant**, 24 May 2005), teenage thugs (**HAPPY SLAP THUG SHOT ME**, 9 June 2005) and other modern folk devils (for instance, kids who wear hooded tops) that act to demonise the working class. One of these examples – **KID SISTERS** – perfectly exemplifies the figure of the 'working class burden'. The lead paragraphs on the front page read:

> Sisters Jemma, Natasha and Jade Williams proudly pose with their tots – after getting pregnant aged 12, 16 and 14. The three girls and the children share a council home in Derby with their twice-divorced mum Julie, 38. None of the toddlers' dads is supporting their children – so the Williams family rakes in £31,000-a-year benefits.

This excerpt includes several of the key 'social defects' routinely employed to derogate the working class. Clearly, 'what we call ourselves and others as well as how these groups are described plays a role in establishing and maintaining hierarchical, valenced relationships' (Moon and Rolison, 1998: 130), and the negative evaluation of this family is discernible in the referential and predicational strategies of the text:

> the Kids; the Grandmoaner; the moaning mum of Williams sisters; Grandma Julie, 38; Twice-divorced Julie; her girls; Julie, who had her first child at 20; Julie, who shares a three bedroom council house in Derby with her three daughters and their children; Natasha had previously had two miscarriages and an abortion

Repeatedly the terms used to name and describe the whole family marks them out as dysfunctional, ignorant, promiscuous, lazy (see Ehrenreich, 1989: 7) and as socially 'lower' than 'Us' – that is, the imagined community of '*The Sun* and its readers' that the newspaper ideologically manufactures. The girls are represented as unnaturally promiscuous and stupid for getting pregnant (repeatedly getting pregnant in the case of Natasha); Julie, the Grandmother, also lacks respectable social values (*twice* divorced, a Grandma *at 38*) and is not only presented as lazy for 'raking in' benefits but also greedy, since she doesn't think that the family receives enough (moaning, *Grandmoaner*). The key paragraph of the article in which the 'greed' of the Grandmother is crystallised and emphasised was printed in italics – a feature which marked it out as textually and ideologically significant:

> *Julie also insisted the £600 a week she and the girls get in benefits is not nearly enough to care for the tots.*[18]

By using the verb 'insisted' to describe Julie's speech act (rather than 'said' or even the more loaded 'claimed') the newspaper constructs a discursive context in which the opinion was offered: a *defence* of her position in response to someone else suggesting the benefits *were* sufficient. The newspaper's support for this counter-standpoint is implicitly revealed through the way that it attempts to undermine Julie's position. This it does in three ways: first, through using the noun phrase '*the £600 a week she and the girls get in benefits*'. Not only is this uncharacteristically long (the article could have said 'her family's benefits' for instance), the total is exaggerated to include rent and council tax subsidies and nursery care that the family don't use. Presenting it in this way enables a rhetorical contrast with her apparent ingratitude: '*she thinks £600 a week isn't enough!*' Second, apparently Julie claimed this £600 'is not *nearly* enough', a standpoint which given the average national wage (see section above) may seem singularly grasping to the working-class target audience of *The Sun*. This is underlined through the use of the adverb 'nearly', which is superfluous to the claim and, when combined with the prior verb 'insisted', suggests that Julie is being unreasonably obstinate. Third, the prepositional phrase '*to care for the tots*' makes her claim that '£600 is not enough' appear even more unreasonable. The rhetorical implication of this (re)phrasing seems to be: How much money does she *need* to pay for three children? Lower down the article, the newspaper acknowledges that the family actually gets a total of £370 per week – money that is significantly lower than the national average and needs to support a family of seven, not simply three 'tots'.

The editorial that accompanied this front-page story was even less equivocal in its condemnation of the family. The rhetoric is so unambiguous it hardly requires further analysis, but I include it here because of the metaphorical framework it uses to represent the family:

> **Vicky clones**
> Little Britain's Vicky Pollard makes us all laugh.
> In her fictional world, having babies and scrounging off the state is perfectly normal behaviour. How sad then that one family has taken this twisted vision of life and turned it into **REALITY**. Sisters Jemma, Jade and Natasha Williams **ALL** have babies and **ALL** are paid a fortune in handouts.
> [. . .] Yet even after hitting the welfare jackpot, they still have the cheek to moan it's not enough! And, of course, it's everyone's fault but their own.

Here *The Sun* employs metaphor to structure our understanding of the family: the girls are 'Vicky clones'. For those unaware, Vicky Pollard is a comic character from the television show 'Little Britain', described by the BBC website as 'a girl who smokes in the swimming pool and has swapped her baby for a Westlife CD'. Selfish, stupid and indifferent, the characterisation is clearly intended to shape not only our view of the girls, but also our perception of how the girls view themselves and what they do: in short, these ignorant girls apparently believe that 'having babies and scrounging off the state is perfectly normal behaviour'.[19] As a parting shot, the girls' failings are then personalised: according to *The Sun*, the 'twisted' lives of these girls are entirely their own fault. We are therefore left with a curiously contradictory representation of working-class life, in which those group members who are picked out and subject to such vitriol are simultaneously archetypal and individual: their failings are somehow *typical of a class* of feckless, child-like drains of society *and* yet are simultaneously *entirely their own doing*. This contradictory quality is the hallmark of an ideological system.

To summarise, mainstream newspapers naturalise class inequality by individualising social dysfunction and blaming the victims of the hierarchical structures of capitalism for their own alienation. In short, inequality is naturalised by making the material conditions of working class *invisible* and by belittling and marking as *hypervisible* the 'socially unacceptable' characteristics of (certain) members of the working class. Such misrepresentations should not only be of concern to those of us who object to exploitation, they also should concern journalists. As Cunningham (2004: 32) points out:

> There are consequences to the fact that millions of people in this country see little of themselves and their lives in the media, unless they are connected somehow to a problem. It may have something to do with why the press is so disliked and distrusted; or why daily newspaper circulation has been in decline for twenty years.

One wonders how long journalists – particularly those working for the popular tabloid press – can go on vilifying the very people that buy their newspapers.

The middle class: a larger slice of the pie

Following the definition of the working class at the start of the last section, Ehrenreich (1989: 12) defines the professional middle class broadly as 'all those people whose economic and social status is based on education rather than on ownership of capital or property [. . .] whose positions require at least a college degree, and increasingly also a graduate degree [. . .] So defined, the professional middle class is a distinct minority, composing no more than about 20 per cent of the population', but a minority that dominates the pages of the press. For reasons explained in Chapter 4, this 20 per cent of the population is the target audience for half of the British national daily newspapers. These five papers – the 'broadsheets' – are particularly voluminous, with their main sections running to around 40 pages and printing at least one and often two additional supplements per day. An adequate analysis of their total contents is therefore out of the reach of this short section. Instead, I will examine a constellation of key ideological themes that characterise the way these newspapers construct the class status of their readerships and the role that their middle-class readers (should) play in the wider capitalist system.

Given that the professional middle class are the managers and overseers of capitalism, it is useful to examine how they represent this position. As stated, there are many texts in which such themes are represented that I could have analysed.[20] However, I chose one particularly instructive column, printed in *The Times*, in which Camilla Cavendish attempted to justify the use of servants. While not typical in focus, her column contains many of the key arguments that the middle class use to support both their position as managers of the working class and the inequalities of capitalism more generally.

Written in response to the book *Global Women* (Ehrenreich and
Russell Hochschild, 2003), the column attempted to diffuse and
counter the book's central thesis – that purchasing others to labour
in your home is exploitative and degrading, made worse by the fact
that many of these servants are immigrants with no employment
rights. The headline – **Why you shouldn't feel guilty about the
au pair** (26 July 2003)[21] – not only provides a précis for the column's
argument, it contains two presuppositions that reveal certain characteristics of the newspaper's target audience: that they *have* au pairs
(the definite article in '*the* au pair' presumes existence); and that
they may be feeling guilty about employing someone in such a way.
Further, with this headline the newspaper is also attempting to subtly
shape audience understandings of this wage relation: the person is
described as an *au pair*, a term that connotes a certain grandeur or
status on the part of the worker, rather than a 'servant' which would
foreground their role and relation to the owner of the house in a
more direct and ideologically uncomfortable way.

The book presents two general arguments, which the column
therefore attempts to counter (though to varying degrees). The first is
that employment of servants is, in itself, exploitative. Such a position
is based on the basic economics of the relationship. We should ask,
why do the middle class employ cooks, cleaners or nannies to look
after their children for 12 hours a day? Take, for example, looking
after children: if we consider this to be a job, a parent could do it and
receive no payment. Or, they could employ a servant, pay them £20
a day and go to work and earn £100 a day, leaving them 'in profit' to
the tune of £80. From such a perspective, the servant is being used
to create surplus value – and that is exploitative. The column doesn't
really engage with this argument and, in keeping with bourgeois
capitalist ideology, instead represents the relationship in terms of a
'free choice':

> The vast majority of women who take jobs in other countries
> are making a deliberate choice to provide their families with the
> security of money. A study in the 1990s found that Filipina secret-
> aries could earn twice as much in Hong Kong, four times as much
> in Rome, or seven times as much in Los Angeles, if they worked
> as maids. [. . .] There is no systematic capitalist conspiracy: there
> are only contracts struck between individuals.

I have already argued against the idea that work is a free choice
(see above), so will say nothing on this point other than to reject

Cavendish's characterisation of the book's standpoint: *Global Women* does not suggest that there is a *'capitalist conspiracy'*, systematic or otherwise. This is a 'straw man argument', used in an attempt to undermine the book's Marxist analysis of the victims of international market forces, and hence is fallacious. Further, Cavendish does not examine *why* a Filipina secretary can earn seven times as much as a maid in Los Angeles, let alone admit that this rate of pay is invariably lower than the rate paid to American citizens for the same job. Instead, she argues that immigrants work as servants (for long hours, often for seven days a week, for very little pay) *because they want to*. In other words, they *themselves* are responsible for their own intolerable material circumstances: *'if they choose to work in these conditions, who are we to stop them?'* While this is on the surface correct – they may not have been forcibly *brought* to 'the West' to work – it clearly overlooks a more accurate systematic truth: that the global economy forces their hand by only offering two 'choices': slave or starve.

The book's second argument develops this point, focusing on the legal and national status of this immigrant 'new servant class'. In the case of the UK (or in the USA, where there are well over 1,000,000 immigrant domestic servants), their continued presence in the country is dependent on their keeping their job. In short, if they leave their job, even to change their employer, they can be deported. In practice, this means that they are indentured to their employers – or, in Toynbee's (2003) term, 'visa-slaves' – a hazardous status that almost inevitably pushes them towards accepting greater indignities than they would if they enjoyed any kind of legal protection. Further, the preponderance of immigrant servants reinforces '"rich kids" views that black means servant: [in the book] a little white girl in a supermarket trolley passing a little black girl exclaims: "Oh look Mommy, a baby maid!"' (ibid.). How does the column deal with these interlocked racisms? The relevant section of the column is as follows (numbered for ease of reference):

1. The fact that so many domestic workers are immigrants helps to fuel [Ehrenreich's] argument, because they are so invisible and therefore vulnerable to abuse.
2. Yet she ignores their fervent desire to use capitalism for their own emancipation. [. . .]
3. Few of the women who travel to the West are leaving anything remotely resembling a nuclear family, where there are two parents who take sole responsibility for the raising of 2.4 children.

4. Their journeys are often courageous bids for emancipation from male-dominated or rigidly stratified societies. [. . .]
5. We must not let simplistic notions of exploitation cut off the lifeline of employment to those who are most in need of it.

In clause 1 of this extract, Cavendish dodges the book's argument about these immigrants' lack of legal status and instead suggests that it is not the workers' lack of basic rights that is the problem, but their social invisibility. It is this 'invisibility' (the fact that they are rarely seen outside their place of work), Cavendish suggests, that allows some employers to abuse their servants, since the servants never emerge from behind the closed doors of their employers' home. This argument is archetypally bourgeois, being based on a fundamental inversion of social reality. First, Cavendish ignores the material factors defining the social and economic relations between employer and worker, replacing them with a-social, a-historic individuals. Such a radical transformation of the working relationship allows her to ignore the indentured status of the immigrant servants, and treat them as 'any other workers'. In fact, it is not the 'invisibility' (nicely euphemistic!) of the servants that makes them 'vulnerable to abuse', rather their invisibility is evidence *of* their abuse. The fact they are never seen outside of their employers' home is *evidence* of their ill treatment (through overwork), not the cause of it – ill treatment they have to endure if they wish to remain in employment and hence remain in this country.

For the remaining clauses in the extract, Cavendish provides a contra-argument. In other words, following her argument against the book's standpoint 'employing immigrant servants is bad' in clause 1, she presents and supports her own standpoint 'employing immigrant servants is good'. In clause 3 she implies that the immigrant women are not really missed as mothers because they do not come from a nuclear family. (This statement draws rhetorically on an example provided earlier in the column: Cavendish refers to 'My friend Imelda', a 'Filipina cleaner' whose children resent her because her sister cares for them.) Because these immigrant servants do not have 'sole responsibility for the raising of 2.4 children', she implies it is OK for them to not see their family for years at a time. Such an argument is asinine in the extreme: the pain a child feels by being separated from its mother is in no way reduced by being cared for by another relative.

Finally, in clauses 4 and 5 Cavendish claims that employment in 'the West' *saves* immigrant women because it allows them to live away from 'male-dominated or rigidly stratified societies'. However, her implicit arguments (that Britain is *not* 'male-dominated or rigidly stratified') are patently false and, under closer examination, actually work to contradict her standpoint. Taking these characterisations of Britain in order: first, the target audience for the column is middle-class women – women who 'feel guilty' about going out to work and paying poorer women 'to clean their houses and look after their children'. Logically, therefore, this entails that child care and domestic work (and therefore the guilt that the column is attempting to assuage) continue to be 'automatically' assigned to women rather than men – otherwise the column would also be rhetorically directed towards the male readership of *The Times*. How is this *not* evidence that Britain is a male-dominated, sexist society? Second, immigrant women are allowed into Britain to work as servants; by Cavendish's admission, many have qualifications to do more rewarding work; but they are denied this opportunity and instead deported back to their country of origin if they work as anything other than a servant. Simply on *this* basis (and ignoring the now negligible level of social mobility in the UK), how is Britain *not* a rigidly (and indeed a *racially*) stratified society?

This column therefore serves as a direct and literal justification for exploitation, social inequality and a capitalist system that milks 'every drop of blood from the weak, wherever they are in the world, whatever they have to sell, even a mother's love' (Toynbee, 2003). It attempts to assuage the 'guilt' of the richest (*female*) sections of *The Times*' readership that currently employ immigrant servants and convince those who do not, that exploitation of this kind is not only a *free choice* on the part of the servant (ignoring the Hobson's Choice of slave or starve) but also that servitude is actually *emancipation*. The claim that '*Arbeit Macht Frei*' is not new, of course. The claim is no less ideological when it appears in a newspaper column.

Summary

In this chapter, I have examined some of the social practices of journalistic discourse. That is, the relationships between journalism and the wider social world analysed in terms of their economic practices, political practices and ideological practices. In doing so, I have hopefully made the case for a materialist approach to CDA to replace the current idealism. By materialism I mean 'an ethnographic eye for the real historical actors, their interests, their alliances, their practices and where they come from, in relation to the discourses they produce' and the social groups (or class) that the discourse is produced *for* (Blommaert, 1999: 7). Such a material perspective allows for an integrated analysis across the three levels required of a CDA (social practices, discursive practices and textual analysis). In examining the social practices of newspaper discourse from a class-conscious perspective, I have drawn attention to (and hopefully helped to reduce) a yawning gap in current CDA literature: the contribution that newspaper discourse plays in the reproduction of capitalist exploitation and class-based inequality. I argued that the representation of class in the newspapers examined exposes the 'institutionalised rules accepted and used by the dominant class to control the discursive actions of the dominated. The ruling class does not need to resort to overt censorship of opposing ideas, as these rules effectively contain inflammatory rhetoric within socially acceptable bounds – bounds accepted by the people who form the community' (McKerrow, 1989: 443). From such a perspective, newspaper discourse helps to ensure and perpetuate the 'situation in which one social class has power over the others is either seen by most members of the society as natural, or not seen at all' (Eagleton, 2002: 5).

Applying Discourse Analysis: Argumentation and Letters to the Editor

Introduction

Newspapers print a wide range of correspondence from their readers. These pages serve as forums for opinion, dialogue and debate; they allow the readership of a paper 'to express their opinions, their fears, their hopes – and, just as important, air their grievances' (Jackson, 1971: 152). Letters' pages aim to *include* readers – both symbolically and literally – who, should their letters be selected for publication, 'feel a sense of importance and special communication' (Wober, 2004: 50). They also play a significant role in communicating the identity of a newspaper given that they attempt to recreate the preoccupations and discourse of their readership, as expressed in their daily postbag. As a consequence, newspaper letters' pages remain one of the most popular features of the newspaper (Kapoor, 1995, cited in Gregory and Hutchins, 2004: 189) and represent an important site for the (re)production and/or resistance of discourse on and around notions of 'We-dom' and 'They-dom' (Hartley, 1992).

In addition, letters to the editor are a powerful feature of newspaper discourse, as revealed in several notable recent case studies. First, on the 14 May 2001, *The Times* printed a letter from 'the chairmen or chief executives of 58 companies, including seven in the FTSE 100 list of top firms [. . .] stating that business should back Labour' (**Top business leaders sign up to Labour**, *The Times*). Exemplifying the 'consensus view' of social relations typical of bourgeois discourse, a closing section of the letter read:

> Economic stability benefits citizen and business alike. We believe that the positive steps taken by the current Government need to be carried forward and developed during the lifetime of the next

Parliament. Consequently, we believe that business should support the party that since May 1997 has done so much to promote stable economic growth and a renewed spirit of enterprise in the British people.

Written at the start of the second week of the 2001 General Election campaign, the letter was clearly intended to have an impact on the voting preferences of Britain's power elite. It is interesting that it was sent to *The Times* – perhaps confirming that it is still the paper of the establishment – but equally importantly, it demonstrates the perceived significance of the letters' page in shaping public opinion.

A second, and more serious, case study reiterates this significance. On 14 October 2003, the *Daily Mirror* and the *Daily Mail* reported that 'US Army spin doctors' (propagandists by any other name) had ghost-written letters sent to local US newspapers that claimed to be from infantry soldiers. The *Mirror* wrote: 'Dozens of letters were sent to newspapers across the US but now it has emerged that the soldiers were given the wording and many did not sign them' (**Iraqi letters of mass deception**, 14 October 2003). The identical letters told of how 'American forces have brought life in the war-torn country back to normal for the local population, with new electricity, water and sewage plants installed' (**Storm over fake letters from US soldiers in Iraq**, *Daily Mail*, 14 October 2003). As Gregory and Hutchins (2004: 194) point out, a prerequisite for the letters' page of a local newspaper is the 'localism or proximity' of the copy and 'a belief in the right of local people to speak in *their* forum'. The US Army recognised and capitalised on this discursive practice, identified the newspapers distributed in the hometowns of the soldiers of the Second Battalion 503rd Airborne Infantry Regiment, and sent them the letter detailing the Army's rosy version of the Iraq occupation. The intention of this was clear: to steer public (mis)understanding of the invasion, at a time when 'a growing number of Americans question the war and the wisdom of a drawn-out occupation of Iraq' (*Daily Mail*).

There are many ways in which letters' pages can be studied (see Atkin and Richardson forthcoming; Bromley, 1998; Gregory and Hutchins, 2004; Lockyer and Pickering, 2001; Lynn and Lea, 2003; Morrison and Love, 1996; Richardson, 2001a; Richardson and Franklin, 2003, 2004; Wahl-Jorgensen, 2001, 2002). I believe that letters to the editor are primarily argumentative: they are designed to convince readers of the acceptability of a point of view and to provoke them into an immediate or future course of action. For this reason, this chapter examines the ways that letter writers use arguments to support these objectives. There are also a great many approaches to the study of arguments.[1] In order to make this chapter manageable, I have elected to focus primarily on the approach to rhetorical argument suggested by Aristotle.

Rhetorical theories of argumentation – or, more openly, theories of argument orientated towards a rhetorical viewpoint – always emphasise the importance of *arguer*, *audience* and *argument* to the success, or otherwise, of argumentative discourse. Each of these three foci – arguer, audience and argument – interact with the other two during argumentation. For example: a logical or valid argument is usually persuasive, but only if the audience can understand it; a skilled arguer will usually win a disagreement, but only if they can properly marshal evidence and use it to their advantage; and an audience is usually receptive to a skilful arguer, but only if they consider them to be trustworthy. I refer to this inter-related three-part structure as 'the rhetorical triangle', and the three elements – arguer, audience and argument – as the three points of the rhetorical triangle. Only a theory of argument that focuses on the triangle as a whole, and that recognises the manner in which the three points connect, interact and cooperate with each other, offers a full explication of persuasion and of argumentative success. Similarly, any investigation of rhetorical argument that doesn't consider the triangle as a whole – in terms of the production and consumption of arguments; in terms of text and context – is empirically and analytically inadequate.

'Getting in': the selection of letters

Letters published in newspapers suggest a great deal about the paper and its readers. First, and most obviously, letters are written by readers, using their ideas, observations and arguments, and these vary substantially across and between newspapers. Second, letters are usually written in response to previous articles in that newspaper; in this respect they therefore also say something about the news values of the newspaper. Third, the editorial staff in that newspaper select and print letters; again, this gives an indication of the newspaper's news values, but also about how the paper wants to represent the opinions of their readers. Fourth, like all editorial content, letters are edited in accordance with the papers' style guide, providing an insight into the interpersonal function of newspaper discourse. Fifth, they are often placed alongside letters that offer different standpoints, in ways that sometimes reveal the editorial line of the paper.

However, as Grey and Brown (1970: 454) have illustrated, 'the letters columns are clearly not representative of public opinion' and in fact more closely reflect the opinions and arguments of an 'articulate minority' (Gallup, 1958). The majority of academic studies into readers' letters have concluded that letter writers tend to be older, better educated, wealthier and more politically conservative than fellow newspaper readers who don't indulge in writing letters to their editor (Grey and Brown, 1970; Renfro, 1979). Such observations beg a number of questions, not least the criteria that newspapers use to distinguish between the letters thought good enough to be included and those to be spiked. On this point, Wahl-Jorgensen (2002) suggests four criteria of 'newsworthiness' which letters' editors use in selecting or rejecting readers' letters. These selection criteria, which are 'shaped in part by concern for the public interest and in part by the need for newspapers to succeed in the market, play a central role in helping letters editors to decide which contributions from readers have a legitimate place in the newspapers column' (ibid.: 73).

First, Wahl-Jorgensen (2002) suggests the rule of relevance, which favours topics that 'have earned a legitimate place in the public debate by virtue of newsworthy events or actions by institutions or other sources of authority' (p. 73). I have already outlined, in Chapter 4, the relationship between news values and newspaper, wherein newsworthiness is the distilled (and somewhat imagined) notion of the kind of stories that interest an identified audience. Of course, letter writers do not necessarily follow a newspaper's *angle* on the news; they are open to comment on, correct or criticise a paper's coverage; but regardless of their judgement of the content of a paper, their letters are coupled to this coverage. In this respect, 'regular citizens' attempts at introducing their own topics to the agenda will almost invariably fail' (ibid.).

Second, Wahl-Jorgensen (2002) suggests the rule of entertainment. Again, notions of what is entertaining differ according to taste, political viewpoint and journalistic genre, but to the extent that all newspapers try to 'turn on readers by offering more sparkly, entertaining op-ed pages and letters sections' (p. 74), they all employ this selection criteria. Of course, 'the punch of hard-hitting entertainment [. . .] might also, by its more agonistic nature, endanger the pursuit of shared understanding and empathy' (p. 75). This is particularly the case when letters argue about disempowered, discriminated or otherwise harassed sections of the public. Third, the rule of brevity favours succinct and punchy letters over lengthy deliberation. Wahl-Jorgensen (2002: 75) shows that this 'bite-size debate approach expresses the desire to hear the opinions of as many persons as possible', but also means that discussion tends to fall within the bounds of 'thinkable thought'. As Chomsky has argued on many occasions, the extreme brevity required of such a format makes it difficult to put forward a radical or even an unconventional standpoint, because of the time or space required to support such atypical conclusions.[2]

Finally, Wahl-Jorgensen (2002: 76) suggests the rule of authority, which letters' page editors use to select 'culturally specific forms of competence for participation'. This authority is displayed in two ways: as textual competence and as personal character. As Bohle (1991; cited in Wahl-Jorgensen, 2002: 77) states, it is not enough to have something to say; a successful letter writer also knows *how* to say it. Therefore all included letters are at the very least competently written: all are grammatically correct, make a relevant point and are 'well versed in hegemonic standards of expression' (ibid.). In keeping with the other selection criteria, the exact form of personal authority alters between newspapers. Wober (2004: 53), for example, argues that the letters' page of *The Times* is dominated by members of the social elites – in other words, MPs, Professors, Officers of Associations (e.g. the Christian Socialists Movement, Dorset Natural History and Archaeological Society, etc.) and 'people in organisations which speak for and try to keep order'. The letters' pages of tabloid newspapers are dominated by individuals drawing on their own experiences and speaking on their own behalf, however they tend to be from the upper end of the readership's socio-economic profile, as evidenced in the way they refer to owning their own homes, use the vocabulary of 'choice' and invoke an individualised power characteristic of middle-class discourse. Therefore, as Wahl-Jorgensen (2002: 77) puts it, the rule of authority

> demonstrates the impossibility of entirely leaving social status out of the public forum: competence is a culturally specific concept, and is closely related to social and economic privilege.

This picture is further complicated when we acknowledge the potential for individuals and groups endowed with sufficient social or linguistic capital (Bourdieu, 1991) to orchestrate letters' campaigns. As mentioned in the Introduction, certain powerful groups are aware of the discourse practices used to select letters for publication, and they construct their correspondence accordingly. The Jewish American pressure group, the Anti-Defamation League

(ADL), is one organisation with some success in gaining access to letters' pages. For instance, the ADL's National Chairman Glen Tobias had a letter published in the *Financial Times* (**Arafat's baffling snub to peace**, 8 February 2001), but almost the entire letter was a press release sent to all news organisations.[3] In fact, this *same* press release was also published in the American newspaper *USA Today* (13 February 2001), under the title **Disillusionment led to Sharon's victory** and bylined to Abraham H. Foxman – this time the 'National Director' of the ADL.[4] How was it that the organisation could get essentially the same letter printed in two different newspapers on opposite sides of the Atlantic?[5] Both letters were bylined to leaders of a prominent organisation (rule of authority), were brief (164 words in the *FT*, 187 words in *USA Today*) and on a punchy, sensational issue (terrorism – the rule of entertainment). However, the key to their inclusion lay in the way they started the two letters:

USA Today, 13 February 2001
A USA TODAY editorial prejudges Israeli Prime Minister – elect Ariel Sharon as an opponent to peace and the cause of continued tension in the region (Israeli election heralds new danger for US, Feb. 6).

[. . .] The Israeli people are increasingly convinced of the need to take a firm stand against Palestinian violence and unrealistic expectations. They have now exercised their democratic right to choose a leader they believe can best deliver peace and security.

Abraham H. Foxman
National Director
Anti-Defamation League

Financial Times, 8 February 2001
Sir, Your one-sided editorial 'Dealing with Mr Sharon' (February 5) shockingly omits any mention of the Palestinian role in the ongoing violence and erroneously places the onus on Arial Sharon.

[. . .] The Israeli people are increasingly convinced of the need to take a firm stand against Palestinian violence and unrealistic expectations. They have now exercised their democratic right to choose a leader who they believe can best deliver peace and security.

Glen A. Tobias
National Chairman
Anti-Defamation League

In both these cases, the ADL used the editorial content of the paper as a 'peg' on which to hang wider arguments in keeping with their agenda – specifically, their unwavering support for Israeli violence (euphemistically described as 'a firm stand') and criticising Yasser Arafat for his claimed involvement in terrorism. The remainder of the letters were identical, aside from slight changes in the ordering of the paragraphs and slight stylistic alterations, most probably in keeping with the respective papers' style guides. The arguments are taken from the ADL's substantive media advocacy campaign, but you wouldn't know this from its manifest content. Of course, such a strategy is not unheard of elsewhere. Richardson and Franklin (2004: 476), for example, demonstrate that 'during the 2001 United Kingdom General Election campaign, the letters pages of local newspapers were colonized by political parties as part of their broader media based campaign strategies'. In keeping with these findings, these letters from the ADL demonstrate that the potential for successfully gaining access to public debate may be increased when letters are written using information provided centrally.

Argumentation

As I mentioned above, I approach letters to the editor as argumentation. Van Eemeren *et al.* (1996: 5) define argumentation as 'a verbal and social activity of reason aiming at increasing (or decreasing) the acceptability of a controversial standpoint for the listener or reader, by putting forward a constellation of propositions intended to justify (or refute) the standpoint before a rational judge.' This definition suggests that argumentation, or argumentative discourse, displays a number of characteristics that I feel are necessary to quickly run through. First, argumentation is *active*. It is an activity in which participants use language to *do* certain things, whether this is advancing their point of view, defending their point of view or attacking that of someone else. On this point, Perelman reiterates that 'it must not be forgotten that all argumentation aims somehow at modifying an existing state of affairs' (1979: 11), whether this be mental, social or political. Second, argumentation is *social*. It is a social activity in which argumentative moves are 'not just the expression of an individual assessment, but a contribution to a communication process between persons or groups who exchange ideas with one another in order to resolve a difference of opinion' (van Eemeren and Grootendorst, 2004: 55). Third, argumentation is a *joint process* between participants. It is an interaction, requiring participants to both produce and consume argumentation; to compose arguments and to analyse those of their opponent; argumentation can only work when participants consent to being persuaded.

In short, argumentation is aimed at resolving a difference of opinion, occurs in a particular material social context, and is real-ised through the participants offering arguments which they believe support their standpoint and which are aimed at exerting an influence on the opinions, attitudes and even behaviour of others. However, argumentation is not a free-for-all, with participants offering any old argument and concluding that they've proved their standpoint. For example, most people would agree it is unreasonable for me to threaten you and then, once you are too scared to defend your standpoint, to declare that I have won the argument – such is the approach of violence not persuasion. Hence, fourth, 'certain stand-ards are required by which the quality of the argumentative language use can be measured' (ibid., 2004: 56). More will be said on these standards – or *dialectical rules* – later on in this chapter. I will therefore dispense with any further discussion at this stage, except to say that these rules should aim to regulate both the *product* of arguments as texts and the *process* of argument as an activity: in other words, to regulate the content of arguments and the conduct of arguers.

Aristotle's *Rhetoric*

Perhaps surprisingly, there have been few accounts of the rhetorical triangle better than Aristotle's *Rhetoric*. Written well over 2000 years ago, the *Rhetoric* is still a leader in the field. For Aristotle, rhetoric should not be a discipline simply aimed at training speakers in verbal skills[6]; nor should rhetoric aim towards producing ornate oration, or what some analysts have termed a 'rhetoric of verbal surface'; nor should rhetoric permit falsehood or distortion, even when directed towards furthering a Platonic ideal of justice. According to the familiar definition (offered early in the *Rhetoric*): 'Rhetoric may be defined as the faculty of observing in any given case the avail-able means of persuasion' (1355b 27–28). It is a *political* facility whose function 'is not simply to succeed in *persuading*, but rather to discover the persuasive facts in each case' (1355b 10–11), to present them in such a way that they convince an audience and thereby to provoke them into an immediate or future course of action. The principle features of Aristotle's theory and practice of rhetoric can now be introduced.

Three divisions of rhetoric

Aristotle identified three varieties of rhetorical discourse: *forensic* or legal rhetoric; *epideictic* or ceremonial rhetoric; and *deliberative* or political rhetoric. Each of these three kinds of persuasive discourse have specific rhetorical goals and hence tend to adopt special topics in articulating, and specific means in fulfilling, such goals. Identifying the division of rhetorical discourse employed is therefore a useful first stage when beginning rhetorical analysis. Taking each in turn: forensic rhetoric covers any form of argumentative discourse in which an arguer – or *rhetor* – condemns or defends someone's past actions. Forensic rhetoric therefore concerns itself with the *past*, its means are accusation and defence, and its special topics are the justice and injustice of actions (allegedly) committed by the defendant.

Second, there is epideictic or ceremonial rhetoric, in which a rhetor is concerned with proving someone or something worthy of admiration or disapproval. Epideictic rhetoric is concerned with the *present*, its means are praise and censure, and its special topics are honour and dishonour. Epideictic rhetoric is intimately associated to the character of those referred: the rhetor attempts to make the audience admire those referred to because of their goodness or dislike them because of their badness. When positive, rhetoric of this kind may be classified as a eulogy; when negative, it is labelled an invective.

Third, there is deliberative rhetoric, which a rhetor adopts when deliberating on the desirability or otherwise of a decision – often a political decision. Deliberative rhetoric is concerned with the *future*, its means are inducement and dissuasion, and its special topics are the advantageous and the disadvantageous. When adopting a deliberative mode of address, the rhetor will urge an audience to do or not do something based on the 'the expediency or the harmfulness of a proposed course of action: if he urges its acceptance, he does so on the ground that it will do good; if he urges its rejection, he does so on the ground that it will do harm' (1358b 22–24). Clearly, deliberative rhetoric only concerns itself with such things 'that ultimately depend on ourselves, and which we have it in our power to set going' (1359a 37–1359b 1). Therefore, matters 'which exist or will exist inevitably, or which cannot possibly exist or take place' (1359a 33) are part of metaphysics rather than deliberative rhetorical debate.

Table 6.1 summarises the foci, means and special topics for each of these three divisions of rhetorical argumentation.

All rhetorical argumentation will correspond with one or other of these divisions – and this is no less true of letters to the editor.

Table 6.1 Rhetorical argumentation

Division	Focus	Means	Special topics
Forensic	Past actions	Accusation or Defence	Justice and injustice
Epideictic	Present character or reputation	Praise or Censure	Honour and Dishonour
Deliberative	Future actions	Inducement or Dissuasion	The advantageous and the disadvantageous

All letters to the editor can be divided into those that discuss past actions (specifically the rightness or wrongness of past actions), those that discuss the character or reputation of someone in the public eye (specifically their probity or their improbity), and those that discuss future actions (specifically the desirability or undesirability of particular actions or activities).

Of course, it is possible for a letter to combine two or more divisions of rhetoric. For example, a letter may argue that Mr Smith shouldn't be voted into public office (deliberative) because he is an unscrupulous character (epideictic), as shown by certain improper actions from his past (forensic). With most letters however, it is possible to discern which variety is the most important – the *key* rhetorical division which directs the argumentation. The key rhetorical division in this imaginary example about Mr Smith is a *deliberative* discourse: Mr Smith's character, and his alleged past actions presented to exemplify this character, are subordinate to the higher deliberative rhetorical function, that it would be disadvantageous to elect Mr Smith to public office. The following example also combines two varieties of rhetorical argumentation:

> Sir, Ahmer Khokhar tells us that his relatives support al-Qaeda and regard its members as martyrs. He confirms my fears on the wisdom of letting large numbers of people of alien culture settle in this country. If we are to make a reasonable extrapolation from his article, many Muslims here support al-Qaeda; of these it is reasonable to suppose that some fraction will want to express that support actively, through violence, since that is what al-Qaeda exists for. [. . .] I reserve an especial contempt for the obscene ingratitude of these people towards a country that affords them the freedom to destroy the freedom they supposedly came for.
>
> John Campion (*The Times*, 10 January 2003)

The key variety directing the argumentation of this letter is a *forensic* rhetoric. In this case, Mr Campion questions 'the wisdom of letting large numbers of people of alien culture settle in this country' (forensic) but does so by using subordinate argumentation which draws on the second Aristotelian rhetorical division *epideictic* rhetoric. In this example, the *epideictic* argument is a negative invective, which attempts to show that 'many Muslims' are loathsome and despicable. Just as a eulogy is based on affirming noble deeds, invectives such as this 'are based on facts of the opposite kind: the orator looks to see what base deeds – real or imaginary – stand to the discredit of those he is attacking, such as treachery' (1396a 16–19). In keeping with Aristotle's advice, Mr Campion misrepresents British Muslims in general as 'alien' immigrants, hostile to the freedoms 'they supposedly came for', 'many' of whom support the violent and militant al-Qaeda. This characterisation is then used to support the conclusion of the key forensic argument: *we should have kept them out!*

Modes of persuasion in letters

Identifying the division, or key division, of rhetorical argumentation that a letter writer employs is only the first step of analysis. At the heart of rhetorical argumentation is the *mode of persuasion* – in essence, the strategy that the arguer takes in persuading the audience. The modes of persuasion form the central basis of the Rhetoric. Indeed Aristotle goes as far as to claim: 'The modes of persuasion are the only true constituents of the art: everything else is merely accessory' (1354a 13–14). In line with the rhetorical triangle introduced above, an arguer can attempt to persuade an audience by leaning more heavily on any of the points of the triangle: the argument, the audience or the arguer herself. Therefore, there are three kinds of strategy open to the arguer:

> The first kind depends of the personal character of the speaker; the second on putting the audience into a certain frame of mind; the third on the proof, or apparent proof, provided by the words of the speech itself. (1356a 2–5)

Taking these modes of persuasion in turn: first, an audience can be persuaded through the character of the arguer, or what is called *ethos*. This mode of proof ties in explicitly with Wahl-Jorgensen's (2002) rule of authority, discussed above. The idea here is that we are more likely to be convinced by someone of 'good character', someone with expertise or someone with firsthand experience. The character of the arguer, or an *ethotic argument*, is a very powerful mode of persuasion when used correctly.[7] Aristotle suggests that an argument drawing on ethos may be particularly persuasive when the 'arguments on different sides of an issue are equally strong [and] the listener has no choice but to consider the speakers and decide in favour of the person who appears wise, virtuous and full of goodwill' (Fortenbaugh, 1996: 151). Therefore, to present an argument drawing on or relying on ethos, the arguer must be able to present herself as a certain type of person and the audience must *believe* that they *are* this certain type of person. When successful, the audience has recognised that wisdom or experience or virtue are grounds for trust and therefore supports the arguer that exhibits these qualities. For example, on 22 May 2004 the letters' page of the *Independent* included letters on Iraq and the international court from a Professor of international law; on Israeli troops killing Palestinian civilians from a group of NGOs working in the West Bank; on the Government's Human Tissue Bill from a Professor of Pathology; and from other authorities on other topics. In each case, the arguments of letter writers are supported by their apparent expertise or firsthand experience: this is a classic ethotic mode of persuasion.

Second, an audience can be persuaded through *pathos*, or emotion, and this can be used explicitly or implicitly in argument. Pathos is used in a rhetorical argument to move the audience from one emotional state to another: pathotic arguments may move an audience to anger (or pity, fear, etc.); alternatively, pathotic arguments can be used to calm an audience down. In both cases, the arguer uses pathotic argumentation to put the audience in a frame of mind that makes them more receptive to what the arguer wants them to believe. As Aristotle put it: 'Our judgments when we are pleased and friendly are not the same as when we are pained and hostile' (1356a 14–15). Take *fear*, for example, which currently dominates political discourse, especially on foreign policy. As Aristotle states:

> If fear is associated with the expectation that something destructive will happen to us, plainly nobody will be afraid who believes nothing can happen to him [. . .] Consequently, when it is advisable that the audience should be frightened, the orator must make them feel that they really are in danger of something, pointing out that it *has happened to others* who were *stronger* than they are, and *is happening*, or has happened, *to people like themselves*, at the hands of *unexpected people*, in an *unexpected form*, and at an *unexpected time*. (1383a 8–12; emphases added)

Fear of 'the Other' is an unwarranted, indeed largely delusional, construction used *ad nauseam* in political discourse. Regardless of this, an arguer can *use* fear – of immigrants, of terrorists, of Muslims – to prime an audience and make them more receptive to the argument's claims and conclusions. When an audience is suitably fearful, they will agree to all manner of conclusion, or questionable governmental policies that they wouldn't usually. Emotions such as anger, love, pity, many others are also used in such a way.

Third, an audience can be persuaded through *logos*, or the logic and structure of the argument itself. In essence, we are more likely to be convinced by an argument supported by evidence and reasoning. *Logos*, and logetic argumentation, cover ways of structuring argumentation that an arguer can use to persuade us that they are correct. There are two essential structures, or forms, which almost all argumentation fits into: deductive arguments and inductive arguments. In the case of deductive arguments, something is asserted in a number of statements, and from these statements there follows a valid conclusion. A good example of this, not from a letter, is:

(a) All cities have corrupt councillors.
(b) Sheffield is a city.
(c) Therefore Sheffield has corrupt councillors.

Here, the conclusion follows the assertions – or what are called the premises: the conclusion cannot be false if the premises are true. However, deductive argumentation very rarely takes on such a complete form, particularly in the case of 'real-world' arguments. What you generally get is a form of *rhetorical* deductive argument where one or more of the premises are missing. So, for example:

(a) All cities have corrupt councillors.
(c) Therefore Sheffield has corrupt councillors.

The middle premise is missing, but the argument is still coherent and perhaps persuasive. Why is this? Because you, the audience, have filled in the missing premise *yourselves*. This particular type of deductive argument is called an *enthymeme*. In an enthymeme, 'the arguer argues A therefore C with the audience filling in the missing premise B to understand how the connection between A and C could be made' (Conley, 1984: 170). Here's another example: a readers' letter printed in the *Daily Mail*:

> Stephen Glover is so wrong about Margaret Thatcher. While she was long serving, that didn't make her a successful Prime Minister. Sadly her greatest achievement was to legitimize greed as a personal and business practice.
>
> A. Swan, Newcastle (*Daily Mail*, 11 August 2003)

This letter is more complicated than the previous example, since it requires several more missing premises to hang together in a coherent way. One way of reconstructing the argument could be:

(a) Thatcher's greatest achievement was to legitimise greed...
    [b great achievements are more important than lesser achievements]
    [c greed is a bad practice to legitimise]
    [d legitimising bad practices is not a sign of a successful PM]
(e?) Therefore, Thatcher wasn't a successful Prime Minister

Here, the arguer omits at least these three premises, perhaps more, that provide the connection between the premise and the conclusion. Because these premises are *absent* in the enthymeme, the argument appears less questionable and therefore more powerful. But, while I broadly agree with the arguer's premise (and, indeed the majority of the deleted premises too), when these deleted premises are reconstructed and we are able to properly interrogate the basis of the argument, the conclusion appears more questionable.

The second structure of argumentation is *inductive* argument. With inductive arguments, specific cases are drawn upon to support a general conclusion. This, in turn, can take three forms: by way of a symptomatic argument; by way of a comparison or analogy; or through arguing a causal relationship. These forms of arguing are more contingent than deductive arguing, with the argument scheme representing a form of *plausible* reasoning rather than being necessarily true. A short discussion of how this can work in real arguments should make this distinction more clear. First, in symptomatic arguments, which are based on a relation of concomitance, association or connection, an individual example is taken to illustrate a wider pattern or trend. A symptomatic relation can be indicated in an argument by terms such as: '... is *characteristic of...*'; '*...is typical of...*'; '*...illustrates...*'; '*...is evidence of...*'; '*...implies...*'; or a variety of other phrases (see Snoeck Henkemans, 2002: 188). Take this letter on the subject of a three-year-old denied a place at nursery because of his local council's decision to give preference to the most disadvantaged children:

> When this Government came to power it emphasised education, education, education – this included nursery places for all children. And now there is another case where a local council gives asylum seekers priority over people born in Britain. [. . .] Discrimination of this type against British nationals is becoming the norm. No wonder extremist parties such as the BNP are recruiting more members to their ranks.
>
> Michael Coates, Stoke on Trent (*Sun*, 2 July 2004)

There were 10 letters on this issue included in this edition of the paper. All of them presented similar symptomatic arguments about this case, aimed at proving 'White people are the true victims of racism'; not one letter argued against this dominant presentation of the case. We can safely assume, therefore, that these letters were published because they accord with the newspaper's racist anti-asylum seeker agenda. Here, Michael Coates takes a single example – admittedly an example of discrimination – and holds it up as representative of discrimination against (White) British nationals. In fact, the boy was discriminated against because his family was perceived to be richer than others – both British and non-British – who also applied for a nursery place. The case is therefore indicative of underfunded, under-resourced nursery provision in the UK, not of anti-White discrimination.

Second, an inductive argument may take the form of a comparison or analogy. A comparative relation can be indicated in an argument by terms such as: '*...equally...*'; '*...similarly...*'; '*...so too...*'; '*...any more than...*'; as well as by using more implicit allusions or evocations. Walton (1989: 256) states: 'Arguments from analogy are often extremely powerful forms of persuasion *to a particular audience* because they compare a [particular] issue to something the audience is very familiar with or has very positive [or *negative*] feelings about.' When the premises of an analogy are successfully adjusted to match an audience's ideological or political commitments, it results in the audience being 'as strongly committed to the conclusion' (ibid.: 15).

Take this example on the subject of Tony Blair's dishonesty in arguing for the invasion of Iraq:

> Tony Blair is sounding more and more like a policeman who, having been found out being selective with the evidence, argues that the suspect was a career criminal and deserved to go down anyway.
>
> Paul Smith, London (*Guardian*, 19 July 2003)

Here, the arguer assumes that the readership of the liberal paper the *Guardian* will have negative feelings about the police being selective with evidence; he then draws a comparison between such a policeman and Tony Blair in order that the audience transfer this negative attitude on to Blair and his actions. The success of this analogy therefore depends, entirely, on the audience sharing the letter writer's view of policemen 'being selective with the evidence'; this argument would be far less successful when directed at more authoritarian readers – who perhaps feel that when a policeman *knows* that someone is a criminal, observing bureaucratic procedures is less important.

Third, we have causal argumentation. A causal relation is indicated in an argument by terms that refer to consequences or outcomes such as: '... *creates* ...'; '... *makes*...'; '... *gives rise to* ...'; and many others. For example, the following letter was written following the killing of two young (Black) women outside a party, as part of a public discussion of the role of guns in British society:

> Let's be honest. The problem starts with the black community. We have to look at the causes. The influences of a music culture that glorifies the gun, homophobic aggression, male chauvinism and drug culture [...] BBC 1xtra has several programmes that play music that encourage gun violence and a general ignorant aggro in the black community. [...]
>
> Neil Fraser, MD, Ariwa Sounds, London
> (*Daily Telegraph*, 10 January 2003)

The argument – that music warps the minds of Black people and turns them to violence – is underlined by the headline of the letter (**BBC encourages violence through ragga**). One might as well suggest 'consuming pasta causes violence', on the basis that violent crime has increased in line with the British diet becoming more cosmopolitan, and the argumentation of this letter would be as laughable were it not based on a pernicious racist assumption: that Black people are so

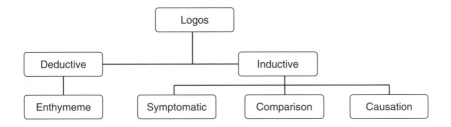

Figure 6.1 Options for a logetic mode of persuasion

stupid that music can drive them to committing violent acts (similar things are also sometimes suggested about working-class White youths, such as following the Columbine school massacre). Given the glut of songs about love, one wonders why we don't all love each other.

To summarise the theory so far, there are three divisions of rhetoric: forensic rhetoric concerning the (in)justice of past actions; epideictic rhetoric concerning the (ig)nobility of present character; and deliberative rhetoric concerning the (dis)advantageousness of future actions. In addition, there are three modes of proof: *ethos*, which relies on the arguer's good character; *pathos*, which draws on emotion; and *logos*, which draws on the structure of the argumentation itself. In turn, logos splits down into further subdivisions (Figure 6.1).

Good rhetorical argumentation will draw on all three of these modes of proof, to varying degrees.

Rules of reasonableness

Therefore, the success, or otherwise, of rhetorical arguments is judged through their material impact on the audience. We can say that rhetorical argumentation is strong or weak by the extent to which an audience agrees that the arguer has supported their standpoint. However, this is less than half of the story. If success is viewed in relation to the audience being persuaded, does this mean that 'anything goes', and that any argumentative process, procedure or product can be used to achieve a persuasive effect? Using fear of asylum seekers to argue for still tighter immigration policies may persuade an audience, but is it *reasonable* to do so? Criticising the *character* of a political opponent rather than her policies may undermine her enough to enable you to win an argument, but is it *reasonable* to do so? Most argumentation theorists would say no: such strategies are unreasonable. To explain why, we need to introduce a more *normative* aspect to our theory of argument which views a reasonable argument, not solely in terms of the end persuasive effect on an audience, but on a proper procedure recognised and adhered to by the participants.

To date, the theory of reasonableness in argumentation that I consider to be the most sophisticated and practicable has been offered by van Eemeren and Grootendorst (1987, 1992, 1994a, 2004). According to their pragma-dialectical theory:

> Argumentation is seen as part of a procedure aimed at resolving a difference of opinion concerning the acceptability of a view or a standpoint. The moves made by the protagonist of the standpoint and those made by – or ascribed to – the real or imaginary antagonist in the discourse are regarded *reasonable only if they can be considered as a contribution to the resolution of the difference of opinion.* [. . .] In order to comply with the dialectical norms of reasonableness [. . .] the speech acts performed in the discourse have to be in agreement with *the rules for critical discussion.* (van Eemeren, Garssen and Meuffels, 2003: 275; emphases added)

These rules for critical discussion 'represent ten different norms which are to be observed for resolving the difference of opinion' (van Eemeren and Grootendorst, 1994b: 63) and are as follows:

1. *The freedom rule*: participants must not prevent each other from putting forward standpoints or casting doubt on standpoints
2. *The burden of proof rule*: whoever who puts forward a standpoint is obliged to defend it if asked to do so
3. *The standpoint rule*: an attack on a standpoint must relate to the standpoint that has indeed been advanced by the protagonist
4. *The relevance rule*: a participant may defend his or her standpoint only by advancing argumentation related to that standpoint
5. *The unexpressed premise rule*: a participant can be held to the premises he leaves implicit; equally, an antagonist may not falsely suggest that a premise has been left unexpressed by the other participant
6. *The starting point rule*: no participant may falsely present a premise as an accepted starting point, or deny a premise representing an accepted starting point
7. *The validity, or logic rule*: the reasoning in the argumentation must be logically valid or must be capable of being made valid by making explicit one or more unexpressed premises

8. *The argument scheme rule*: a standpoint may not be regarded as conclusively defended if the defence does not take place by means of an appropriate argument scheme that is correctly applied
9. *The closure rule*: the failed defence of a standpoint must result in a protagonist retracting the standpoint, and a successful defence of a standpoint must result in an antagonist retracting his or her doubts
10. *The ambiguity, or usage rule*: participants must not use any formations that are not sufficiently clear or confusingly ambiguous, and they must interpret the formations of the other participant as carefully and accurately as possible.

(from van Eemeren and Grootendorst, 2004: 190–196)

Only when these 10 rules are observed is a reasonable resolution of a difference of opinion possible. Conversely, violations of these rules produce unreasonable argumentation of various kinds in the form of fallacies that derail the possibility of achieving a full and sincere resolution. As Reisigl and Wodak (2001: 71) point out, when analysing 'the persuasive, manipulative, discursive legitimation of racist, ethnicist, nationalist, sexist and other forms of discrimination [. . .] one encounters many violations of these 10 rules'. For instance, 'the populist and very often racist or ethnicist argumentation that the increase in unemployment rates within a specific nation state is the consequence of the growing number of immigrants' (p. 73) is fallacious because it violates rule 8: the argument scheme rule. Popularly known as a *post hoc, ergo propter hoc* fallacy, such argumentation confuses a chronological relation ('after this' – *post hoc*) with a causal relation ('therefore because of this' – *ergo propter hoc*). Although causal argumentation is an acceptable argument scheme, presenting immigration as a *single causal* factor in unemployment rates 'completely ignores all the complex economic relationships and relevant economic, political and social factors responsible for unemployment' (ibid.).

Fallacies

Integrating this model with Aristotle's rhetorical theory, although each of the modes of proof can be used in a reasonable way to support an arguer's point of view, they can also be used *incorrectly* – or, in technical terms, used *fallaciously*. Each of the three modes of proof has corresponding fallacies – fallacies that 'kick in' when they are used incorrectly. Take arguments relying on an *ethotic* manoeuvre, for example. In many cases, there is no choice but to accept the opinion of experts or eyewitnesses – indeed Aristotle claimed that *ethos* was the most compelling mode of proof. But we must watch out for cases in which someone claims to have authority or expertise but either doesn't, or that their expertise is irrelevant. This is called the fallacy of abuse of authority or, in more formal terms, an *argumentum ad verecundiam*. For instance, someone may say 'I'm a professor, so I know about the benefits of privatisation', but they're may be actually a professor of Egyptology, so their status is probably irrelevant on this subject.

Second, there are the pathotic fallacies where an arguer will base argumentation on arousing emotions, specifically the *manipulation* of emotion, in order to distort perception or impair the audience's critical faculties.[8] Common pathotic fallacies include scare tactics – often involving exaggeration and hyperbole – and sentimental appeals. Another significant pathotic fallacy is called the 'bandwagon fallacy' (the *argumentum ad populum*), where an arguer will claim their conclusions should be accepted because so many people agree with it. For example:

> The public, I suggest, want to see [. . .] an acknowledgement that there is a problem with asylum seekers which needs urgent attention. This is not a racial issue at all, but common sense. Dash it all, this country is full.

> Concerned (*Mirfield Reporter*, 25 May 2001)

Here, the arguer attempts a deductive argument but uses a fallacious argument. Even assuming that 'the public' *do* want 'a problem with asylum seekers' to be acknowledged, this in no way proves that there actually *is* any 'problem with asylum seekers', merely that a group of people *believe* it to be the case. The fallaciousness of the move is better revealed with a more extreme case. Imagine the letter read: 'the public want an acknowledgement that there is a problem with talking frogs that needs urgent attention'. The arguer tries to use the apparent popularity of public perception to convince us that what the public *perceives* to be the case does in fact exist – and that is a fallacious move.

In the build up to the 2005 General Election, Michael Howard and the Conservative Party adopted an identical argumentative approach. The campaign was actually fought under the slogan 'Are you thinking what we're thinking?' demonstrating the communion between the argument and audience that the Party were attempting to establish. One of their five key election policies centred on reducing immigration. On this issue Howard argued:

> I think most people would agree that Britain has reached a turning point. They know that our communities cannot successfully absorb newcomers at today's pace. [. . .] So people will face a clear choice at the next election: unlimited immigration under Mr Blair or limited, controlled immigration with the Conservatives. (Speech at Conservative Campaign Headquarters, 24 January 2005)

On other occasions Michael Howard justified his anti-immigrant electioneering by arguing that the public want their worries and fears about immigration to be acknowledged. Such a rhetorical strategy clearly makes a mockery of Howard's claimed forensic skill. To reiterate the point: believing something is real does not mean it *is* real; the public 'believing' that immigration is a problem (even assuming that it does believe this) does not *make* it a problem. A more acceptable response to public concerns about the number of immigrants would therefore be to *tell the truth* about migration:[9] that immigrant children improve British schools (**Immigrant children make learning a richer experience for all, study shows**, *Independent*, 26 June 2004); that migration benefits the capitalist economy (**Myth of Migrants: UK better off by £500k a week**, *Daily Mirror*, 8 July 2004); and that it is non-White Britons who are more likely to fear crime and to be a victim of crime.[10]

Finally, there are logical fallacies. There are many, many ways in which arguers can misuse or twist reason that are fallacious, so I will only discuss a couple of the more recurrent fallacies here.[11] First, letter writers frequently commit the fallacy of hasty generalisation. The fallacy of hasty or overgeneralisation occurs if, when using a symptomatic argument, a conclusion is a generalisation based upon examples that are unrepresentative or insufficient. For example:

> The Organisation of the Islamic Conference recently met. On the agenda were the usual anti-US and anti-Israel rants, but not one mention of Islamic terrorism. If the larger Islamic world is serious about tackling Islamic terror, then surely it should bother to discuss it.
>
> Michelle Moshelian, London (*Guardian*, 5 May 2004)

Here, on the basis of a single event, the arguer makes a general point about the conduct of the Organisation of the Islamic Conference (OIC) and expands this further to make a still more general point about 'the larger Islamic world'. This is a generalising synecdoche, typical of racist discourse, in which the characteristics of a part are incorrectly transferred to the whole. It is unreasonable to make a general point about the willingness, or otherwise, of the OIC to tackle 'Islamic terror' on the basis of one meeting. The observation is *not representative*, since the OIC has explicitly condemned such activities in the past. Further, it is *insufficient* to use the actions of the OIC to make a general point about the 'Islamic world' (whatever this is supposed to be – are British Muslims part of 'the Islamic World'?). The OIC does not represent the views of many Muslims – particularly given that many of its members are Heads of States of regimes responsible for some horrendous violations of *Muslim* human rights. In sum, the supporting premise is neither representative nor sufficient and hence the argumentation is fallacious.

Logical fallacies can also be committed when an arguer defends a standpoint using an analogy. For example:

> Tolerance works both ways (When the veil means freedom, January 20). It is no more intolerant to require Muslim women not to wear *hijab* in a non-Muslim country than to require non-Muslim women to wear a headscarf in a Muslim country.
>
> Robin Gill, Oxford (*Guardian*, 22 January 2004)

Here, the analogy fails because the components of the analogy are not sufficiently comparable: forcing Muslim women not to wear the veil is not the same as forcing non-Muslim women to wear it. Muslim women who wear the veil do so for reasons of modesty: they consider it to be immodest to expose certain parts of their body (their torso, their head or in some cases their face) to either men they're not married to, or male non-family members. Put this way, the modesty of Muslim and non-Muslim women is, at heart, not that dissimilar: non-Muslim women also wear clothes to cover their bodies. A more fitting analogy could therefore have been: 'It is no more intolerant to require Muslim women not to wear the veil than it is to require non-Muslim women to go topless'. When reformulated in this way, the unreasonableness of the argument is clearly evident.

Kilroy-Silk and anti-Arab racism

In line with the approach to CDA that I have been arguing for in this book, and the discursive practices of newspapers in particular, rhetoric should be viewed as the process of 'analysing the material effects of particular uses of language in particular social conjuctures' (Eagleton, 1981: 101). The material effects of language are particularly important to consider when argumentation may have a detrimental effect on the welfare of others. I view my job, as a socialist and a critical discourse analyst, to 'expose the rhetorical structures by which non-socialist works produce politically undesirable effects, as a way of combating what is now unfashionable to call false consciousness' (ibid.: 113). Take, for example, the presence of prejudicial or racist views in readers' letters. Racist rhetoric not only reflects the extent to which such views have 'become part of what is seen as 'normal' by the dominant group' (Essed, 1991: 288), but also is (re)productive and transposable, modifying material power relations in other fields (Bourdieu, 1991). Such rhetoric should be met head-on and confronted without equivocation.

On 4 January 2004, the British tabloid newspaper the *Sunday Express* printed a column written by Robert Kilroy-Silk. The column, headlined **We owe Arabs nothing**, created a political storm for the newspaper and especially its author, though exactly the same column had been printed in April 2003 under the headline **Us, loathsome? Shame on them**. Kilroy laid out his rhetorical argument in plain language from the outset:

> WE ARE told by some of the more hysterical critics of the war on terror that 'it is destroying the Arab world.' So? Should we be worried about that? [...] After all, the Arab countries are not exactly shining examples of civilisation, are they?

Lower down, amongst other points, he asked:

> We're told that the Arabs loathe us. Really? [...] What do they think we feel about them? That we adore them for the way they murdered more than 3,000 civilians on September 11 and then danced in the hot, dusty streets to celebrate the murders? [...] That we admire them for being suicide bombers, limb-amputators, women-repressors? I don't think the Arab states should start a debate about what is really loathsome.

In the subsequent furore, Kilroy was sacked from his presenting job at the BBC and launched a political party called *Veritas* that campaigned on a single-issue anti-immigration platform. The argumentation of the column contains simple errors (he claims Iran is part of 'the Arab World' when it is Persian; and that Syria supported Saddam Hussein when they were enemies), commits numerous fallacies[12] and is clearly and obviously racist. However, the details of the column don't really interest me (see Halliday, 2006 for a critique); what interests me is the *response* that the column generated in the letters' pages of newspapers *other than* the *Daily Express*. The response of the *Express* was to be expected: their letters' page was dominated by readers supporting the printing of the column and defending Kilroy's standpoint. Over three days (13–15 January 2004), of the 15 letters which were printed on the subject of Kilroy's column, only three attacked him for his views and these were all included on the first day of 'the debate'. This, of course, is the customary reaction: a newspaper usually feels compelled to defend its own coverage, particularly right-wing populist newspapers like the *Express*, even when exposed as objectionable. I find it more interesting, therefore, to examine the argumentation of the letters printed in other newspapers, given that they had less of an ideological stake in defending or attacking Kilroy's position.

The letters printed on this topic took one of two global standpoints: 'Kilroy was right' or 'Kilroy was wrong'. In this respect, the whole debate can be classified as fitting with a *forensic* division of rhetoric: it was concerned with the past; characterised by accusation and defence; and its special topics were the justice and injustice of actions (allegedly) committed by the defendant. However, the letters printed did not equally represent each standpoint, and instead letters' pages of the majority of the newspapers were either strongly against Kilroy's argumentation, *accusing* him of writing an unjust argument (e.g. the *Guardian*, the *Independent*) or strongly in favour of him, defending him against his persecutors in the BBC, 'politically correct people' and the derogatively named 'race relations industry' (e.g. *The Times*, the *Sun* and the *Express*). Only two newspapers presented a close-to-equal number of letters from either standpoint: the *Daily Telegraph*, which across three days published four letters defending Kilroy and three against, ending the coverage of the story with a letter against; and the *Daily Mirror* which printed in two letters defending and three letters criticising the publication of the column. That said, even in these cases of relatively balanced representation of these two forensic standpoints, the discursive agenda of each newspaper was still evident. The *Mirror's* letters (13 January 2004), for example, were collected under the headline **Kilroy's attack on Arabs is hypocrisy**, despite this only summarising the argumentation of the first of its five letters. Further, the letters alternate between letters attacking and defending Kilroy, ending with a letter that clearly states, 'Kilroy was wrong. His comments with regards to Arabs were spiteful and thoughtless.' Though not as strongly put as labelling his arguments racist, the letter concludes the debate, implying that those critical of Kilroy 'won'.

Of course, it is insufficient for a discourse analyst to simply state that a letter 'defended' or 'attacked' Kilroy without looking at *how* this was achieved. The following letter (third from the five printed in the *Mirror*) attempted to counter Kilroy's argumentation:[13]

Kilroy-Silk was wrong to ask what the Arabs have ever done for the world. They were developing the principles of astronomy, mathematics and medicine centuries before the first Europeans arrived in America to steal land from its native people. The Arabs had a cultured civilisation when Europe's barbarians were burning people alive in the name of religion.

Robert Brown, Manchester (*Daily Mirror*, 13 January 2004)

The key division of this letter is *forensic* rhetoric (revealed in the statement 'Kilroy was wrong'), but this is achieved through drawing on a second Aristotelian rhetorical division – *epideictic* rhetoric – that praises Arab civilisation. The letter writer then provides reasons for praising Arab civilisation – thereby employing a logetic mode of proof – and, specifically, refers to key achievements that he suggests are a reflection of the contribution of Arab civilisation (symptomatic argumentation). If we were to present the argumentation schematically, it could appear something like that show in Figure 6.2.

The argumentation therefore directly counters Kilroy's standpoint that Arabs have not contributed anything 'to us'. This is achieved through using two rhetorical figures. First, the frequently used 'rule of three' ('astronomy, mathematics and medicine') lends a sense of completeness to the list that providing two or four 'Arab achievements' wouldn't.[14] Second, the writer uses antithesis – a form of parallelism characterised by 'a compact expression of contrast or opposition' (Jasinski, 2001: 544) – in order to emphasise these achievements. It is interesting that the writer drew on *historic* examples of '*European*' barbarity, rather that a *contemporary* example of *British* barbarity (e.g. the immorality of British policy in Iraq and Afghanistan, or British support for repressive governments in Israel,

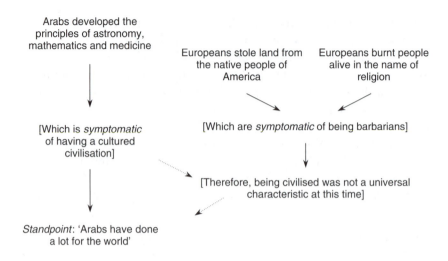

Figure 6.2 Rhetorical argument scheme

Russia, Turkey, Saudi Arabia, Columbia, etc.) to press this rhetorical point. In this respect, the letter, while countering Kilroy's standpoint, in fact is underwritten by a similar ideological assumption: the myth that British foreign policy is well meaning and, while not always achieving this, nevertheless strives to promote moral principles.

The *Sun's* letters' page covering the 'debate' (14 January 2004) was similarly typical of the agenda of the paper. Of the 11 letters printed, 10 defended the 'right' of Kilroy to write what he did (eight of the letters also agreed with his standpoint, labelling it 'the truth'), in one case suggesting 'this hypocrisy and bias towards non-Christians and non-whites is typical of this country today.' Only one letter didn't defend Kilroy, and even here the writer tempered the accusation by stating 'we are all entitled to our views' and that 'It's a shame that his show has been taken off'. While an extreme case, the way the *Sun* constructed its letters' page in response to this news event was a crystallisation of three strategies adopted by those who agreed with Kilroy and supported the publication of his racist argumentation:

- that he spoke the truth about Muslims;
- even if you object to his views you should not silence him; 'free speech' means all are free to express their view, no matter what;
- and even if it *was* racist, certain Muslims also write racist things about Whites/Christians/Jews, so it's discriminatory to only restrict White racism (this strategy is reflected in the page's collective headline: **If Abu Hamza can speak out, so can Kilroy**).

The first of these forensic argumentative strategies is a denial of racism – all he said was 'true' and therefore cannot be racist. A paradigm example of this, written by 'Commander H.L. Foxworthy (retired)', read: 'Is there actually anything in Mr Kilroy-Silk's article which is factually incorrect?' (*The Times*, 12 January 2004). As indicated above, a *great* deal of the column was factually inaccurate, not to mention unreasonable and morally questionable. The second and third argumentative strategies are justifications for racism: in essence, an argument to the effect that Kilroy acted properly because 'we', the ethnic managers of Britain, have a *right* to be racist. Both the letters' pages of *The Times* and the *Sun* presented such argumentation, and it is useful to compare the ways that it manifested itself in the two newspapers:

The Times	*Sun*
If Kilroy-Silk had made such comments about Christians and the Church, the BBC would not have suspended his programme. [. . .] The BBC needs more balance; either there should be more respect for us all, or all should be open to criticism.	What has happened to our free speech? Kilroy spoke his mind and his programme has been taken off, yet we allow people like the Hook to rant and rave and nothing is done to him.
David Winkworth, Farnborough	William Dargan, Hants

Clearly there are some stylistic differences between these two letters, as one would expect when comparing the contents of broadsheet and tabloid newspapers. The broadsheet letter poses a hypothetical analogy ('If. . .') while the tabloid presents a categorical analogy ('we [do] allow'); the broadsheet analogy refers to the BBC while the tabloid refers to the folk-bogeyman Abu Hamza ('Hook' is a metonymic referential strategy used by the *Sun*, based on the fact that he has metal prosthetic hands); the broadsheet letter uses the credentialising double barrel name 'Kilroy-Silk' while the tabloid refers to 'Kilroy'; and so on. However, they are both based on the same assumption: that all 'criticisms' (again, note the referential strategy: Kilroy's column was a diatribe, not criticism) are the same, regardless of the medium or context of the attack and regardless of who or what is being attacked. In fact this is not the case. Abu Hamza 'ranting and raving' to a small assembly of his followers is not the same as a rant from Kilroy printed in a mainstream, mass circulated newspaper.

This is not to say that either rant is acceptable argumentation; but purely in terms of the (potential) audience affected by the prejudicial outbursts, the two are not comparable. Second, regarding the target of invective, we must consider material realities and social power in particular. In relation to the criticism of religions specifically, Robin Richardson argues:

> A criticism which appears evenhanded across two or more religions has differential impacts, according to where the adherents of a religion are positioned in unequal power relations and patterns of discrimination, and according to the extent to which religion is seen as a marker of identity and belonging rather than a system of belief. (**Liberal responses to Islam**, *Guardian*, 20 August 2004)

Clearly social context needs to be taken into consideration when making such an observation: the strident criticism of an Arab in a Jordanian newspaper will not have the same potential for encouraging anti-Muslim prejudice as the strident criticism of an Arab in the *Express*; similarly, the strident criticism of a Jew in a Jordanian newspaper holds more potential for encouraging racist social outcomes than identical criticisms in an Israeli newspaper. The common differentiator is social context: declaring open season on the criticism of already disempowered social out-groups is not the same as criticising members of the majority in-group.

Summary

This chapter has examined letters to the editor as an argumentative discourse genre. Letters' pages remain important to both newspapers and their readers, representing a key site in which the identities of the readers – as both producers and consumers of news discourse – are constructed by the newspaper. While there are many ways to examine letters to the editor, I maintain that a crucial one should be an analysis of argumentation. Argumentation should be regarded as a joint enterprise between participants – that is, between the arguer and the audience, the antagonist and the protagonist, or between the *producer* and the *consumer* of an *argument*. I labelled these three elements *the rhetorical triangle*, and each must be borne in mind when analysing *any* discourse, not just argumentative discourse. The key to an examination of rhetorical argumentation is the identification of the mode of proof. In what ways does the arguer rely on an *ethotic* mode of proof, for instance stating that they have expertise, firsthand experience of the issue, or imply that they are trustworthy? In what ways does the arguer rely on a *pathotic* mode of proof, in which emotion is used to put you, the audience, into a particular emotive state? What kind of argument schemes does the arguer rely on? Do they use a symptomatic argument (indicated by a term such as 'is typical of'), a comparison argument (indicated by terms such as 'likewise' or 'equally'), or a causal argument (indicated by terms such as 'creates' or 'leads to')? In each case, the analyst needs to ask: Do these (occasionally implicit) rhetorical strategies *successfully* and *reasonably* support the standpoint? Breaking argumentation down in this way will help to better understand the ways that arguers deliberate controversial or contentious standpoints, employ propositions intended to justify (or refute) such standpoints (van Eemeren *et al.*, 1996) and use language to justify and encourage divisive or intolerable beliefs.

Critical Discourse Analysis: War Reporting

Introduction

> The Americans and Blair decided to go to war in March 2002. You need to look at everything that happened after that in the context of that decision and how they were organising what was going on [...] And they embarked upon what I would call the most centralized political propaganda campaign in modern history to shape the run-up, the conduct and the aftermath of the war. (Tim Ripley, Freelance for the *Scotsman*, the *Financial Times* and *Janes Defence* magazines, from **Pieces in the Jigsaw of War**, *Journalist*, October 2003: 11)

Tony Blair had been gunning for Iraq for a long time before Britain finally invaded in March 2003. Indeed, the length of time that Blair had been arguing for the desirability of bombing Iraq should demonstrate the inaccuracy of the popular perception that he is 'Bush's poodle'.[1] As early as 1998, near the end of the UNSCOM crisis, Blair was repeatedly quoted arguing for 'doing something' about Iraq, and about Saddam Hussein more specifically. For example, a report in the *Financial Times* quotes him saying 'if he [Saddam Hussein] isn't stopped – and stopped soon – the effects will be worse for the whole of the region in the long term' (**Blair joins US in warning Iraq over hidden weapons**, 29 January 1998). With the plan to invade in place – which, as Ripley indicates above, was agreed by 2002 at the very latest – it was necessary to convince the general public of the need for such an invasion: and for that, a propaganda campaign was required and developed.

A conventional propagandistic technique used during the pre-invasion propaganda campaign was to reduce options and possibilities to an 'either/or' position. Typically war propaganda describes 'conflict in a radically polarized way – as a struggle between the 'good guys and the bad guys' and in black and white. So, a discourse dominated by propaganda will consequently only allow two positions: for and against. Attempts or claims to take a third position – a distanced, neutral or critical standpoint – will be effectively suppressed' (Nohrstedt *et al.*, 2000: 384). In the case of the invasion of Iraq however, propagandists pushed the discourse a stage further than simply limiting the argumentative positions to 'for war' and 'against war', maintaining that the choice was for *action* (i.e. invasion) or for complete *inaction*. Opening the campaign for invasion in March 2002, President Bush declared that when it came to 'the threat posed by weapons of mass destruction [. . .] "inaction was not an option"' ('**Inaction is not an option**', *Guardian*, 12 March 2002). Rarely, however, was the strategy expressed with such clarity as when the then Labour Chairman, John Reid, stated:

> A great moral choice has been put before us by the people on the march yesterday. It is not a choice between peace and war. It is a choice between doing something and not doing anything. If you take the view that we should not do anything, you too have a moral responsibility, because by doing that you are sustaining the status quo under which people are being murdered, tortured and dying and starving. (**War is an ugly thing but you just have to trust Tony**, *Daily Express*, 17 February 2003)

When expressed like this, the 'choice' seems stark: either support war or support the continued murder, torture and so on of Iraqi citizens. However, the argument makes a number of unwarranted inferential leaps, made visible when laid out schematically, as shown in Figure 7.1.

Presenting the crisis in such a way is not only a paradigm example of what Orwell called 'the defence of the indefensible' ('not going to war is undesirable'), it is purposefully designed to close down

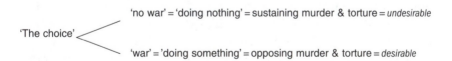

Figure 7.1 'The choice', as presented in pro-war propaganda

debate and disguise an abundance of possible political responses. For instance: Was the Hussein regime the *sole cause* of the appalling humanitarian crisis in Iraq? Was war the only way to oppose the status quo in Iraq? Was war the only way to stop people 'being murdered, tortured and dying and starving'? Would war *reduce* or *increase* the number of people 'being murdered, tortured and dying and starving'? All of these necessary questions, and their messy and problematic answers, were disregarded in favour of Reid's Manichean response: our way is good and any other way perpetuates murder.

In this final chapter, I will attempt to draw together some of the major threads thus far introduced and discussed in an analysis of war reporting. More specifically, this chapter will examine the way the recent US/UK invasion of Iraq was reported, focusing primarily on British newspapers. The discussion will focus on the relationship between the representation of the invasion and the strategic interests of governmental sources in these two countries. However, there is a clear problem in a chapter such as this, which needs to be acknowledged at the start. Specifically, it is difficult to analyse the invasion of Iraq completely given that it is, to all intents and purposes, still going on. At the time of writing, Iraq is still under an army of occupation, soldiers and many civilians are being killed everyday[2] and the compelled conversion of Iraq from a planned to a market economy is still being driven through. This chapter, therefore, focuses predominantly on the period immediately prior to the invasion and the six-week conflict prior to when Bush declared 'mission accomplished'. Rather than speculating on the 'true motivation' of governmental or military actors, I have attempted to keep my analysis focused on material concerns: in other words, what was said and by whom with what rhetorical effect during the pre-invasion period; the contents of reporting during the invasion; and the relationship of text-contents to the social and discursive conditions in which such reports were produced.

Social and discursive practices: propaganda and journalism

During wars, journalists are exposed to propaganda from all sides, most notably from organisations and institutions with a stake in the killing. Unfortunately, journalism becomes *shaped* and *driven* by this propaganda. To explain how this occurs we need to look at the interaction between the discursive practices of journalism and the social practices of the world. The key social practices, or the key social forces, to consider are the governmental and military organisations involved in the conflict. Journalism is a powerful genre of communication which, through employing argumentation – predominantly rhetorical moves placed in the normative framework of objective reporting – can help organise people's understandings of the world. Powerful institutions, in this case governments, the military and the rest of the security state, want to use journalism to promote their version of the war to the world and hence shape the behaviour of the public in their favour.

Nohrstedt *et al.* (2000: 384) argue, 'The context for war correspondents and media coverage of military operations in international conflicts is flooded by propaganda.' By propaganda they mean 'the deliberate and systematic attempt to shape perceptions, manipulate cognitions, and direct behaviour to achieve a response that furthers the desired intent of the propagandist' (Jowett and O'Donnell, 1992: 4). It is important to note that propaganda is *not* necessarily built on lies; nor does successful propaganda involve the closure of newspapers or the direct control of what is printed. As Knightly (2000: 478) points out:

> a democratic government cannot afford to be as crude as that. It never goes in for summary repression or direct control; it nullifies rather than conceals undesirable news; it controls emphasis rather than facts; it balances bad news with good; it lies directly only when it is certain that the lie will not be found out during the course of the war. This [is] the method that Britain chose.

In British propaganda of the First World War, for instance, '[f]acts were deployed selectively yet rationally, while falsehoods were eschewed in the belief that they would ultimately be exposed and thereby jeopardise the credibility of those facts that had been released' (Taylor, 1995: 3). Hence, propaganda usually operates by utilising established facts, building on conventional (but often mythic) beliefs and, in particular, playing on the fears or desires of the target audience. Indeed, 'Propaganda is as much about confirming as about converting public opinion' (Welch, 1993: 9).

'Our propaganda' is given a variety of names: 'public relations', when political beliefs are propagated in domestic audiences; 'public diplomacy', when beliefs are propagated in foreign audiences (see Snow, 2004); or 'psychological operations' (PsyOps), when beliefs are propagated in 'Enemy audiences' (see Taylor, 2003). Contrary to popular assumptions, it is amongst *democracies* and not dictatorships that propaganda continues to be most frequently used – emanating from the powerful in order to sediment their hegemony. As Taylor (1995: 4) explains, 'In pluralistic democracies, which purport to exist on the basis of consensus rather than coercion, persuasion [. . .] becomes an integral part of the political process.' More critically, political discourse in Western democracies demonstrates that '[t]he less the state is able to employ violence in defence of the interests of elite groups that effectively dominate it, the more it becomes necessary to devise techniques' (Chomsky, 2002: 19) that help propagate expedient public opinion.

Propaganda emanates from *all* interested parties during wartime, and perhaps *especially* during *the run up* to wars. 'Almost every news source, PR officer or politician have, in one way or another, vested interests in relation to the conflict and will only inform about things that presumably support their strategic and tactical objectives' (Nohrstedt *et al.*, 2000: 384). These propaganda campaigns filter into news journalism in a number of ways that relate directly to the discursive practices of journalism. It is towards these discursive practices that we now turn.

Propaganda and the discursive practices of journalism

In Chapter 4, I introduced certain key professional and occupational practices that shape journalism as a discourse process and therefore help to account for the products of newspaper discourse. Of these, four have direct influence in assisting the success of propaganda campaigns. First, and in the most general sense, a declared war that involves 'your country' is a highly newsworthy story. Indeed, a declared war could easily satisfy all 10 of the news values suggested by Harcup and O'Neill (2001): reference to the power elite (individuals, organisations and nations); reference to celebrity (e.g. 'Saving Private Jessica Lynch'); entertainment (e.g. human interest, drama); surprise; good news (e.g. rescues, personal triumph); bad news (e.g. tragedy, accident); magnitude; relevance (involvement of 'Our boys', political importance); follow-up stories; and the newspaper's agenda. On this basis, it seems inconceivable that a UK national, or even a local newspaper, could not report a declared war that involved, or may potentially involve, British soldiers.[3]

Second, all objective journalism needs sources to quote and to base stories on, and this is no less true when covering a declared war. An 'authoritative' source is one that is assumed to have practical knowledge of the reported event. Unfortunately, during wartime, the mainstream media interpret this to mean military or governmental sources – basically, people who are involved in killing or who help to justify the killing – and 'compliant journalists get a steady drip-feed of exclusive stories from official sources' (Lynch, 2003: 114). However, according to the 'Alice in Wonderland' logic that pervades main-stream journalism, avoiding such sources and seeking out individuals and groups without a (financial or political) stake in the killing can leave a journalist open to accusations of bias. As Jake Lynch has stated:

> If say, for example, you cease to base your news agenda on the words and deeds of official sources, of the Prime Minister, of the government, and start to base it instead on gathering alternative perspectives, on gathering news from unconventional sources, then you will be somehow exposing yourself to the risk that you'll be accused of bias.[4]

The reliance on such militaristic sources skews reporting in pretty predictable ways, ensuring that 'spin-doctors [i.e. government propagandists] get a reliable conduit for their message to enter the public realm' (ibid.).

These first two characteristics of newspaper discursive practices almost inevitably result in journalists and media organisations negotiating access – access to the story, access to sources and access to the battlefield – and this negotiated access always comes at a price. This was illustrated faultlessly by the way the reporting of the Falklands War of 1982 was controlled. The islands themselves are particularly isolated – 400 miles from the Argentine mainland and 8000 miles from the UK. Therefore, 'in return for access to the action the correspondents had to accept the MoD ground rules. These were crippling' (Knightly, 2000: 478). There are four points to make here:

1. no correspondents other than British were allowed to accompany the task force; there was to be no room for impartial or neutral reporters.
2. the individual reporters were vetted, with certain reporters being refused accommodation on the grounds that there was no room. There was, however, enough room for the Navy to take 3 million chocolate bars.
3. the correspondents who were allowed accommodation had to sign forms to accept censorship at source by the six MoD 'public

relations officers'. There was no way round this as, in addition to controlling access, the MoD also controlled the broadcast and communications facilities.

4. shaping agenda: all correspondents were issued an MoD booklet which informed them that they would be expected to 'help in leading and steadying public opinion in times of national stress or crisis' (all from ibid.: 478–479).

The only other source of information was the MoD briefings in London – which, unsurprisingly, were evasive and not particularly helpful. This herding of journalists was incredibly successful: the MoD censored, suppressed and delayed what they considered 'dangerous news', released 'bad news in dribs and drabs in order to nullify its impact' and simultaneously presented itself 'as the only real source of accurate information about what was happening' (ibid.: 481). And, due to the two constraints of journalistic discourse outlined above – the need to report the story and the need to access sources significant to the story – the news media complied. Indeed, 'the MoD could not have achieved what it did without some compliance from the British media' (ibid.). This success of the MoD in controlling the way the conflict was reported has gone to set the standard for all successive conflicts from the US invasions of Granada in 1983, Panama in 1989, the Gulf conflict in 1991 and most recently the invasion of Iraq.

Third, as Okrent (2004) has put it, 'newspaper people live to be first', and in the rush to publish or broadcast scoops, the appropriate caution and scepticism can be 'drowned in a flood of adrenalin'. This is a particular problem for television news, especially 24-hour rolling news channels, whose haste to broadcast a scoop frequently meant 'that military claims [were] relayed instantly to millions without being confirmed or verified only to be refuted later by reporters on the ground' (**When are facts facts? Not in a war**, *Guardian*, 25 March 2003). For instance, Tony Maddox (Senior Vice President of CNN International) has acknowledged that during the invasion of Iraq he came across:

stories where there were lots of sources of information that were very difficult to check, and you were in the process of having to say, well do we sit on this until we check it out, in which case others are going to run with it and we'll get the blame if it turns out to be true, or alternatively we pump it out there and we reserve the right to pull it back afterwards? (in Lynch, 2003: 119).

Richard Sambrook, Head of BBC News, was similarly supportive of his journalists going 'live on air telling the world about [a story] before they really know what is going on', because 'what we said was what we thought we'd been told at the time, and if it turned out to be wrong we had to go back and correct it' (ibid.). In practice, broadcasters retracted or corrected stories so often that they started to look ridiculous: the battle to take control of the port Umm Qasr was a case in point. By the afternoon of Sunday 23 March, the port 'had been "taken" nine times. By Sunday night there were *still* ugly skirmishes between coalition forces and irregulars loyal to Saddam' (**When are facts facts? Not in a war**, *Guardian*, 25 March 2003). More serious was the impact on the audience of such frantic propagandising. As the Cardiff Study (Cardiff School of Journalism, 2004: 39) of the reporting of the invasion demonstrates, the general public were

> much more likely to remember the original incorrect story than the subsequent retraction. So, for example, 81% remembered Tony Blair's condemnation of the execution of two British prisoners of war, but of those, only 13% recalled that this accusation turned out to be untrue. Similarly, 25% were able to recall Iraq being reported as firing Scud missiles into Kuwait, but only 15% of these recalled that these claims turned out to be unfounded.

The demand to be first, a reflection of the logic of the capitalist market, therefore allows propagandists to create a fictional version of the war – a version that, despite being retracted or revised in future broadcasts, nevertheless persists in the memories of the audience.

Fourth, there's the pressure from the audience either in the form of perceived audience sensibilities (resulting in an absence of images showing the bloody aftermath of bombing) or their perceived political viewpoints. Rarely, however, is it acknowledged that the *vast* majority of people, and not just in the UK, were *against* the invasion in the form that it took – as high as 73 per cent according to one poll (YouGov poll from 23–24 January, cited in *The Sunday Times*, 26 January 2003). In direct contrast, Danny Schechter (Executive Editor, MediaChannel.org) argues that the prevalent perception amongst American media executives was 'we can't get ahead of our audience. *The audience was gung-ho for the war*, therefore we have to give the audience what it wants' (in Lynch, 2003: 124; emphasis added). This acute misperception had such a profound effect on coverage that, in the words of Schechter, it resulted in 'an abdication of journalistic responsibility' (ibid.). That said, once a war starts, the newspaper buying public are notoriously unreceptive to reporting critical of 'Our boys', or even stories unsupportive of the war. For instance, on 11 April 2003, it was announced that the circulation of the anti-war tabloid, the *Daily Mirror*, 'had fallen below the two million mark and that its anti-war stance had contributed to this decline' (Freedman, 2003: 104). In response, the editor, Piers Morgan, was pressured into lessening 'the paper's critical coverage of the war and to shift the war off the front pages' (ibid.). As Freedman (2003: 107) explains:

> when military action started and opinion polls revealed a more ambivalent attitude towards the war amongst both its own readers and the general public, the *Mirror* was less willing to be identified with what it saw as minority views. Constrained by a 'responsibility' towards the bottom line, the paper was unable to maintain a consistent opposition towards the war and was forced to 'ameliorate' its coverage. Such is the logic of the newspaper business.

Therefore, these final two characteristics of newspaper discursive practices – a desire to be first with a story rather than watchful of propaganda and the pressure to avoid stories or views critical of 'Our side' – conspire to reduce war journalism to being a conduit for the views of the powerful.

Manufacturing consent: modes of proof in the 'pre-war' period

Rhetoric is never just talk. Rhetoric is political language designed and therefore with the capacity to shape public belief and the decisions and behaviour of an audience; it always aims at inciting action in an audience, or at least the disposition to act. As discussed in Chapter 6, Aristotle suggested that there are three modes of proof, or strategies, that an arguer can use to persuade an audience:

1. *logos*, the structure of an argument and the way a good argument draws upon reasoning in order to support a conclusion;
2. *ethos*, the character of the arguer or the way that we are more inclined to believe people who we perceive to be trustworthy or are knowledgeable about the matter under discussion;
3. and *pathos*, the use of emotional themes or emotional language to make an audience more receptive to your conclusion.

All three of these modes of proof were used during the build-up to the invasion of Iraq; all three were used in an attempt to shape the public belief that war was necessary and desirable. Interestingly, however, they tended not to be used together. In fact the build-up to the invasion seemed to go through three phases in which each of the modes of proof successively predominated the rhetorical argumentation used in an attempt to justify the war.

First, the US/UK alliance used reasoning – the first mode of proof. They said that we should go to war for two reasons: first because Iraq had these 'bad bombs', which are both against the relevant declarations and also threatening to peace and stability; and second, because of the links (or perhaps just the *potential* for links in the future) between Iraq and al-Qaeda. For instance, Tony Blair said the following in the House of Commons, 3 February 2003:

> Even now, I hope Saddam can come to his senses, co-operate fully and disarm peacefully, as the UN has demanded. But if he does not, if he rejects the peaceful route, then he must be disarmed by force [. . .] Saddam's weapons of mass destruction and the threats they pose to the world must be confronted.

The above excerpt is riddled with presuppositions functional to Blair's standpoint that 'Saddam' (note the personalisation, *he*) 'must be disarmed by force': that Saddam possesses threatening weapons, that he has lost his senses and is not co-operating with the UN. To underline the badness of these bombs, a new term was brought into popular usage: Weapons of Mass Destruction, later shortened to the more catchy and memorable 'WMD'. In fact, the correct term for these weapons is 'nuclear, chemical, bacteriological (biological) and toxin weapons'.[5] Although the term 'WMD' has been a part of military jargon for some time, prior to this propaganda campaign, such bombs were called 'non-conventional weapons' when journalists referred to Iraq's alleged (indeed *non-existent*) arsenal as a whole, or 'biological weapons', 'nerve agents' or else by a name (e.g. anthrax) when they were being more specific. Even during the UNSCOM crisis 1997–98, which centred on the inspections regime, the term 'WMD' was never used (see Richardson, 2004). A search of the *Guardian* website, for instance, shows that there were only 13 articles that contained the phrase 'weapons of mass destruction' in 1998, all in November and December, the first dated 14 November, a month before the US 'Desert Fox' cruise missile attacks on Iraq. This number rose to 75 articles in 1999, 204 in 2001, 2070 in 2003 and then dropped off to only 251 in 2005 (to the time of writing). The prominence of the phrase, as reflected in the frequency it was used in newspaper reports, is therefore directly related to the propaganda of the US/UK regimes: necessary for policy aims in 2003, embarrassing in 2005.

It should be stressed that while using chemical, bacteriological (biological) and toxin weapons are appalling methods of killing people, they are not methods that kill people in large numbers; hence they do not bring 'mass' destruction. Nuclear weapons *do* produce mass destruction of course, but the vast majority of nuclear ordinance in modern warfare are depleted uranium (DU) artillery rounds, used by *American* and *British* tanks and battlefield artillery. The pressure group of the International Physicists for the Prevention of Nuclear War warn that 'DU weapons indiscriminately contaminate the places in which they are used, and the contamination persists long after the conclusion of hostilities, adding to the radioactive and toxic burden imposed upon civilians, wildlife, and ecosystems.'[6] Based on this, there is therefore a strong argument that 'DU munitions, as radiological and toxic weapons, are in violation of the United Nations Charter, the Geneva Conventions, the Conventional Weapons Convention, and the Hague Conventions, which forbid the use of "poison or poisoned weapons" and "arms, projectiles or materials calculated to cause unnecessary suffering".'[7] In other words, certain weapons that 'We' habitually used during the invasion are *illegal WMD*. The ideological nature of the noun phrase 'WMD' is therefore revealed by the fact that 'We' don't have them, only 'They' do.

A second reason employed to support the standpoint 'we should go to war' (which was used far more prominently in America than in the UK) were alleged links between Iraq and al-Qaeda. President Bush used the opportunity of his 2003 State of the Union address to 'reveal' (not 'claim' or 'allege' which sound much less categorical) that he was in possession of 'Evidence, from intelligence sources, secret communications and statements by people now in custody [that] reveal that Saddam Hussein aids and protects terrorists, including members of al Qaeda.'[8] The link between terrorism and the Government of Iraq almost entirely centred upon one man – Abu Musab al-Zarqawi – who at this time was based in the Kurdish Autonomous region in the North of Iraq, in other words, an area *not* under the direct control of the Iraqi government. With respect to the 'statements from people in custody', as Mahajan (2003) put it: 'Given the condition al-Qaeda detainees are being held in and the obvious incentives for them to tell a story the US government wants to hear, this is very far from being actual evidence.' Blair was much more guarded (or perhaps stealthy) in the way he presented the 'link' between Iraq and 'international terrorism':

> I know that many of you find it hard to understand why I care so deeply about this. I tell you: it is fear. Not the fear that Saddam is about to launch a strike on a British town or city tomorrow or the next day. Not a conventional fear about a conventional threat. But the fear that one day these new threats of weapons of mass destruction, rogue states and international terrorism combine to deliver a catastrophe to our world; and the shame then of knowing that I saw that threat, day after day, and I did nothing to stop it.[9]

This excerpt contains many rhetorical tropes and figures (the rule of three (or *tricolon*), parallelism, *anaphora*, *antithesis*) that contribute to the success of his argument. However, I will only examine one here: his use of *prolepsis*. As Jasinski (2001: 554) explains, *prolepsis* involves 'responding to the anticipated objections of one's opponents'. Here, it is the *way* Blair represents the views of his imaginary antagonists that is of significance. Opening his argument with the viewpoint of an imagined interrogator is highly functional to Blair's standpoint, since it allows him to falsely present an accepted starting point for discussion. Specifically, he states those of us who oppose the proposed invasion are having difficulty understanding why he *cares so deeply* about Iraq's weapons; in fact most opponents of the war *doubted the existence* of such weapons. His fallacious move allows a radical transformation of the speech act of the imagined antagonist from an assertive to a directive. In other words, a transformation from a more accurate rendering of an opposing standpoint, for instance:

ASSERTIVE: *expressing a standpoint*: For example, 'Iraq has no battle operational non-conventional weapons.'

to a benign request:

DIRECTIVE: *requesting argumentation*: 'Why do you care so deeply about this?'

The difference between these two speech acts is profound: the assertive entails opposition to Blair's argumentation while the directive requests and therefore implies that we are amenable to his standpoint; the assertive places the imagined antagonist in a relation of opposing equals within the critical discussion while the directive implies a hierarchical relation, in which 'Tony teaches us why he cares'. From this starting point, and specifically the way it disavows any burden of proof, Blair is able to talk about *his fear* that *one day* these threats [may? might? could? will?] combine, rather than having to prove the 'bad bombs' exist and then demonstrating the likelihood that his feared 'catastrophe' will actually occur.

Both of these reasons for invading Iraq were regularly questioned in the press.[10] For instance, the *Daily Mirror* quoted the opinion of 'Falklands Hero Simon Weston':

> Blair says there's evidence of a worldwide terror network and Saddam Hussein has evil weapons of mass destruction. Saddam may well have these weapons but where's the proof? Where's the evidence? At the moment Blair hasn't given us any, just trite statements asking us to believe him. (**We Need Proof**, *Daily Mirror*, 22 January 2003)

Such a viewpoint was typical of reporting in the period prior to the invasion, particularly that of the anti-war tabloid, the *Daily Mirror*. The governmental and military planners, therefore, shifted their argumentative approach to emphasise an *ethetic* mode of proof, or one that relied on the character of the arguer. This was most notable in the prominence of General Colin Powell during the build-up to war – a man who, despite rising to prominence by attempting to cover up US war crimes in Vietnam, including the massacre at My Lai – was represented as a 'Dove', as a diplomat, as a moderate and reasonable man whose views are to be trusted.[11] On 5 February 2003, Powell gave a 90-minute presentation to the UN Security Council, in which he made the case for invading Iraq using transcripts of tape recordings, satellite photographs and 'reconstructed' (read *imagined*) computer images. None of these sources were conclusive – as one commentator put it, 'Just because there are trucks around a site doesn't mean they're transporting warheads' (**Flawed War**, *Daily Mirror*, 6 February 2003) – and as a result, his performance had to lean heavily on his personal character. Christopher Hitchens, writing in the *Mirror* on the same day argued, 'Colin Powell's words carry more weight [than most] coming as they do from a former sceptic' (**Yesterday's Drama at the UN**, *Daily Mirror*, 6 February 2003).

But Powell's presentation was *not* convincing, as evidenced by the reaction of a range of sources. A week after the presentation, Hans Blix spoke out against Powell's 'evidence' at a press conference at

UN Headquarters, stating that they did not prove Iraq was clearing the site of 'bad bombs': 'The reported activity of munitions at the site could just as easily have been a routine activity as a movement of proscribed munitions in anticipation of an imminent inspection' (**Blix queries US 'evidence' on Iraq**, *Guardian*, 14 February 2003). Recognising their rhetorical flaw, propagandists moved on to rely on *pathos* – using emotion to try to sound plausible. Again, it is useful to quote Blair's argumentation, this time addressing Party activists in Glasgow, describing the Iraqi victims of the Hussein regime:

> These victims will never be seen on our screens. They will never feature on our TV screens to inspire millions to take to the streets. But they exist nonetheless. Ridding the world of Saddam would be an act of humanity. It is leaving him there that would be inhumane.

It is significant that such an argumentative line was adopted on the day of the anti-war demonstrations in London. Echoing John Reid's implicit attack on the protesters, Blair (again assuming that only two options are available: total war or acquiescence) suggests that the only way to stop the deaths of innocent Iraqis is to bomb Iraq – strategically described as 'Ridding the world of Saddam'. This *was* a successful rhetorical strategy. Arguing that the real reason for invading Iraq was to save Iraqis – what has been called *the rhetoric of military humanism* (Chomsky, 1999) – simultaneously made the Western audience feel bad for Iraqis, good for ourselves and drew on an imagined and vaguely racist legacy of the way 'the West' has historically positioned itself as being responsible for 'civilising the world'. This *pathotic* strategy was successful because it appealed to a wide range of political backgrounds. First, it appealed to the political right and neo-conservatives who feel that the way to promote international security is to remove distasteful dictators (at least those who stand in the way of 'our national interest'). More interestingly, the propaganda also convinced a significant number of liberal journalists to use their columns to argue that we have a civilising duty to 'free Iraqis' by bombing their country and killing potentially thousands of innocents. Ed Herman (2002) has called such people the '"cruise missile left" (CML) because of their alignment with power and their eager support of external violence'. In the UK, this group included David Aaronovitch, who argued that we should bomb Iraq 'for the sake of the Iraqi people who cannot lift this yoke on their own' (*Observer*, 2 February 2003). Elsewhere he argued that Iraqis were currently being killed, so we might as well invade and remove Saddam since either way (i.e. if we invade or 'do nothing') 'we would have blood on our hands' (*Guardian*, 11 February 2003). On the day that around 2 million people demonstrated in London against the potential invasion, Johann Hari also argued that war was the answer,

> not because of the dangers of weapons of mass destruction; nor for any of the other ridiculous reasons that have been given in the past few months. No. The only moral factor in this war should be the Iraqi people, and their needs – and the Iraqi people's greatest need is for our help to get rid of one of the worst dictators on earth. (*Independent*, 15 February 2003)

Similarly, as early as 11 August 2002, Nick Cohen in the *Observer* (**Who will save Iraq?**) berated 'Noam Chomsky and his supporters' for their knee-jerk opposition to whatever the USA proposes and hence becoming 'the mirror image of the hypocrisies of American power'.[12] Reading such argumentation, it is clear that the 'CML' were content to ignore not only the intrinsic illegality of what they propose, but also the injurious effect that encouraging unilateralism has on international law. As Chomsky has put it, no 'state, certainly not one with the record of the United States, should be given any authorisation to act independently, violently, on the basis of its own leadership groups. That's ridiculous. We don't allow it to anyone else, why to the United States?'[13]

Of course, the *actual* way that the military perceived Iraqi civilians was revealed over and over again during this period. In what was described as a 'warning to Mr Hussein' (not a 'threat' of course), British Air Marshall Burridge said 'We do not want to give the impression that he can move his armour around and put it in places where he thinks we wouldn't strike' (**Allies prepare opinion for heavy loss of life**, *Financial Times*, 15/16 March 2003). In other words, if Iraqi military personnel are camped in civilian areas, we'll bomb them anyway. General Tommy Franks was, aptly, more frank in his appraisal, simply stating that civilian targets were not 'off limits', even if this involved bombing targets 'close to hospitals and close to schools and close to mosques and that sort of thing' (ibid.). Abdicating any responsibility for killing innocent Iraqis, Franks stated: 'The one who holds the key to civilian casualties [. . .] inside Iraq is Saddam Hussein.' Essentially, Franks' argument is as follows: Saddam is breaking the law; Saddam needs to be stopped; bombing will stop him; any war crimes that *we* commit while stopping Saddam breaking the law are Saddam's fault. That such an ideological conclusion wasn't treated with the contempt it deserved demonstrates the realisation of a successful propaganda campaign: the only way to save Iraq was to bomb it; all other possible avenues are expurgated, even if Iraq is destroyed in the process. As Blair put it, repeating the mantra of the pre-invasion campaign, 'doing nothing is not an option' (*The Mirror*, 8 April 2002).

Discursive practices: shepherding journalists

Once the invasion started, a key requirement to succeeding in 'the information war' was controlling, or shepherding, journalists. This is because, in the words of Webster (2003: 58), there is still 'an ethic of resistance to manipulation of news in warfare'. Limiting the information available to journalists – both those in the field and the 2000 or so journalists stationed at Doha – was the primary method in which the military propaganda campaign was achieved. The majority of journalists in the field were what were called 'embedded' journalists – that is, they lived with a regiment of soldiers. As the Cardiff Study (Cardiff School of Journalism, 2004) states, 'The Pentagon saw the embed programme as part of a well-planned, co-ordinated media and "Psych-Ops" strategy [. . .] as part of the military campaign' (p.16). For the Pentagon, 'the intended journalism was not one which would investigate the reasons for the war or the justifications for it. It was a journalism designed to keep public opinion on the side of the US forces and to minimise the possibility for analysis or criticism of policy, politics or reasons for war' (ibid.: 22).

Embedding of journalists had two principal effects: first, as in the past, the journalists grew to identify with the men they were living with. In such an arrangement, a 'psychological identification [. . .] grows between the embedded correspondent and the soldiers he is with [demonstrated by] the use of the "we", we're doing this, and we're doing that' (from Lynch, 2003: 122). As Larson (2004) explains, 'Danger, or the threat of danger, is a great bonding mechanism' (p. 128) that caused him to lose 'some or all of my neutrality' while he reported the invasion. Going on, he admitted, 'I was an American, I was with American soldiers and people from another country were trying to kill all of us' (p. 127). This psychological identification was anticipated by military, and so they encouraged close contact between soldiers and journalists. The press reporting of the invasion was replete with indicators of this identification, even in the ostensibly anti-war *Daily Mirror*. For instance, Tom Newton Dunn (embedded with 40 Commando regiment) wrote of the moment he realised 'how close *we* were to getting to war' (**Into Iraq**, *Daily Mirror*, 22 March 2003). A deictic pronoun like 'we' is, of course, indefinite and could refer to a range of collectives: does he mean 'we' the nation or 'we' the men he is travelling with? The answer was provided two paragraphs lower down:

> I stood *with the rest of* the 900 Royal Marine Commandos in a wide circle as Lt Col Gordon Messenger addressed *us*. [...] I had been told that the most dangerous time *for any of us* was the 20-minute helicopter ride over to Al Faw, 40 miles away from our position. If *we* got past the anti-aircraft guns by the shoreline, and the shoulder-fired surface-to-air missiles and landed safely, *we* would probably – just probably – be OK. (emphases added)

Here, 'we' is being used in a restricted sense of the men in the regiment – a group that the reporter clearly feels he is part of. Such personal identification inevitably results in an abandonment of journalistic objectivity and the co-option of the journalist into the military's public relations (read *propaganda*) machine. As Larson (2004: 129) put it, 'If you are friends with somebody, then you don't want to write anything that would make that person look bad. [...] Even though I wasn't friends with the senior officers [in contrast to the enlisted soldiers], I still developed a concern for their well-being and the reputation of the unit. I didn't want to report anything that would make the unit as a whole look bad.'

Second, embed journalists only had a very small pool of sources to draw upon and could only present a very small-scale, fragmented view of the war. As Audrey Gillan (embedded with the Household Cavalry for the *Guardian*) put it, in an embedded relationship 'you do not have very much freedom of movement, [or] ability to go off and interview who you like. We have no translators with us, basically no control, we're seeing what they want us to see' (from Lynch, 2003: 122). Journalists who were in Iraq only knew of events that happened to them: they had no TV and often little contact with anyone outside of the regiment they were covering. Their perspective on the war was therefore incredibly limited. Even the Cardiff Study (Cardiff School of Journalism, 2004) – which inexplicably claimed that 'the use of embeds [...] meant that broadcasters were *less* dependent on military briefings and

better able to offer *independent* accounts of the military campaign'
(p. 4; emphasis added) – acknowledged that the limits imposed onto
journalists' 'freedom of movement amounted to a form of censorship'
(p. 10) and therefore that 'however independent they attempted to
be, their reports would only give a partial, one-sided view of the war'
(p. 11). This restricted view was an *explicit aim* of the propaganda
campaign. As Colonel Paul Brook, the Assistant Director of media
operations for the MoD, put it, the embeds' view of the war was to be
'like looking through a smartie tube . . . through a net curtain . . . at
night' (ibid.: 17). This view is supported by the journalists in Iraq.
For instance, Gillan stated:

> We [embeds] missed the war. I didn't even know who Comical Ali
> was until my Dad picked me up from Glasgow airport and told
> me about this hilarious guy. The foreign desk asked me to write
> a piece about what the troops thought about Saddam Hussein's
> statue toppling over in Baghdad and we didn't know. (from **Pieces
> in the Jigsaw of War**, *Journalist*, October 2003: 10)

But, if journalists did still feel that they were going to kick against
the system and present a critical view of the war, they were limited
in another far more explicit way: through the rules of the embedding
relationship. First, it was the US Assistant Secretary of Defence for
Public Affairs that granted permission to who was allowed in and
who wasn't. This is why potentially awkward journalists like those at
al-Jazeera weren't admitted; as in the Falklands conflict, there was
to be no room for 'impartials'. Second, embedded journalists had
to sign a contract with their military 'hosts' accepting a number of
conditions – what were called the ground rules.[14] Central to this
contract was the requirement that journalists

> [. . .] follow the direction and orders of the Government related to
> such participation. [. . .] The media employee acknowledges that
> failure to follow any direction, order, regulation or ground rule may
> result in the termination of the media employee's participation in
> the embedding process.[15]

These ground rules included restrictions about certain *stories* and
certain *details* that were *always* out of bounds (principally those
that would 'endanger operational security'). Significantly, journalists
were restricted from reporting the 'rules of engagement' – that

is, who the military thought were legitimate targets, the method the troops used for distinguishing between targets and innocent civilians and the ways of dealing with legitimate targets. In addition to the self-censorship generated by adhering to the ground rules, the military also used more direct forms of censorship. Audrey Gillan, for example, states 'I know a lot of journalists who were censored; I was censored, sometimes quite rightly where I was in breach of security and could have brought us into great danger. Other issues were simply stylistic, things like "running for cover" was changed to "dashing for cover" because running for cover implies cowardice' (from Lynch, 2003: 122). Such stylistic alterations are not benign. Brian Appleyard (1991), writing in *The Sunday Times* during the Gulf conflict of 1991, argued that war inevitably *involves* and *colonises* language, and that each war demands a brand new linguistic style register in order to express its own uniqueness. On the one hand this style register 'should resonate [...] ethical correctness, clean-liness and scientific efficiency, and, on the other hand, glamour, machismo and derring do' (from Walsh, 1995: 12). As this example shows, military sources felt that the processes used to describe Our ('valorous') actions were important enough to warrant direct inter-ference; as I demonstrate lower down, headlines were similarly influ-enced by such stylistic concerns. And if all else failed, the agreement stated that 'Unit commanders may impose temporary restrictions on electronic transmissions for operational security reasons',[16] a rule that saw journalists having their mobile phones blocked for unex-plained reasons.

What this understandably did was put journalists on their toes – not wanting to cross the line by reporting *too much* detail of what was happening, or reporting the *wrong* details about what was happening. Quoting the contract: 'Violation of these ground rules may result in the immediate termination of the embed and removal from the AOR [area of responsibility].' In order to ensure that this didn't occur, journalists checked their reports with the military. In the words of Richard Gaisford, a BBC embed: 'We have to check each story we have with them. And if they're not at the immediate level above us – that's the Captain who's our media liaison officer – he will check with the Colonel who is obviously above him and then they will check with Brigade headquarters as well' (BBC News 24, 28 March 2003).[17] What this illustrates is that these embeds were actually integrated into military command structures: checking their copy, not with their editors but with the military they were supposed to be reporting (Miller, 2003).

Reporting the invasion: action and agency in headlines

An examination of the content of the headlines is a useful first approach to the analysis of newspaper outputs. Headlines are a 'part of news rhetoric whose function it is to attract the reader' (Bell, 1991: 189). More specifically, headlines perform a double function: 'a semantic function, regarding the referential text, and a pragmatic function regarding the reader (the receiver) to whom the text is addressed. The two functions are simultaneous', in as much as the headline acts 'to alert the reader (receiver) to the nature or the content of the text. This is the pragmatic function of the headline, and it includes the semantic one' (Iarovici and Amel, 1989: 441–443). Here, I will focus specifically on the transitivity of the headlines reporting the invasion. According to systemic functional linguistics, 'transitivity is the *foundation* of representation: it is the way the clause is used to analyse events and situations as being of certain types' (Fowler, 1991: 71). As discussed in Chapter 3, the various types of verb process (mental, verbal, relational, transitive and intransitive action) aren't just syntactically different, they also carry differences of *meaning* – that is, semantic differences – between these processes and hence between differing clauses. Further, CDA maintains that 'since transitivity makes options available, we are always suppressing some possibilities, so the choice we make [...] indicates our point of view' (ibid.) – a point of view that may be ideologically significant.

To explore these issues, I chose to sample eight newspapers – four tabloids and four broadsheets – on alternate days for the first six weeks of the invasion. Only coding alternate days meant that I could sample the whole of the six weeks while keeping the data set to a manageable size (2107 headlines). My code sheet recorded 16 variables, including the newspaper, the page of the article, the type of clause (noun phrase, verb phrase or other), the type of process, the construction (active, passive) and the nationality of agent and object. Coding and quantifying the content of headlines can clearly cause certain problems for CDA and for ideological analysis in particular, as I explained in Chapter 2. That said, the data produced by coding do provide us with a useful starting point for analysis, since they reveal some interesting patterns of meaning *across* texts. In line with Simpson's (1993: 88) suggested approach, the following analysis focuses on the *participants* involved in the process, the *process* itself and the *circumstances* associated with the process.

Participants

Although it is clumsy to simply associate 'Iraq' with the 'Them' position on the ideological square (given that the majority of Iraqis were victims of the regime) and 'US/UK' with 'Us', it is nevertheless useful to first examine the frequency that national actors are referred to in the sampled headlines. Table 7.1 below cross-tabulates the nationality of cited actors with the newspaper that the headline appeared in.

Table 7.1 suggests some interesting things about the way these sampled newspapers represented the invasion of Iraq. First, and most striking, is the almost complete absence of the UN as an actor – or the *complete* absence, in the case of the tabloids. Although war clearly signals the failure of diplomacy (and hence the marginalisation of the UN), this textual exclusion stands as an index of the way that international law was positioned throughout the build-up and implementation of the invasion: as insignificant and hardly worth mentioning. Second, it is necessary to comment on the number of actors of 'Unknown' nationality. The 'Unknown' nationality was the product of two semantic-syntactic features that conceal agency: the use of passive verbs with deleted agents (used in 155 headlines, 7.3% of total); and the number of headlines that used personal pronouns such as 'I', 'me' and 'we'. Some examples of personal pronoun usage included:

> **'I never want to hear that sound again'** (*Guardian*, 31 March 2003)
> **We can't wait to get her home** (*Daily Express*, 3 April 2003)
> **We're here to stay** (*Daily Mirror*, 7 April 2003)
> **Hello... Is it me you're looking for?** (*Sun*, 11 April 2003)
> **I was not involved says businessman** (*Daily Telegraph*, 23 April 2003)

Deictic indicators of person such as these (also 'us' and 'you') necessarily strip any sense of nationality from a headline, since their meaning is fixed by time, place and the participants in communication (Fowler, 1991: 63). This construction was noticeably higher in the tabloids than the broadsheets (with the exception of the *Guardian*). This finding supports Dor's (2003: 697) argument that 'tabloid headlines rarely summarise their stories [...] and in many cases are not even informative'. Instead, headlines in tabloids – and, interestingly, the increasingly 'broadloid' *Guardian* – 'present the readers with a "fairly complex riddle" which, first, triggers frames and

Table 7.1 National actors, according to newspaper

	USA N	USA %	UK N	UK %	UN N	UN %	Iraqi N	Iraqi %	Other N	Other %	N/A N	N/A %	Unknown N	Unknown %	Total
Daily Express	7	4.4	38	23.9			30	18.9	27	17.0	20	12.6	37	23.3	159
Daily Mail	16	8.5	37	19.7			40	21.3	33	17.6	18	9.6	44	23.4	188
Daily Mirror	18	8.2	41	18.6			30	13.6	37	16.8	28	12.7	66	30.0	220
The Sun	10	4.3	67	28.5			36	15.3	30	12.8	18	7.7	74	31.5	235
Financial Times	93	23.3	48	12.0	5	1.3	33	8.3	179	44.8	7	1.8	35	8.8	400
Guardian	49	16.3	53	17.3	1	0.3	44	14.7	49	16.3	36	12.0	69	23.0	301
Independent	48	18.5	62	23.9	2	0.8	42	16.2	63	24.3	19	7.3	23	8.9	259
Daily Telegraph	53	15.4	81	23.5	1	0.3	71	20.6	80	23.2	16	4.6	43	12.5	345
Total	294	14.0	427	20.2	9	0.4	326	15.5	498	23.6	162	7.7	391	18.6	2107

belief systems in the reader's mind, and, then, gets resolved in the ensuing text' (ibid.). The reader would have to read on to find out who, or what, these pronouns refer to.

Third, both numerically and proportionately, tabloid headlines represent the USA as an agent significantly less frequently than the broadsheets. For instance, across the six weeks of the sample, only seven headlines printed in the *Daily Express* (4.4%) represented the USA as an actor – in other words, as the agent of a verb, doing, saying or thinking something. The presence of British action and actors was a great deal higher in tabloid headlines: in the *Sun's* headlines, for instance, Britons were represented as actors over six times more frequently than Americans. This ratio is highly misrepresentative, given the scale of US military involvement in the invasion. The active military might of the USA was reflected a little more realistically in the headlines of the broadsheets, though the majority still foregrounded the actions of Britons (speaking, attacking, advancing, considering, etc.) more frequently than those of Americans. The exception to this pattern was the *Financial Times*, which positioned the USA as an actor in a little under a quarter of their headlines ($n = 93$, 23.3%) and Britons in 12 per cent ($n = 48$). However not even the *Financial Times* could bring itself to foreground Iraqi action: with the anomalous exception of the *Daily Mail*, the headlines of all newspapers represented the actions of Britons more frequently than those of Iraqis.

What this demonstrates is that, like with the reporting of international sporting events, 'It is almost taken for granted that media coverage [. . .] will assume spectators' main interest' is in the 'team' representing 'Us' (Brookes, 2002: 83). Little matter, it seems, that the vast majority of the invasion (i.e. *the actual story*) involved Americans invading Iraq, the American military bombing Iraqis and the American military announcing their achievements; British newspapers, with the exception of the *Financial Times*, were preoccupied with the actions of a minority of British troops. Such a preoccupation is not only revealing of British newspapers' overwhelmingly nationalist news agenda, it also serves to bolster the ideological notion that the invasion was undertaken by a coalition of equals.

Looking in a little more detail at the sample, as expected and in accordance with the ideological square, the referential and predicational strategies chosen by the sampled newspapers almost ubiquitously presented 'Us' in a positive manner and 'Them' in a negative manner. For the tabloids, British troops were labelled with terms that denoted intimacy, ownership ('our'), implied that 'We' share a familial relationship ('boys'), or else elevated 'Us' to a position of greatness. For instance:

Barely 18, Our Youngest Soldier in the Conflict (*Daily Mail*, 1 April 2003)
Crusade for all our war heroes (*Daily Express*, 15 April 2003)
Hero Brits Mourned (*Sun*, 18 April 2003)
Free Our Men (*Daily Mirror*, 29 April 2003)

The broadsheets rarely adopted such affected rhetoric, but often their headlines were no less ideological. Take this headline printed in the *Daily Telegraph* at the start of the invasion (21 March 2003):

Actor	Verb	Object	Prepositional phrase
Allies	**launch**	**their onslaught on tyranny**	**from air, land and sea**

Here, the *Daily Telegraph* creates a degree of distance from the reported action through using the possessive 'their' to qualify the object. However, the remainder of this noun phrase is clearly intended to structure a positive understanding of 'Our' involvement in the conflict. Through choosing to use the phrase 'onslaught on tyranny', over alternatives such as 'their invasion', 'their onslaught *on Iraq*' or simply 'their onslaught', the newspaper not only provides a justification for the attack but also demonstrates that it considered the invasion to be just and principled.

'Our positivity' was also maintained via backgrounding the negative consequences of 'Our' actions. In this sample, this occurred through the use of metonymy and other ideological ascriptions of agency that diminished 'Our' active role in killing innocents. For example:

Missiles hit Red Crescent maternity hospital (*Independent*, 3 April 2003)
Maternity Unit bomb kills three (*Daily Mirror*, 3 April 2003)
Rocket kills teenager in Iran (*Financial Times*, 9 April 2003)
Grenade kills two soldiers (*Daily Telegraph*, 15 April 2003)

In each of these headlines, a metonym is used to shield 'Our' agency: in each, the user of an object is replaced by the object itself. It was US forces that launched all of these missiles, bombs and rockets (in the case of the fourth headline, the grenade was both thrown by and killed US soldiers) but you wouldn't know this to look at these headlines. These headlines were the product of an editorial choice; we should remember they didn't have to appear in the above form. Taking the second example: 'Maternity Unit bomb kills three' concertinas two processes (US bombs a maternity unit and kills three people) into a clipped noun phrase that retains their contextual sense (a bomb, a maternity unit, three people killed) but removes any sense of responsibility.

Arguably, headlines are constructed to be short and punchy, and we should therefore expect clipped or compound noun phrases to be used over longer (and less striking) full clauses that properly ascribe agency. However, nowhere in this sample did any headline state, entail or even imply that 'Allied soldiers' had acted in an intentionally negative way. On occasion, sub-editors had to perform significant linguistic labour to achieve this. Take the headline **Talks on new regime exclude UN and are boycotted by Shia group** (*Guardian*, 15 April 2003), for example. In using this construction, the sub-editor chose to present 'Talks on new regime' *as the agent*, a representation that removes any sense that it was *the invading forces* (principally the USA) that were responsible for excluding the UN from the talks. The USA did this because their plans for the new Iraqi regime were at odds with international law. In contrast, where they appeared in headlines, the negativity of the Iraqi military forces was emphasised through the way they were referred to:

> **Troops on alert for Saddam's suicide squad** (*Independent*, 26 March 2003)
> **A vile enemy** (*Sun*, 28 March 2003)
> **Saddam brute is quizzed** (*Sun*, 23 April 2003)

The negative nominalisations in these headlines hardly require further analysis.

Processes

As with the participants above, it is initially useful to quantify the types of clause and verb processes used and their distribution across the sampled newspapers.

Table 7.2 clearly demonstrates the principal difference between tabloid and broadsheet headlines: the ratio of noun phrase

Table 7.2 Headline type to newspaper

	Type of headline						Total
	Noun phrase		Full clause		Other		
	Count	(%)	Count	(%)	Count	(%)	
Daily Express	38	23.9	121	76.1			159
Daily Mail	44	23.4	142	75.5	2	1.1	188
Daily Mirror	52	23.6	165	75.0	3	1.4	220
The Sun	66	28.1	167	71.1	2	0.9	235
Financial Times	11	2.8	389	97.3			400
Guardian	18	6.0	283	94.0			301
Independent	10	3.9	249	96.1			259
Daily Telegraph	20	5.8	322	93.6	2	0.6	344
Total	259	12.3	1838	87.3	9	0.4	2106

(NP) headlines to those containing full clauses. Some examples of NP headlines from the sample included:

Saddam's Last Stand (*Sun*, 25 March 2003)
Bloodbath in Ambush Alley (*Daily Express*, 26 March 2003)
Wailing Children. The Wounded. The Dead (*Guardian*, 3 April 2003)
The Ultimate Humiliation (*Daily Mail*, 10 April 2003)
Iranian Rebel Army Threat (*Daily Mirror*, 30 April 2003)

None of the above headlines use a verb; they are all noun phrases. Noun phrases are usually identifiable by being able to precede them with an indefinite ('a') or definite article ('the'), for instance: '[the] bloodbath in ambush alley'. The exception to this is the first example, since the head of the noun phrase ('last stand') is already modified by the possessive 'Saddam's . . .'. The compound noun in the fifth example is a peculiarity of news-speak rarely if ever used in everyday speech. The headline could even be extended further to produce increasingly convoluted noun phrases such as '*Fanatical Iranian Rebel Army Threat*'; '*Fanatical Iranian Rebel Army Threat Shock*'; and so on. Providing a name for an action or an event obscures agency, and hence the perpetrators' rationale and responsibility, from the reported process. Tabloid newspapers are on average over five times more likely to include a nominalised headline than a broadsheet newspaper (tabloid 24.7% NP headlines; broadsheet 4.5%). The difference between the two genres of newspaper is so

Table 7.3 Newspaper format and process type

	Tabloid Newspapers		Broadsheet newspapers		Total	
	N	(%)	N	(%)	N	(%)
Verbal process	43	5.4	216	16.6	259	12.3
Mental process	39	4.9	60	4.6	99	4.7
Relational process	157	19.6	232	17.8	389	18.5
Transitive action process	234	29.2	481	36.9	715	33.9
Intransitive action process	124	15.5	255	19.5	379	18.0
Noun phrase	198	24.7	59	4.5	257	12.2
Other	7	0.9	2	0.2	9	0.4
Total	802	100.0	1305	100.0	2107	100.0

marked that the use of nominalised headlines should be considered a stylistic characteristic of tabloid reporting.

In more detail, Table 7.3 above shows the frequency and proportion of four main verb processes, across the two institutional genres of newspaper.

Following on from the discussion above, Table 7.3 demonstrates that broadsheet newspapers use their headlines to represent action far more often than tabloids, whether verbal, transitive or intransitive action processes. Indeed the only process that was included in proportionately more tabloids than broadsheets were relational processes – that is verbs such as 'is', 'was', 'are' and so on. The significance of relational processes is discussed below. The much higher incidence of verbal processes in the headlines of the sampled broadsheets are also worthy of note:

> **War May Be Longer Than You Think, Says Hoon** (*Daily Telegraph*, 21 March 2003)
> **ITN Says Veteran Reporter is Dead** (*Financial Times*, 24 March 2003)
> **Blair Pivotal in Bush Policy says Ex-Envoy** (*Guardian*, 4 April 2003)
> **War is Madness Judge Tells Rally** (*Independent*, 7 April 2003)

Looking at the second of these examples, a tabloid would most probably distill this headline down to a relational process: 'Veteran Reporter [is] Dead'. As the examples show, broadsheets more typically retain the source responsible for the statement. This is only partly explained by the tabloid preference for shorter, punchier headlines, and seems to indicate another key differentiation between tabloid and broadsheet reporting: for middle-class broadsheet audiences, a statement is newsworthy not merely for its manifest content or truth value, but also because of the social standing of the speaker. The professional middle classes worship social status above all things, and hence when reporting an accusation, pronouncement or other speech event, broadsheets identify the utterer in the headline, often through reference to his/her job description or by using other markers of social class ('Judge'; 'Ex-Envoy').

Going further, we need to consider the processes chosen in the sampled headlines and their possible ideological import. First, and most obviously, verbs may be more or less euphemistic, or carry more or less negative meaning. The ideological square predicts that positive words will be used more frequently to describe 'our' actions, and negative words will be used more frequently to describe 'theirs'. This was exactly what the sample recorded. For instance:

Our boys go in to defeat the snipers (*Sun*, 25 March 2003)
UK marines finally calm the port that proved so resistant
    (*Independent*, 26 March 2003)
UK cleric butchered at Shrine (*Sun*, 11 April 2003)

The *Independent's* use of 'calm' as a verb, in the second of these examples, is highly ideological: babies are calmed, animals may be calmed; the Iraqi port in question was conquered by force. The third example is included to demonstrate the strength of the ideological square when interpreting ambiguous statements, in this case a passivised verb without agent: on reading this headline, who do you assume did the 'butchering'? Although it is possible that the 'UK cleric' referred to was 'butchered' by British or American troops, I contend that this would not be the first guess of the majority of readers: butchery, slaughter and indeed killing, in general, are reportedly not activities that 'We' committed during the war and, when combined with a British victim, the implicature will always be that 'they did it', whoever 'they' happen to be at any one time.

More interesting, at least from the perspective of transitivity, are examples in which the choice of process is ideological. In this sample, this predominantly occurred in two ways: first, the reported event was represented as a state of affairs rather than a transitive action process:

Baghdad Burning (*Sun*, 21 March 2003)
A volatile region is in chaos (*Daily Mirror*, 26 March 2003)

As stated above, relational processes were the only verb process used by tabloids more often than broadsheet newspapers. The first of these examples, from the front page of the *Sun* on the first day of the invasion, represented a fundamentally transitive event – to invade, attack or bomb – as a relation: 'Baghdad [is] burning.' While it is inconceivable that any reader of the newspaper would be unaware that Baghdad was burning because the US had bombed it, nevertheless, the headline acts to background this politically uncomfortable fact: US bombs were burning Baghdad, razing its civilian infrastructure, its schools and its homes. Similarly, an alternate construction of the second headline above – perhaps 'US bring chaos to Middle East' rather than simply stating the region '*is in* chaos' – could have foregrounded the negative effects of 'Our' presence in Iraq in a much more direct way rather than the politically timid option they chose.

Second, sub-editors frequently chose to use the intransitive verb 'to die' over the transitive 'to kill':

Two die at checkpoint (*Daily Mirror*, 15 April 2003)
13 Iraqis die as US troops fire into crowd (*Daily Telegraph*, 30 April 2003)

The headline from the *Daily Mirror* is not only uninformative it also misrepresents these two deaths: the two (Iraqi) victims did not simply 'die', they were *killed*. Similarly, with the second example, the 13 Iraqi civilians referred to did not simply 'die'; these US soldiers *killed* them. The prepositional phrase 'as US troops fire into crowd' acts to provide *context* to the reported event, rather than an explicit ascription of agency: the preposition 'as' entails that these two events occurred simultaneously ('this occurred *while* that occurred') rather than one being the direct consequence of the other. Hence, while this construction implies that it was US bullets that killed these people, it simultaneously structures our comprehension of the event: this was an unforeseen, unfortunate accident, as if the soldiers involved did not understand that firing live ammunition into a crowd of civilians would bring about death.

Following on from this point, responsibility for killing people (at least when the killers were American or British) was also disavowed through the use of passivised agent deletion. For example:

ITN Man Killed in Crossfire (*Daily Express*, 24 March 2003)
Two cameramen killed as US shell hits hotel (*Guardian*, 9 April 2003)
Three Foreign Journalists Killed in Office Attacks (*Financial Times*, 9 April 2003)

For each of these headlines we should ask: killed by whom? The example from the *Guardian* follows the pattern identified above: the prepositional phrase 'as US shell hits hotel' is used to provide context for the reported deaths, not responsibility for them. The ITN man referred to in the first headline – Terry Lloyd – we now know was killed by the US, though this was arguably not definitively accepted at the time. In response to his death, television news producers, who felt their three-to-four-man crews were prone to being targeted by the US military, 'shelved plans to send up to 100 more staff into Iraq because of fears for their safety' (Plunkett, 2003). Of course, this was 'mission accomplished' for the US military, who succeeded in limiting reporting from 'unilaterals' and hence shutting down possible unhelpful – that is 'off message' – voices. The dishonest vagueness in the third headline is less easily excused. Covering this event the day before, CNN online reported 'U.S. military attacks killed three journalists in two different buildings in Baghdad Tuesday, raising questions about the tactics of U.S. troops trying to take control of the Iraqi capital' (**US attacks kill three journalists**).[18] The facts of the event were therefore well known by the time the *Financial Times* went to print.[19]

Circumstances

The circumstances associated with the processes also contribute to an ideological representation of the invasion. In the sampled headlines, circumstances were predominantly provided through the use of prepositional phrases. Prepositional phrases can be used to modify both noun and verb phrases, providing extra details on the time, place or the manner in which the action described in the process occurred; they are marked by a preposition (e.g. 'as', 'in', 'on', 'to', 'amid' and many others) and an object (e.g. '*as* we went', '*in* the box', '*amid* the chaos', etc.). Most frequently, the sampled headlines used prepositional phrases to modify the verb phrase of the clause. Given that some of these are examined above, I'll only add three more here. In each case, the prepositional phrase is underlined:

> **Two RAF Tornado crew die <u>in US missile blunder</u>** (*Daily Telegraph*, 24 March 2003)
> **Children killed <u>in US assault</u>** (*Guardian*, 2 April 2003)
> **Eighteen Kurdish soldiers killed, many injured <u>in US 'friendly fire'</u>** (*Financial Times*, 7 April 2003)

The use of the preposition 'in' in each of these headlines is highly ideological. When examining the second and third examples above we should ask: Why was the preposition 'in' used instead of 'by'? It would be more accurate to state 'Children killed *by* US assault' or 'Eighteen Kurdish soldiers killed, many injured *by* US "friendly fire"'. More forcefully, the sub-editor could have written 'US kill children *in* assault'. Any of these headlines could have just as easily fitted into the space filled by the chosen headlines,[20] but were not used, presumably to avoid catching any flak from the US Army. The first headline is even more ideological: the sub-editor not only substituted 'by' for 'in', but also swapped the transitive verb 'killed' for the intransitive 'died'.[21] Again, the prepositional phrase 'in US missile blunder' is used to provide context to the reported event (i.e, the wider event that these deaths were part of) and not agency (in other words, *responsibility* for these deaths).

On occasion, a prepositional phrase was used to modify a noun phrase. Take, for instance, the headline of a report printed in the *Independent*: **British surround city in grip of Saddam's militia** (1 April 2003). First, according to this representation of the war, Iraqi soldiers were now a 'militia' and not 'soldiers' at all (but not yet fedayeen or insurgents); more interesting, however, is the way that this term is used in the prepositional phrase of the headline. If the first part of the clause – 'British surround city' – stood alone as the headline, as it could given its structure is grammatically correct (S:NP VP O:NP), the headline could prompt a negative impression of the described action. In other words, the readers of the *Independent* may conclude that 'Our' described actions were aggressive. But by modifying the noun 'city' with the prepositional phrase 'in [the] grip of Saddam's militia' the sub-editor provides a justification for the British action: the siege is necessary to *liberate* the city (metonymically standing in for Iraq) from the 'grip' of Saddam and his mercenaries. As with all ideological representations, this headline turns reality on its head.

Cracks in the hegemony

While it would be wrong to claim that *all* the sampled headlines accorded with the ideological square, the vast majority *did*, making exceptions to the rule all the more conspicuous. Take the headline **Brit kills Brits** (*Daily Mirror*, 26 March 2003), for instance: Not only was this the first transitive action process printed in the *Daily Mirror* (five days into the invasion), it was also an exceptionally direct representation of what the remaining newspapers called 'friendly fire' or else only implied through the use of prepositional phrases. Nowhere else across the sample was being killed by a member of your own Army described with such candour. However the most anomalous headline in the sample was printed in the *Financial Times*: **US-backed militia terrorises town** (9 April 2003). First, it is highly unusual for 'Our' actions to be described as 'terrorising'. It is even more unusual for 'Our terror' to be represented using a transitive verb with an active voice (more typical would be a passive voice: 'Town terrorised by US-backed militia'). It is significant, however, that the agent in this case was apparently not the USA but a 'US-backed militia', a distinction that provides a little ideological distance. It is striking that in a sample in which 539 of the headlines (25.6%) contained active transitive processes, reporting an invasion that resulted in the deaths of tens of thousands of Iraqi civilians, countless Iraqi soldiers and was justified by lies and deliberate falsehood, that this is as close as *any* newspaper headline got to directly criticising the actions of the US/UK invaders.

Pro patria mori: heroes, villains and the marshalling of morality

The remainder of the chapter will examine how the ideological square was reflected in the body of news reports.

Us and Them: 'Iraqi savages'

The ideological square predicts that the way that two sides are represented – that is, the way 'We' are represented and the way 'They' are represented – will be radically dichotomised. Of course, such polarisation serves political as well as rhetorical ends. As Gerbner (1991: 3) puts it, 'Calling some people barbarians makes it easier to act barbarian to them. [...] Labelling a large group "terrorists" seems to justify terrorising them. [...] Calling some people crazy or

insane makes it possible to suspend rules of rationality and decency.'
In short, when 'the enemy' are rhetorically constructed and dehu-
manised, it becomes possible to treat them in an inhuman way and
still retain 'Our' sense of moral superiority.

The most obvious way that this occurred was the ways that 'Our
side' and 'Their side' were named. As discussed in the analysis of
headlines above, British and Americans were described using terms
that conferred status, prestige and professionalism: they were 'coalition troops', 'ground forces', 'servicemen', 'the allies', or else were
described by regiment – for instance '3 Commando Brigade Royal
Marines', or 'The 7th US Cavalry in Abrams main battle tanks and
Bradley personnel carriers' (all from the 'anti-war' *Guardian*, **Ground
forces push into Iraq**, 21 March 2003). Such descriptions are
truthful of course, but rarely were *Iraqi* soldiers described in such
terms – indeed they were rarely called 'soldiers'. In keeping with the
reporting patterns of other recent wars (see Allan, 2004), newspaper
reports referred to Iraqi troops using terms that entailed they were
amateurish or unprofessional ('militia', 'irregulars') or else that they
were suicidal zealots, for instance *'fanatical security forces'*, 'hundreds
of *volunteer fanatics* prepared to sacrifice themselves to kill coalition troops' (all from *Sunday Mirror*, 30 March 2003). Instrumental
in this characterisation of the Iraqi Army was the use of two additional referential strategies: *fedayeen* and the ultimate Muslim folk
devil, *the suicide bomber*. A single incident – four American soldiers
were apparently killed by Ali al-Noamani who was then awarded two
posthumous medals by Saddam Hussein – was all the proof that
some journalists needed to argue that Iraqis were in fact 'terrorists'
and 'suicide bombers', and not soldiers at all. For instance, in a
column about a week before the fall of Baghdad, Melanie Phillips
wrote:

> people [. . .] said that there was no evidence Saddam was involved
> in terrorism. They were proved wrong in the most gruesome way at
> the weekend when four soldiers were killed by a suicide bomber.
> The Iraqis now say 4,000 Arabs, *including hundreds of Palestinians*,
> have come to Iraq to form human bombs, 'the first on the glorious
> path of jihad (holy war) against the invaders'. [. . .] The war against
> Iraq is turning very graphically into a war against terror. (**Grow
> up or shut up. This war simply must be won**, *Daily Mail*,
> 31 March 2003)

While undoubtedly an unconventional way to kill the enemy, such a 'suicide attack' could never be accurately described as 'terrorism' given that the victims were soldiers. However, two days later – tucked away at the bottom of an opposing page in the *Sun* – came the admission that the 'suicide bomber' who killed these Americans 'was an innocent taxi driver blown up by remote control' (**Taxi bomb detonated by remote**, *The Sun*, 2 April 2003). Ironically, therefore, this *was* a criminal act because Ali al-Noamani was an innocent victim; however, as the *Sun* rightly pointed out, the finding made 'nonsense of the claim that 4,000 fanatics [were] ready to die for Saddam'. Unfortunately, as with other audience members, the US Army proved that they were more inclined to believe the initial incorrect version of events. That same day, the US Army killed ten unarmed women and children at a checkpoint when their car failed to stop; a heightened 'fear of terrorism' was the cited explanation.

Second, the representation of 'Our' and 'Their' actions was similarly dictated by the ideological square. This occurred at the level of the process chosen (as demonstrated in the discussion of headlines above), but it also determined the events held to symbolise 'Our' values and character and 'Theirs'. For instance, the day after al-Jazeera broadcast footage which showed dead and captured American soldiers, *The Sun's* front page read: **AT THE MERCY OF SAVAGES: Terrified US troops captured and paraded on TV by cruel Iraqis** (24 March 2003). Inside, the opening of a two-page article read (noun phrases underlined; verb phrases italicised):

GLOATING BASTARD

A gloating Iraqi thug *disgusted* the world last night by *manhandling* American soldiers on TV.

Six brave US troops killed in battle were *shown stripped and lying* in pools of blood on the floor of a makeshift morgue.

The smirking Saddam henchman *dragged* one corpse along the floor by the arm and *twisted* its head so the cameras could get a better shot.

And in a further example of Iraqi savagery, shaken US prisoners were *forced to face* a merciless TV grilling in defiance of the rules of war.

Set out like this, the dichotomisation is clearly apparent: in each clause Iraqis are represented as agents doing (repulsive) things to American soldiers [objects]; in each clause Americans are cast as victims, helpless to resist 'Iraqi savagery' because they are either dead or traumatised by their ordeal; in each clause, the referential and predicative strategies underline the depravity of the Iraqis (gloating Iraqi thug, manhandling, smirking Saddam henchman, dragged, twisted, forced, merciless) and the innocence of the Americans (brave, killed in battle, stripped, shaken, forced).

US Defence Secretary Donald Rumsfeld was said to be furious with al-Jazeera for broadcasting the footage and, in a display of startling hypocrisy, accused them of violating the Geneva Convention, which lays down the rules for the treatment of prisoners of war. As an al-Jazeera spokesman said at the time: 'Look who's talking about international law and regulations.'[22] American indifference for international law (at least when inconsistent with their goals) was underlined the following day, when the US bombed Iraqi State Television in a(nother) clear breach of the Geneva Convention. Of course, the USA was unfazed by its own criminal actions, openly stating, 'it had deliberately targeted Iraqi television and satellite communications' in an effort to damage 'the regime's command and control capacity' (**State TV back, but satellite still down**, *Guardian*, 26 March 2003). The same day, both the English and Arabic language websites of al-Jazeera were forced down by hackers in an attack widely thought to have originated in America.[23] A week later, Americans shelled 'The Basra Sheraton, whose only guests [were] al-Jazeera journalists', despite al-Jazeera informing the US military of the location of its Basra headquarters.[24] More seriously, six days after this attack, US troops bombed the Baghdad offices of al-Jazeera and Abu Dhabi Television 'killing Tareq Ayyoub, a Palestinian Jordanian journalist working for al-Jazeera'.[25] Again, the US had been told the Global Positioning Systems co-ordinates of the office, leading the International Federation of Journalists to state that a 'sinister pattern' was developing, in which the US military was killing journalists whose reporting was contrary to their preferred view of the invasion.[26]

Two further articles, from the same page of the free daily commuter newspaper *Metro* (2 April 2003), demonstrate the kind of reported events used to underline the dominant representation of Iraqi and 'Allied' military forces:

A. I saw children used as human shields

1a. Paramilitaries used children as human shields in a shoot-out with British tanks, writes Martin Bentham.

2a. Sgt David Baird, 32, who commands a Challenger 2 tank with the Royal Scots Dragoon Guards, said he saw at least four or five children aged between five and eight grabbed by the scruff of the neck and held by Fedayeen fighters as they crossed the road in front of his tank.

3a. [. . .] He said: 'I am married with a son of nine months and I felt disgusted. In this part of the world it seems that life is not held in the same way as we regard it. It was terrible'.

B. Tears for Dead Baby

1b. Soldiers buried a baby facing Mecca after finding her in the middle of the road.

2b. Her tiny, mangled corpse was discovered by a US tank unit as it entered Kifl – a village 130 miles south of Baghdad – in the aftermath of a fierce battle.

3b. Chaplain Glenn Palmer [. . .] said: 'You would have thought she was a doll, until you got closer.'

4b. Distressed soldiers said a Muslim prayer and put a makeshift marker on her grave.

5b. Mr Palmer said: 'I'm sure she was Muslim and we respect that tradition'.

It is clearly no accident that these two articles appeared on the same page. Placed side by side in this way, it becomes apparent that they have been written in such a way as to convey the kinds of qualities that apparently characterise 'Us' and those that characterise 'Them'. Indeed, the reports imply that 'Their values' are the mirror opposite of 'Ours': we are sensitive soldiers, they are callous fedayeen; we try to protect children, they endanger children; we respect life, they hold it in contempt; we are friends to the Iraqis, they are their enemies. Such sentiments are encapsulated in paragraph 3a, a direct quote from the 'witness' to Iraqi 'Fedayeen fighters' (not soldiers of course) jeopardising the lives of children. Compare this to 'Our' treatment of the dead infant in paragraphs 1b and 4b. Conspicuously absent from report B is any sense that 'We' (and Our superior values) may have been responsible for killing this Iraqi infant. The report simply states she was 'discovered [. . .] in the aftermath of a fierce battle' – that is, a battle in which the US had bombed and shelled the village before 'entering' it. As Ellul (1965: 58) has pointed out, a successful propaganda campaign necessarily requires that the propagandist insists on the purity of 'Our' actions, whilst simultaneously accusing the enemy of 'the very intention that he himself has'. That is, 'He who wants to provoke a war not only proclaims his own peaceful intentions but also accuses the other party of provocation. [. . .] He who wants to establish a dictatorship always insists his adversaries are bent on dictatorship' (ibid.). And those who view the Iraqis as expendable, as 'mere Muslims', whose deaths are an irrelevance when viewed in relation to 'freeing the country', always accuse their enemies of holding these same beliefs.[27]

Brits and Yanks: Who are the better imperialists?

As Preston pointed out at the time, once the war started, ' "Our boys" worked much of their familiar leader-writing magic' and effectively finished off open journalistic resistance to the invasion.[28] Reporting the invasion was therefore problematic for newspapers that had previously declared they were 'anti-war'. How do you present 'Us' in a good light (and hence stay on side with the newspaper buying public) without (1) an abrupt reversal of your pre-war editorial position and (2) justifying the slaughter of innocent Iraqis? As discussed above, deictic pronouns, such as 'Us' and 'Them', 'Our' and 'Their', do not have any meaning other than their immediate application: their meaning is constantly negotiated and renegotiated in the context of specific reports. Therefore, actors included within the ideological 'We' in some reports are positioned as 'They' in others. With the outbreak of hostilities, what developed in the 'anti-war newspapers' (i.e. the *Independent*, the *Guardian*, and most prominently the *Daily Mirror*) was not opposition to the invasion *per se*, but criticism directed almost exclusively towards the actions of American troops: 'Our boys' were represented as making the best of the bad situation dealt them by Blair and the distasteful aspects of the invasion were projected onto the Americans.

This rhetorical – and ideological – partition of responsibility occurred in three ways. First, criticism was made implicit through the way newspapers highlighted events in which Americans had (inadvertently or otherwise) killed civilians and other non-combatants. For instance, the *Guardian* reported that the US had killed 34 civilians when their missiles 'hit the wrong target' (**This makes us love Saddam, not America**', 24 March 2003). The gist of the article read: 'As volunteers pulled corpses and body parts from the smouldering ruins of the compound yesterday, Mr Saeed's widow Aisha and

10 children wanted to know only one thing: *why had America killed him?*' The answer, the rest of the article implied, was that he had simply gotten in the way. As Tommy Franks stated prior to the war, no civilian target was to be considered 'off limits'. In contrast to the broadsheet, the tabloid *Mirror* newspapers were more prone to editorialising when reporting civilian atrocities. For instance, the injuries suffered by one Iraqi, 14-year-old Zaina Kadim, were described and explained as follows:

> An arm and a leg ripped open by flying shrapnel. A gaping wound beside the right eye of her otherwise beautiful face. *The Americans call it collateral damage. The doctor treating her called it slaughter.* (**Carnage on the day for prayers**, *Sunday Mirror*, 30 March 2003; original emphasis)

First, the claim 'The Americans call it collateral damage' is significant since it logically entails that the Americans had indeed classified this victim's injuries 'collateral damage'. In turn, this entails that they were *aware* of the victim and, logically, that they acknowledge that they were *responsible* for amongst other things, the 'gaping wound beside the right eye of her otherwise beautiful face'. Second, the term 'collateral damage' is infamously regarded as signalling a blasé attitude towards killing innocents during wartime. Through the immediate contrast with 'slaughter' (the assessment of a *doctor*), the article additionally implies that the Americans are unmoved by the consequences of their actions. Whenever events such as these were reported, newspapers used the modifier 'American' (thus 'American attack', 'Americans say'), rhetorically implying that this was, somehow, not 'Our' war.

Second, newspapers partitioned and disavowed British responsibility through quoting sources that were not only critical of US but also contrasted 'Our' actions in Iraq with 'Theirs'. The following example, criticising the American justification for their troops killing 10 unarmed women and children at a checkpoint, was typical of the *Mirror's* approach:

> A senior British source said the killings showed the inexperience of American troops in dealing with urban warfare. 'It is the old British saying about Americans: All the gear and no idea'. (**We're sorry: US say checkpoint shootings by kid soldiers are a tragedy**, *Daily Mirror*, 2 April 2003)

Here, the reporter used an *indirect* quotation that explicitly shapes our understanding of the *direct* quotation that follows it: they have 'no idea' because of their 'inexperience'. Again, broadsheets were a little more reticent about using such interpretative devices to direct audience understanding, relying instead on highlighting the views of British soldiers that accorded with their editorial commitment:

> Air Trooper Kevin Asquith "I didn't like hearing about those seven women and children [shot by US forces]. We are supposed to be helping them, not killing them. The Yanks have always been gung-ho. I would ask George Bush 'Is it worth it? Who is next?'" (**Behind the lines, stoicism and humour in a soldier's life**, *Independent*, 5 April 2003)

The quote was included twice in the above article: once as part of a list of 'views from the troops', and again as a 'pulled quote', in a much larger font as part of a coloured sidebar running down the side of the report. This reveals the importance that the newspaper placed on the viewpoint and, when combined with the other pulled quotes (for instance 'a Lance Corporal' is quoted saying 'We are wasting valuable soldiers for something that is not our fight'), indicates the editorial view of the newspaper. While journalists often quote sources whose views accord with their own or their newspaper's view of an event (see Tuchman, 1972), this second strategy for disavowing British responsibility is qualitatively different from simply reporting civilian deaths that were the consequence of American attacks. Reporting the deaths of civilians, even critically, would not necessarily foster a negative view of American actions in the eyes of an audience. As was oft-repeated during the invasion, 'unfortunate things occur during war' and therefore deaths of civilians can be put down to accidents or human error. Such a rationalisation is less plausible when the 'inexperienced', 'gung-ho' American troops are explicitly compared with the more knowledgeable and restrained British troops. The reporting implicitly asked: if the British can act 'appropriately', then why aren't the Americans?

Third, newspapers used their op-ed pages to, often forcefully, back up the viewpoints of quoted sources presenting an Us/Them representation of American and British actions. For instance, following the speech of Lt Colonel Collins – a speech that Butt *et al.* (2005) point out received widespread and laudatory international coverage – the *Daily Mirror* offered the following assessment of his views.

After all the jingoistic nonsense from George Bush and his warmongering political cronies, take time to read the words of Lt Colonel Collins and understand why the British Army is the finest, most admired and most compassionate military force in the world. (**Heroes led by a man of principle**, *Daily Mirror*, 20 March 2003)

Note, again, the Orwellian use of language in this excerpt: What does the newspaper *mean* when it claims 'We' have the 'most compassionate military force in the world'? That they kill your family then attend the funeral the following day and offer condolences? The *Mirror* also printed forcefully argued columns that claimed to identify the reasons why 'We Brits' are so much better at conquering Iraq than the US. For instance:

The American military machine is the most sophisticated and lethal weapon system in the world [. . .] But US military thinking – strategy and tactics – is driven by their technology. They are not superior thinkers. They just have greater assets to play and experiment with. Unfortunately the British army does not have this level of hardware. [. . .] But the Brits have something no amount of computer chips or satellites can compensate for. These brave young men have hard-earned experience passed down from generation to generation in basic and bloody fighting. (**USA has all the gear, but we've done the practice**, *Daily Mirror*, 26 March 2003)

Thus a relation of opposites is set up in these series of propositions, generalised into an overarching gist in the headline (see Tomlin *et al.* (1997) for a discussion of such transformations): they have 'assets to play [. . .] with', we do not; we have 'experience [. . .] in basic and bloody fighting', implying that they do not; they 'are not superior thinkers', implying that we are. In short, the apparent over-reliance on military hardware – caricatured as 'computer chips' and 'satellites' – is the failing of American military, while 'Our' dependence on 'basic and bloody fighting' is a much better way to fight *and win* the invasion. Hence, because the apparent problem lies with the way that the Americans were conducting the invasion, not with the invasion itself, newspapers avoided having to print criticisms of British troops that 'the audience' assumedly find so offensive.

It should be noted that underlying this criticism of the US was not the brutal and appalling effects that US weapons and tactics were having on Iraqi civilians, but the effect that they were having on the war effort – in other words, on the hard work 'Our Boys' were putting in winning over 'hearts and minds.' In other words, once the war started, the dominant argument of reporting in the previously anti-war newspapers was: '*We British are much better at imperialism than the Americans.*' For instance, following the massacre of 10 women and children at a checkpoint, the *Daily Mirror* uncritically conveyed the British Army's

> [. . .] *irritation* that it happened on the day that British troops began patrolling in berets rather than helmets, which UK commanders had hoped would be a propaganda coup showing parts of the country returning to normality. (**We're sorry: US say check-point shootings by kid soldiers are a tragedy**, *Daily Mirror*, 2 April 2003; my emphasis)

Never has the meaning of the phrase 'returning to normality' been so abused: the reporter implies that he thinks it is normal for Iraqis to be under the control of an occupying army – at least when these imperialists are *British*.

Each of the strategies detailed above enabled the 'anti-war' newspapers to ideologically maintain opposition to the *invasion* but support for British troops *involved* in the invasion. When examining the Us/Them manner in which the imperialist activities of American and British troops were represented, the words of John Pilger are useful to bear in mind: 'British troops may be better trained than the Americans; but this does not alter the fact that they are part of, indeed essential to, a criminal invasion of a country offering us no threat' (**The War for Truth**, *Daily Mirror*, 5 April 2003).

Summary

The first stage in this propaganda war, directed at justifying war against Saddam Hussein, his 'bad bombs' and his potential future collaboration with enemies of freedom, wasn't successful: it failed to convince the lion's share of the general public of the necessity of invading Iraq. However, once the invasion started, a second phase in the propaganda war was instigated. This second stage was a great deal more successful because military and governmental sources are better adept at controlling the media during wartime conditions than they are in 'peace time'. Governmental propagandists are fully aware of the discursive practices of journalism – the kinds of stories that will appeal to journalists, the kind of information that they need, in the required format and the time of release that will optimise the probability that their unadulterated message will enter the public realm. It was this awareness of the discursive practices of journalism, and the way that they were used by the military and security state *against* journalism, that ensured journalists' coverage of the invasion was to the liking of their military supervisors.

Conclusion

With this book, I have discussed a theory and a method of analysing newspaper discourse. Throughout, I have made a number of assumptions about newspaper discourse, which, at this point, it is perhaps useful to reiterate. First, discourse should be defined as *language in use*. Second, and consequently, newspaper discourse should be approached in such a way that assumes that it is an activity, or a practice. Newspaper discourse is directed at doing something – even if this is only informing you of what is going to be on the TV tonight, it is active. Third, that as a practice, newspaper discourse must necessarily be situated in a context – in a social setting. There can be no practice detached from a social context, and no social context is ever wholly neutral: certain ways of acting are considered more appropriate and ways of speaking or writing have become entrenched into styles and genres. Hence, the social setting *frames* and *structures* the language used – in some cases *controlling* the language used – enabling certain people to speak and restricting others; certain words or phrases will be obligatory, or considered more suitable, and others words or phrases will be prohibited. The relevance of this to newspaper discourse is clearly demonstrated in sourcing routines and the existence (and the contents) of newspaper style guides. Finally, the theoretical model introduced assumes that newspaper discourse – this language in use – can, in turn, have *effect* on the social context of its use, via shaping the ways that the consumers of newspapers perceive themselves, perceive others and, most importantly, differentiate (and *rank*) themselves relative to others.

If we take this to be an acceptable way to situate newspaper discourse, then in addition to examining the form and function of journalistic texts, it becomes necessary for our analysis to take into account the social *contexts* in which journalistic language is used and the social *consequences* of its use. Clearly, these two aspects of language use are *intimately* related to power. Power is an essential issue to acknowledge because, as most of us probably believe, journalism has more power to shape our understanding about events, ideas, people and the relationships between people, than many other forms of communication.

This is what this book has been emphasising: if we believe that language is social, that speaking or writing are activities intended to do things, and that journalism is a powerful form of communication, how does all this tie together? How does the language of journalism work? How does it function and how can it act upon us? Questions like this may be considered at a large scale and at a smaller scale. At a large scale we can ask: in what social circumstances do journalists work and what are the relationships between journalism and these social circumstances? In tackling such questions, we could examine the effects of material social conditions on the way that journalists go about their job (i.e., economic and political practices); and we can look at the way journalism may reproduce these social conditions (e.g. by naturalising them) or can challenge them, by showing that social change is not only possible but *inevitable*. At a smaller scale we could ask: How does this text achieve its function (i.e. its argumentative or communicative goal)? Here, we could look at how the text hangs together cohesively; how it represents social action or actors (through referential or predicational strategies); the kinds of sources referred to or quoted; which source is held up as being the most authoritative or believable and how this is achieved; how the author uses modes of proof to support a conclusion; and the range of text-discursive features discussed in Chapter 3.

Clearly these are big questions to ask. But the model of CDA proposed by Fairclough, and applied and developed here, is useful in approaching them. It is useful because although it acknowledges the scale and complexity of the dialectic – where society affects journalism and journalism can affect society – it allows us to break it down into smaller sections, in order to make our analysis easier. For purposes of analysis, newspaper discourse can be divided into 'a complex of three elements: social practice, discursive practice (text production, distribution and consumption), and text, and the analysis of a specific discourse calls for analysis in each of these three dimensions and their interrelations' (Fairclough, 1995b: 74). Taking each in turn, social practices are the 'outside' influences that shape the production and consumption of news, just as they shape the production and consumption of other texts (including the one you're currently reading). Social practices are 'the social phenomena existing prior to, and hence shaping, impinging upon and accessible to journalistic practice' (Richardson, 2004: 5). Journalism is inescapably connected to the social, political and cultural context (etc.) in which it is written and consumed, and hence needs to be (re)located in these contexts during analysis. Some questions to consider when examining the social practices of newspapers include:

- Where has the information in this article come from?
- Is there a reason why this information was provided to journalists on the day, or the instant, that it was? Does releasing *this* story cover up a *more significant* story?
- What are the relations between this text and systems such as markets, ownership, advertising, government, the law and religious beliefs?
- How much power and social influence do the cited/quoted sources have?
- How much power and social influence does the focus, or *subjects*, of the story have?
- Is there a customary or habitually used constellation of representations associated with stories on this subject? Are these negative or positive?
- Who, if anyone, is 'othered' by the reporting? That is, whom does the report construct as 'Us' and who are 'They'? Are any of 'Them' represented as part of 'Us' in *other* reporting contexts? What are the possible reasons for this?
- What are the possible social consequences of reporting?
- Specifically, who benefits and who loses – or may be *harmed* – from coverage of this sort?

In short, as Fairclough (1995a: 202) puts it, we need to ask 'What wider socio-cultural processes is this text a part of, what are its wider social conditions, and what are its likely effects?'

Second, since '*society*' and '*culture*' don't write the news, we also need to examine the practices of news organisations and the processes of production, including news-values, the pursuit of journalistic objectivity and structuring influence of the audience on news discourse. We should remember, 'News is not a natural phenomenon emerging straight from "reality", but a *product*. It is produced by an industry, shaped by the bureaucratic and economic structure of that industry, by the relations between the media and other industries and [. . .] by relations with government and with other political organisations' (Fowler, 1991: 222). It is useful to assume that there is always a *reason* for a news-text being the way that it is. The text, indeed the newspaper as a whole, is the result of journalists making a multitude of choices between alternatives, including: between covering event A or event B; between putting story A on the front page or story B;

between quoting this source or that; between this way of referring to said source or that; between using headline A or headline B; and so on. Some more productive questions to bear in mind when considering the discursive practices of journalism include:

- Why, out of all the events in the world and all the information received by a newspaper on a particular day, was this story selected?
- What was it about this reported event that the newspaper thought would interest its readers? Why was it included on this particular page? Why was it given the space it was allocated – why wasn't it longer or shorter?
- Is the 'natural history' of this report discernible? Was information given to the journalist as an 'off the record' briefing, in a public meeting (where the source could have been open to cross-examination), in a press release (entailing a one-way dissemination of information) or in some other form?
- Does any formal or informal agreement exist between source and journalist (or newspaper) regarding the way that information can be collected, processed or presented? Would the journalist be rewarded – in *any* way – for favourable coverage, or chastised – in *any* way – for negative coverage?
- Stylistic choices: Does the newspaper employ a linguistic style that is familiar or more formal? How is this style achieved? How is the 'brand' of the newspaper communicated through story selection, layout, the use of 'white space', headlines, fonts and assorted furniture?
- Does the text achieve the primary goal of journalism? Does it help you better understand the world and your role in it?

Taking only one of the points above, the study of linguistic style tells us that the way that people speak or write is fundamentally related to the audience they are speaking or writing *for*. So, if we assume that certain words are there for a reason, that they were thought to communicate what the journalist wanted to say *to this particular audience* better than other words or better forms of expression, what does this tell us? Does it tell us something about the status of the audience? Or something about the relationship between the audience and the journalist? Or something about the politics of the paper? Or perhaps it tells us something about the relationship between the paper and wider society?

Third, there's analysis of the content of texts themselves, where analysis should aim to show *HOW* meaning is communicated. At this level, Fairclough (1995a: 202) argues we should ask 'How is the text designed, why is it designed in this way, and how else could it have been designed?' (ibid.) This analysis of text should be *playful*, in which the analyst fools around with the wording, composition and layout of the text to expose how it conveys its messages. As stated above, we should approach texts as the result of a series of many choices, including:

- Choices between referential and predicational strategies: What explicit and implicit meanings are conveyed by the words chosen to refer to people, places, concepts, events and processes?
- Choices between forms of expression (or syntactic choices): What semantic meanings are represented by syntactic choices? How are agency and responsibility represented through the use of different verb processes, particularly for negative social actions?
- Does the journalist use direct or indirect quotation? What effect does this have on reader perceptions of the source and her/his viewpoint?
- Choices between argumentative techniques: How are the three points of the rhetorical triangle (arguer, argument and audience) manoeuvred in defence of a standpoint? Does the arguer rely on arguing from example, analogy or causation? Are any rhetorical tropes used? What is the relationship between such argumentative moves and the imagined audience?
- Choices in text structure: Does the order in which sources are referred to have any effect on your view of their opinion? How is this achieved? Are contrastive words like 'but', 'however' and 'yet' used to undermine a source?
- Choices in the layout and juxtaposition of texts: Are two articles on a similar subject placed adjacent, or near to each other? How does this affect your reading of either or both texts?

When analysing the text-discursive features of newspapers, you should look at texts and think: *How could this have been different?* Would the whole gist or tone of the text change if we were to swap a particular word with another one, or rephrase a particular sentence, or take out a sentence entirely? How could this story have been written if the audience was richer (or poorer), or less English, or less male, or less white, and so on?

Finally, our examination of newspaper discourse as a whole needs to be explicitly related to power, ideology and hegemony. CD Analysts need to *'reverse the taken-for-granted'* stance and 'ask whether a particular sense or reading of a particular word, phrase, or larger segment of text relies on an assumption' (Woods and Kroger, 2000: 94) about the gender, 'race', religion, nationality, class (etc.) of those referred to. Most importantly, analysts should ask:

- How does reporting relate to, and *reflect*, wider structural and social inequalities?
- In what ways do the hierarchies of capitalism – in which the rich are valued more than the poor – permeate coverage? Does reporting bolster the power of the dominant classes?
- How, if at all, does the report deal with power abuse such as discrimination, dominance and exploitation? Is racism encouraged? Is class exploitation ignored, justified or denounced?
- Does the report deny the possibility of meaningful social change? Is the public represented as passive and apathetic, or active, involved and critical? Is the 'historically transient' capitalist social order 'represented as eternal, natural, inevitable or "rational"' (Jones, 2001: 227)? In short, is capitalist exploitation presented as a natural, enduring social reality?

Remaining focused on these questions will help produce analysis that is *understanding* of the often-difficult material conditions in which journalism is produced, *sensitive* to the intricacies of how texts function and *critical* of any detrimental effect – ideologically and materially – of contemporary newspaper reporting.

Notes

1 Introduction: newspaper discourse

1. Of course, this is not the end of the capitalist exchange system. The distribution company could then sell the figurine, perhaps to a British retail outlet, for £5, who may then sell it for £10 in their shop. Once the end sale is taken into account, the worker was exploited for 19/20 of the working day.
2. **A Rising Tide?**, *Washington Post*, 12 March 2006, http://www.washingtonpost.com/wp-dyn/content/article/2006/03/11/AR2006031101051_pf.html, accessed 14 March 2006.
3. More astute readers may have picked up on this example and the way that it enacts my identity: at the very least it entails that I go to the pub; this implies that I drink alcohol; and may additionally imply that I drink in the same pubs as my students.

2 Analysing newspapers: context, text and consequence

1. This is not to suggest, of course, that ideology is 'the sole element in which the reproduction/transformation of the relations of production of a social formation takes place; that would ignore the economic determinations which condition that reproduction/transformation' (Pêcheux, 1994: 141).
2. I place 'choice' in inverted commas because such variation is by no means 'free' or 'arbitrary', for reasons discussed later in this chapter and, particularly, in Chapter 4.
3. While Jones (2001) offers this point as a criticism of the approach to ideological analysis in cognitive linguistics, I feel that it is also applicable to the *logocentric* approach of much (critical) discourse analysis.

3 Analysing texts: some concepts and tools of linguistic analysis

1. While Mohammad is a name intimately associated with Islam, not everyone called Mohammad is Muslim. Hence, this use of the name *implies* that the hypothetical average terrorist is assumed to be Muslim, but does not *entail* it.
2. These 'accusations' came from four newspapers: the *Sun*, the *Daily Mail*, *The Times* and the *Daily Mirror*. The *Mail*'s criticism was the most strident. They argued: 'The public no longer knows what to believe. When this government is so distrusted, can anyone be blamed for the

jaundiced view that the confused and confusing crime figures are just another example of lies, damned lies and statistics?'
3. Taking these '-gates' in turn: in Irangate, the USA sold weapons to Iran and diverted the funds to the right-wing Nicaraguan Contra guerrillas. An examination of those involved reveals a startling number of people who were also involved in the Watergate scandal. Lewinskygate, followed Monica Lewinsky's sexual relationship with Bill Clinton; in Rathergate, reporter Dan Rather broke the story of Pres. George W. Bush's dereliction of duty during the Vietnam War using documents that were proven false. In the UK, Camillagate involved a taped telephone conversation between Prince Charles and Mrs Camilla Parker-Bowles; Cheriegate concerned Cherie Blair's association with Carole Caplin; and Squidgygate involved a taped telephone conversation between Diana, Princess of Wales, and 'a male friend'. Hansiegate was a cricket match-fixing scandal involving South African captain Hansie Cronje.
4. See Chapter 2 for a discussion of the coherence relations of pronouns.

4 Discursive practices: producing print journalism

1. According to the International New Safety Institute, at least 1300 news media personnel have been killed in the last 15 years because of, or whilst at, work. In 2004, journalists were killed in: Africa (2); Venezuela (1); Peru (2); Paraguay (1); Nicaragua (2); Mexico (4); Haiti (1); Dominican Republic (1); Columbia (1); Brazil (2); Serbia and Montenegro (1); Russia (3); Belarus (1); Saudi Arabia (1); Israel and the Occupied Territories (1); Iraq (23); Sri Lanka (3); Philippines (11); Pakistan (1); Nepal (2); India (3); and Bangladesh (4). Almost all were murdered.
2. Data available at http://www.statistics.gov.uk/CCI/nugget.asp?ID=2& Pos=1&ColRank=1&Rank=192, accessed 7 April 2005.
3. See EthicNet (http://www.uta.fi/ethicnet) for details of the codes of practice in place in 36 European countries and the International Federation of Journalists.
4. See http://www.nuj.org.uk/inner.php?docid=59 for the full NUJ code of conduct, accessed 1 July 2005.
5. See http://www.uta.fi/ethicnet/ifj.html for the full IFJ Declaration of Principles, accessed 1 July 2005.
6. For instance, while the content of Article 19 of the Universal Declaration of Human Rights is well known (that 'Everyone has the right to freedom of opinion and expression . . .'), Article 29 (2) states: 'In the exercise of his rights and freedoms, everyone shall be subject only to such limitation as are determined by law solely for the purpose of securing due recognition and respect for the rights and freedoms of others and of meeting the just requirements of morality, public order and the general welfare in a democratic society.'

7. *BBC Monitoring* is a subscription news and information service that provides news briefings and analysis for its customers. In the words of its website, *BBC Monitoring* 'selects and translates news from radio, television, press, news agencies and the Internet from 150 countries in more than 70 languages'. *BBC Monitoring* is part of BBC World Service, which is funded by the Foreign and Commonwealth Office. The material they produce is bought by subscribers, mainly governmental and quasi-governmental organisations.

8. Reported 12 April 2005 (see http://news.bbc.co.uk/1/hi/world/middle_east/4436119.stm), accessed 15 April 2005.

9. On this point, Iggers (1999: 92) argues that 'few journalists are prepared to actively defend objectivity as an epistemological doctrine'. Despite this, 'the underlying, corresponding theory of truth remains embedded in the way concepts such as facts, distortion and bias are used in journalism' (ibid.).

10. Here I mean prejudicial in the legal sense of the publication of information that creates a substantial risk that the course of justice in particular proceedings will be seriously prejudiced or impeded. Criminal proceedings become active once an arrest warrant or summons is issued, or an arrest has been made. Anything that directly links the suspect or defendant to the alleged crime, or any suggestion that he/she is guilty (including reference to past convictions) is likely to be taken as prejudicial. And the intention of whoever published the material is irrelevant – if a judge rules that the published matter creates a substantial risk of serious prejudice to active proceedings, it does not matter if they meant to risk impediment. (Many thanks to Mark Hanna for this definition.)

11. The Press Complaints Commission (PCC) 'received 10 complaints from the public, a significant amount given that the offensive wording was changed for later editions' (Kelso and Byrne, 2003: 4). Typically though, the PCC didn't take any action since the complaints came from third parties. Unfortunately, the PCC interprets the Code of Conduct in a remarkably restrictive, individualised (indeed bourgeois) way: only the individual(s) directly affected by a report may complain. This has historically meant that despite widespread racist reporting of 'immigrants', minority ethnic communities and most recently 'asylum seekers', particularly in tabloids such as the *Daily Express*, *Daily Mail* and the *Sun*, not a *single* complaint on the grounds of racist reporting has *ever* been upheld by the PCC (Frost, 2004; Petley, 2006).

12. Accordingly, a few days later the editor of the *Sun*, Rebekah Wade, met with Marjorie Wallace to discuss the affair: 'Rebekah Wade asked me to lunch and she said, "Why couldn't I use bonkers and what else would do?" What I said there was really simple. I remember having the same conversation with her predecessor, David Yelland. He said: What's a three letter word I can put in a headline rather than nut or mad? I said, "What about ill? Because that's what it is – ill. Someone's

ill and they go to hospital." [Rebekah] sort of said, "Well yeah, maybe"'
(available at www.bbc.co.uk/ouch/news/btn/bruno_sun.shtml, accessed
17 May 2005).
13. *The Times'* style guide is available at: http://www.timesonline.co.uk/
section/0,,2941,00.html, the *Guardian*'s is available at http://www.
guardian.co.uk/styleguide/0,5817,184913,00.html both accessed 1 July
2005.
14. The *Guardian* prefers 'forenames' to 'Christian names' – again, note
the referential strategy and what this suggests about the identity of the
newspaper.

5 Social practices: journalism and the material world

1. For instance, the Sheffield *Star*'s Sorake Beach Appeal produced
18 feature articles between its launch on 29 December 2004 and
10 February 2005 – one every two days. The appeal was intended
to rebuild 'the paradise Indonesian village of Sorake Beach, *home of
former Sheffield woman* Jo-Anne Wau, which has been shattered by
the deadly tsunamis' (http://www.sheffieldtoday.net/mk4custompages/
custompage.aspx? pageid=48146, accessed 2 June 2005).
2. Only the officially declared campaigns will be examined here. The
campaigns of local regional UK newspapers are archived at http://www.
holdthefrontpage.co.uk/campaigns/campaignsindex.shtml. In limiting
myself in such a way, my analysis necessarily ignores 'below the line'
campaigning that occurs when a newspaper runs on a story every day
but doesn't declare this as 'a campaign'. For example, my analysis misses
campaigns such as the highly racist anti-asylum seeker campaign of the
Dover Express (1998–99). On 1 October 1998, the *Dover Express* ran
an editorial headed **We want to wash dross down drain**. The editorial denounced 'illegal immigrants, asylum-seekers, bootleggers (who
take many guises) and the scum of the earth drug smugglers who have
targeted our beloved coastline. We are left with the back draft of a
nation's human sewage and no cash to wash it down the drain.'
3. See Temple (2004) for an overview of campaigns ran by local evening
papers, 2000–2004.
4. Despite this, profits from local newspapers continue to rise. For instance,
the group operating profit of Archant (who own 27 regional newspaper
titles in and around London) was up 20.7 per cent in 2004 to £32.7m;
Northcliffe increased its operating profit by 7 per cent to £100.5m;
Johnston Press' profits rose 18 per cent to £150.6m; and profits for
Trinity Mirror's regional division rose almost 25 per cent to £150.6m in
2004 (all from www.holdthefrontpage.co.uk, accessed 3 June 2005).
5. The distribution of the *Leicester Mercury* overlaps with the *Nottingham
Evening Post* and the *Derby Evening Telegraph*; the *Derby Evening*

Telegraph also overlaps with the *Nottingham Evening Post*; and the *Nottingham Evening Post* also overlaps with the *Lincolnshire Echo*.

6. Quoted in http://www.holdthefrontpage.co.uk/campaigns/2004/07july/040721text.shtml, accessed 3 June 2005.

7. For instance, the *Western Morning News'* campaign against 'the impetuous rush to build hundreds of monstrous, noisy, ugly and massively intrusive wind turbines across one of Britain's most beautiful landscapes', quoted in http://www.holdthefrontpage.co.uk/campaigns/2004/06june/040610wind.shtml, accessed 8 June 2005.

8. http://www.holdthefrontpage.co.uk/campaigns/2005/01jan/050125birm.shtml, accessed 7 June 2005.

9. http://www.holdthefrontpage.co.uk/campaigns/2004/05may/040526 yobbo.shtml, accessed 7 June 2005.

10. http://www.newsshopper.co.uk/news/shopayob/, accessed 7 June 2005.

11. http://www.holdthefrontpage.co.uk/campaigns/2004/05may/040525 west.shtml, accessed 7 June 2005.

12. http://www.holdthefrontpage.co.uk/campaigns/2004/08aug/040806 brave.shtml, accessed 7 June 2005.

13. http://www.holdthefrontpage.co.uk/campaigns/2004/09sep/040913rada.shtml, accessed 8 June 2005.

14. http://www.nomisweb.co.uk/reports/lmp/la/2038431861/report.aspx?pc=NW3, accessed 8 June 2005.

15. Lecture at *Symposium on Images of Islam in the Media*, Al-Khoei Foundation and The Islamic Educational, Scientific and Cultural Organisation (ISESCO), 25 October 1999.

16. As explained in the Introduction, to this I would also add that the working class are those people who have little-to-no autonomous control over their working day: they 'punch in' rather than arrive at work; they are supervised by 'team leaders', foremen and managers rather than being trusted and self-directed; and they are required to work in a predetermined location rather than working from home (as I often do).

17. In fact job protection can be very good for business and the economy. France, for instance, restricts medium and large business to a maximum 35-hour week and has a higher per capita productivity rate than Britain where workers can labour for 50 hours a week.

18. Here, 'tot' is used partly as a colloquial term of endearment to refer to the children (in accordance with *The Sun's* style) and partly to differentiate them from 'the girls'.

19. The character Vicky Pollard has become an immediately recognisable stereotype, leading to many young women being branded 'the real-life Vicky'. For instance, see **Judge bans real-life Vicky Pollard from her own home** (*Guardian*, 10 May 2005, http://www.guardian.co.uk/uk_news/story/0,1480080,00.html, accessed 24 June 2005).

20. On this point it is interesting that while the anti-social behaviour of the poor is always made hypervisible, the anti-social behaviour of the

rich is not only *excused* but also actively *encouraged*. For instance: **Super-rich lobby to save tax loophole** (*Guardian*, 13 April 2002) details but doesn't criticise the selfish attempts of the rich to avoid paying tax; **Hain forced to retreat on rich tax** (*Guardian*, 21 June 2003) illustrates the Blair government's complicity in such behaviour; **Keeping it in the family** (*Financial Times*, 27 November 2004) attempts to educate the rich about how to avoid paying inheritance tax; and **Tax breaks are steadily chiselled away** (*Financial Times*, 22/23 January 2005) in which the journalist complains that the opportunities for such selfish greed are slowly being closed. Paying tax is a social responsibility that should be linked directly to the ability to pay; tax avoidance makes the middle class just as anti-social as the cast of 'yobs' paraded in tabloids on a daily basis. Indeed they are arguably *more* anti-social since tax avoidance denies essential public services the funds they need and hence has a greater negative social effect.

21. Column available at http://www.timesonline.co.uk/article/0,,1072-755767,00.html, accessed 24 June 2005.

6 Applying discourse analysis: argumentation and letters to the editor

1. For an introduction to some of the more influential contemporary theoretical and analytical approaches, see van Eemeren *et al.* (1996; 1997).
2. For instance, in a recent interview for the *Sunday Herald*, Chomsky stated: 'If you're gonna be asked a question, say, about terrorism and you're given three sentences between commercials, you've got two choices. You can repeat conventional ideology – you say, "yeah, Iran supports terrorism". Or you can sound like you're from Neptune. You can say, "yeah, the US is one of the leading terrorist states." The people have a right to ask what you mean' (see http://www.sundayherald.com/48388, accessed 31 March 2005).
3. See http://www.adl.org/presrele/IslME_62/3750_62.asp, accessed 31 March 2005.
4. See http://www.adl.org/israel/letter_usa_today.asp, accessed 31 March 2005.
5. For the record, the letter was also printed in *The Valley Independent* (Pennsylvania, USA), by-lined to Joel Ratner and Joseph Friedman. Here the opening read: 'Charley Reese continues to propagate his one-sided view of the Israeli–Palestinian conflict and accuses Israelis of voting "for war and against peace" by electing Ariel Sharon ("Israel has chosen national suicide")' (see http://www.adl.org/israel/letter_valley_independant.asp, accessed 31 March 2005). The remainder of the letter reproduced identical material.

6. On this point, Aristotle warns: 'the more we try to make either dialectic or rhetoric not, what they really are, practical faculties, but sciences, the more we shall inadvertently be destroying their true nature; for we shall be re-fashioning them and shall be passing into the region of sciences dealing with definite subjects rather than simply with speeches' (1359b 11–16).

7. I prefer to use the term 'ethotic' in preference to 'ethical' to avoid terminological confusion; I prefer 'pathotic' over 'pathetic' and 'logetic' over 'logical' for identical reasons.

8. Again, I use 'pathotic fallacy' in preference to 'pathetic fallacy' used in literary theory, where it refers to a device in which objects or abstract concepts are described as if they have thoughts or feelings, or else seem to be in tune with the feelings of a character (e.g. rain used to signify a character's emotions).

9. Of course, it is erroneous to claim that it is *numbers* of immigrants that are most commonly perceived as the problem. The threat that racists perceive in immigration is articulated in a number of key thematics – crime, disorder, disease, 'our way of life' – that are related to, but by no means reliant upon, a large number of 'immigrants'.

10. See www.statistics.gov.uk/cci/nugget.asp?id=467 for details.

11. For longer discussions of logical fallacies see: van Eemeren and Grootendorst (1992); Hamblin (1970); and Hansen and Pinto (1995).

12. In my estimation, the column commits at least the following fallacies: *argumentum ad hominem*, attacking arguers' characters rather than standpoints (rule 1); evading the burden of proof (rule 2); attacking a fictitious standpoint (rule 3); non-argumentative means of persuasion, emotional play on fear and loathing (rule 4); falsely presenting a premise as a shared starting point (rule 6); fallacies of composition and division (rule 7); fallacy of hasty generalisation (rule 8); fallacy of declaring successful defence (rule 9).

13. The letters *defending* Kilroy in the *Mirror* did not contain particularly good argumentation. More than likely, this was due to the newspaper's own agenda against Kilroy. Therefore I will ignore these two pro-Kilroy letters in favour of letters that supported this standpoint in a more convincing way printed in other newspapers.

14. The rule of three – or *tricolon* – is ubiquitous in political discourse, from 'life, liberty and the pursuit of happiness', through Gaitskill's 'We shall *fight* and *fight* and *fight* again to save the party that we love' to New Labour's 'Education, education, education'.

7 Critical discourse analysis: war reporting

1. For example, see http://www.theage.com.au/articles/2002/08/12/1029113894507.html, http://www.socialist.net/content/view/410/31/, http://www.cnn.com/2004/WORLD/meast/12/21/britain.iraq/ and http:

//www.slate.com/id/2070857 for a range of international sources that refer to, or agree with, the characterisation. Many more exist.

2. See **A quiet day at the morgue, just 20 new bodies to deal with**, *Guardian*, 26 August 2005, http://www.guardian.co.uk/Iraq/Story/ 0,2763,1556795,00.html, access 26 August 2005.

3. Throughout this discussion, I have repeatedly and intentionally used the term 'declared war' to distinguish such events from covert wars or proxy wars. In contrast to the prominent reporting of declared wars, it is rare for either covert or proxy wars to receive any coverage at all, for reasons spelled out in great detail in Chomsky (2002), Herman (1992) and Herman and Chomsky (1994).

4. Jake Lynch, Freelance reporter, BBC, quoted in *Weapons of Mass Deception* (2005), a documentary film directed by Danny Schechter (www.fair.org).

5. Cf. the Convention on the Prohibition of the Development, Production and Stockpiling of Bacteriological (Biological) and Toxin Weapons and on Their Destruction (1972), http://fas.org/nuke/control/bwc/text/ bwc.htm, accessed 23 August 2005. See http://www.stimson.org/ cbw/?sn=CB2001121890 for details of Chemical weapons conventions (accessed 23 August 2005).

6. From http://www.ippnw.org/DUStatement.html, accessed 23 August 2005.

7. From http://www.ippnw.org/NukeNPTPrepCom2003EPWs.html, accessed 23 August 2005.

8. Quoted in **Saddam is 'deceiving, not disarming'**, *Guardian*, 29 January 2003, www.guardian.co.uk/usa/story/0,12271,884498,00.html, accessed 29 January 2003.

9. Quoted in **Blair dismisses Saddam's 'games'**, *Guardian*, 28 February 2003, http://politics.guardian.co.uk/foreignaffairs/story/ 0,11538,904909,00.html, accessed 28 February 2003.

10. For an article demolishing the key claims of Powell's speech, see **AP Staffer Fact-Checks Powell's UN Speech**, http://editorandpublisher.com/eandp/news/article_display.jsp?vnu_content_id=1971092, accessed 25 August 2005.

11. Describing American war crimes in his 1995 memoir, *My American Journey*, Powell offers the following justification: 'I recall a phrase we used in the field, MAM, for military-age male [. . .] If a helo spotted a peasant in black pajamas who looked remotely suspicious, a possible MAM, the pilot would circle and fire in front of him. If he moved, his movement was judged evidence of hostile intent, and the next burst was not in front, but at him. Brutal? Maybe so. But an able battalion commander with whom I had served at Gelnhausen (West Germany), Lt. Col. Walter Pritchard, was killed by enemy sniper fire while observing MAMs from a helicopter. And Pritchard was only one of many. The kill-or-be-killed nature of combat tends to dull fine perceptions of right and wrong.'

12. Going on, Cohen states that the 'bad faith of the anti-war movement' is such that 'If the US encourages the persecution of Palestinians, but belatedly fights against Serbian ethnic cleansing, they will support freedom in the West Bank but not in the Balkans.'

13. Quoted at http://lrp.greenrd.org/2004/09/are-cruise-missile-left-blind-to.html, accessed 23 August 2005.

14. See http://www.militarycity.com/iraq/1631270.html for full details of the 'Public Affairs Guidance on Embedding', including the ground rules and http://lists.stir.ac.uk/pipermail/media-watch/2003-March/000522.html for a discussion of their implications (both accessed 30 August 2005).

15. From http://www.journalism.org/resources/tools/ethics/wartime/embedding.asp, accessed 30 August 2005.

16. From 'Public Affairs Guidance on Embedding', http://www.militarycity.com/iraq/1631270.html, accessed 30 August 2005.

17. From Miller (2003).

18. http://www.cnn.com/2003/WORLD/meast/04/08/sprj.irq.hotel/, accessed 11 August 2005.

19. Since the US Army killed these journalists, the family of one of them – José Couso of the Spanish network Telecinco – has launched a criminal lawsuit for war crimes against three US soldiers, which alleges that they knew that journalists were in the Palestine Hotel.

20. The standard defence for ideological headlines that I have repeatedly heard from journalists is that more truthful alternatives could not have fitted on the page. In these cases, such a prosaic explanation simply does not stand up to scrutiny.

21. Once the verb 'died' was selected it would be unusual to write 'by' given that intransitive processes only involve an actor, not an actor and an afflicted. Thus, we may say 'X killed Y'; 'Y was killed *by* X'; or more imprecisely 'Y died', but not 'Y died by X'. I say that it would be unusual to use 'by' to modify an intransitive verb, rather than grammatically incorrect because there are cases in which it may occur. For instance, if I wanted to sound rather literary (or pompous) I could say 'Y died *by X's hand*'.

22. From **Al-Jazeera causes outcry with broadcast of battle casualties**, *Guardian*, 24 March 2003.

23. See **Al-Jazeera website 'hit by hackers'**, *Guardian*, 26 March 2003

24. http://media.guardian.co.uk/broadcast/story/0,,928144,00.html, accessed 1 September 2005.

25. http://media.guardian.co.uk/broadcast/story/0,,932458,00.html, accessed 1 September 2005.

26. For a recent report demonstrating the US continues to eliminate journalists and others that attend to the deaths of innocent Iraqis, see Klein (2004).

Glossary

This final section should be viewed as a preliminary guide to how certain terms and concepts have been interpreted and applied in this book. They are only intended to provide a starting point for aiding understanding. Other definitions of the entries that follow also exist and readers should seek these out as part of a critical reflection on language and journalism.

Adjective: A part of speech which modifies a noun, describing it or making its meaning more specific (e.g. the *tall* chair). Adjectives can usually be intensified (e.g. the *very tall* chair).

Adverbs: A part of speech that modifies any other part of speech, with the exception of nouns (which are modified by adjectives). In general, adverbs provide information such as 'how?', 'when?', 'where?' and 'how often?'. They are often derived from adjectives, through adding the suffix '-ly' (e.g. 'happy' – 'happily').

Agent: The participant of a situation that carries out an action. For instance, in the active sentence 'John kicked the ball', 'John' is the agent; similarly, in the passive sentence 'The ball was kicked by John', 'John' is still the agent.

Anaphora: A rhetorical scheme involving the repetition of the same word or group of words at the start of sentences. For example: '*We are a people in* a quandary about the present. *We are a people in* search of our future. *We are a people in* search of a national community' (Barbara Jordan, 1976, Democratic Convention Keynote Address).

Antithesis: A rhetorical scheme involving 'a compact expression of contrast or opposition' (Jasinski, 2001: 544) that is usually combined with a form of repetition or parallelism. Marx was especially fond of using antithesis (perhaps a by-product of his Hegelian philosophical roots), and one of his more famous examples is: 'It is not the consciousness of men that determines their being, but, on the contrary, their social being that determines their consciousness' (from *A Contribution to the Critique of Political Economy*, 1859).

Causal argument: An inductive argument in which a standpoint is defended 'by making it understood that there is a relation of *causality* between the argument and the standpoint' (van Eemeren and Grootendorst, 1992: 97). For instance: 'Lydia must have weak eyes, because she is always reading in poor light (And reading in poor light gives you weak eyes)' (van Eemeren, Grootendorst and Snoeck Henkemans, 2002: 100).

Comparison argument: An inductive argument based on a relation of analogy. An arguer defends his/her standpoint by showing that what is stated in the argument is similar to that which is stated in the standpoint 'and that on the grounds of this resemblance the standpoint should be accepted' (van Eemeren, Grootendorst and Snoeck Henkemans, 2002: 99). For instance: 'Why shouldn't students at good universities have to pay higher tuition fees? It costs more to live in a nice area of town' [and paying to live in 'a nice area of town' is comparable to paying for a 'good education'].

Content analysis: A research method based on the assumption that the words, phrases, themes, actors (etc.) mentioned most often in an analysed sample of texts are those that reflect the most important aspects of these texts. Content analysts, therefore, devise variables that aim at counting these most important textual features, and attempt to do so in an objective and systematic way. According to Berelson's (1952: 262) classic chapter on the subject, content analysis should be limited to counting '*the manifest content* of the communication' rather than 'the *latent intentions* which the content may express nor the latent responses which it may elicit'.

Conversation Analysis: As a starting point, CA can be described as the study of talk in interaction. It aims 'to provide an elaborate and systematic account of the way in which talk, especially talk-in-interaction, is constructed and understood by speakers' and, in doing so, hopes 'to develop an understanding of the underlying structural organisation of naturally occurring conversation' (Kitzinger and Frith, 1999: 299). Although many of its findings can be incorporated into a textual analysis (the first third of a complete critical discourse analysis), much CA is incompatible with the wider theory and method introduced in this book given its reliance on Idealist philosophical assumptions. Specifically, CA maintains that individuals and groups participate in the creation of their perceived reality through talk: hence, consciousness determines reality. To this extent, CA is based on ontological assumptions (in other words, assumptions about 'what exists?') that are the exact opposite of a Materialist standpoint.

Critical Discourse Analysis: Generally speaking, CDA is interested in linking linguistic analysis to social analysis. More specifically, CDA is interested in social problems such as dominance, power abuse, discrimination (racist, sexist, nationalist, ethnicist, etc.) and the role that language plays in reproducing, or resisting, such iniquitous social realities.

Deductive argument: An argument whose conclusion – or standpoint – must be true if its premises are true. For instance: 'All humans are mortal; Aristotle is a human; therefore Aristotle is mortal.'

Deliberative rhetoric: One of the three divisions of rhetoric suggested by Aristotle. Deliberative rhetoric is focused on the future, and debates the desirability, or undesirability, of possible future actions. It operates through encouragement or dissuasion, and its special topics are the advantageous and the disadvantageous.

Discourse: An endlessly debated term. This book takes it to refer to 'language in use'. In a lot more detail, van Dijk (1998) offers several definitional approaches to the concept. First the '*extended* primary meaning', designating a 'specific communicative event' usually involving, for example, 'a number of social actors, typically in speaker/writer and hearer/reader roles (but also a number of other roles such as observer or over-hearer), taking part in a communicative act, in a specific setting (time, place, circumstances) and based on other context features' such as power, privilege and other hierarchical constellations (p. 194). Second, the '*restricted* primary meaning', designating the abstract 'verbal dimension of the spoken or written communicative act' thereby referring to 'the accomplished or ongoing "product" of the communicative act' (ibid.) – in other words, the actual text produced by communication. These are the most commonly adopted referents of the term 'discourse'. Third, we can refer to a 'token' of a *specific* discourse (of the extended or restricted primary meanings) taking place between *these* specific actors in *this* specific setting. By this meaning of discourse, 'indefinite or definite articles or demonstratives are applied', referring to 'the discourse', 'that discourse', 'those discourses' (etc.) (van Dijk, 1998: 194–195). Fourth, we can conceptualise discourse as 'type', corresponding with the notion of a genre. Therefore, we can talk about the 'discourse of news reporting' in general. Fifth, there is the notion of 'social domains' of discourse such as 'medical discourse', 'political discourse' and so on (van Dijk, 1998: 196). Such domains usually draw upon a number of (discursive) genres – for example, 'political discourse' is constituted by genres such as 'political speeches', 'press conferences', 'government legislation' and several others. And lastly, there is the more Foucauldian notion of an 'order of discourse', referring to 'all the text and talk, or the discourses of a specific period, community or a whole culture' or 'the very abstract and general notion of the "discourse" of that period, community of culture' (ibid.).

Given the discussion above, it may seem simplistic to define discourse as 'language in use'. However, this definition is sufficiently precise to locate *language* as the centre of discourse, yet still flexible enough to be able to denote 'language in use' in general (extended primary meaning), 'this particular *example* of language in use' (token) and the written or recorded *text* of language in use (restricted primary meaning).

Enthymeme: A rhetorical syllogism (a three-part deductive argument), in which one premise is unstated. So, while a deductive syllogism may be structured: 'A, B, therefore C', an enthymeme dispenses with either the major premise 'A' or the minor premise 'B'. For example: 'All humans are mortal; therefore Aristotle is mortal', deletes the minor premise 'B' (Aristotle is a human) and argues 'A therefore C'. Equally: 'Aristotle is a human; therefore Aristotle is mortal' deletes the major premise 'A' (All humans are mortal) and argues 'B therefore C'. In an enthymeme, you, the reader, fill in the missing premise yourself in order to make the argument coherent.

Epideictic rhetoric: One of the three divisions of rhetoric suggested by Aristotle. Epideictic (or 'ceremonial') rhetoric is focused on the present and is concerned with proving someone or something worthy of admiration or disapproval. It operates through praise or criticism, and its special topics are the honourable and the dishonourable.

Ethos: One of the three modes of rhetorical proof suggested by Aristotle. In the words of Aristotle, an ethetic proof 'is achieved by the speaker's personal character when the speech is so spoken as to make us think him credible. We believe good men [*sic*] more fully and more readily than others' (1356a: 2–5). Specifically, to successfully evoke an ethetic proof, Aristotle suggests that a speaker must show wisdom (*phronêsis*), be virtuous (*arête*) and demonstrate goodwill (*eunoia*) towards the antagonist or audience.

Felicity conditions: A feature of speech act theory (an approach to linguistic philosophy that pointed out there was more to language use than propositions that may be true or untrue. For instance, sentences like 'Good luck' or 'Well done' are not true or false; they are, as Austin suggested, 'words that do things'). Felicity conditions are those features, or aspects, of a context that must exist for an utterance to successfully count as a speech act (or, more formally, to have any illocutionary force). Broadly, these amount to social identity and social setting, and the relations between these two things. As Mey (2001: 96) puts it, 'we have to be certain that the person enunciating these words actually has the power to do so, and second, we have to have the right circumstances for the uttering'. So, I may shout 'Out!' at a cricket match, but unless I am an Umpire my speech act has no illocutionary force.

Forensic rhetoric: One of the three divisions of rhetoric suggested by Aristotle. Forensic (or legal) rhetoric is focused on the past, and is concerned with the rightness or wrongness of someone's past actions. It operates through accusation and defence and its special topics are justice and injustice.

Idealist philosophy: An ontological perspective in which consciousness is taken to determine social being. Idealists start with human consciousness and proceed from this to an investigation of material reality; they argue 'human beings collectively and individually created their own reality in response to changing circumstances' (McLellan, 1986: 7). This approach is opposed by materialism, in which the world is held to exist prior to and independent of our knowledge.

Ideational function: One of the three major functions of language use, posited by Systemic Functional Linguistics. In addition to the interpersonal and textual functions (see below), language serves to communicate ideas about concepts, events and processes, and the actors (people, institutions, laws, etc.) involved in these.

Ideological square: A concept, developed by Teun van Dijk, that predicts that prejudicial discourse will be characterised by a positive characterisation of the self (the in-group; Us) and a simultaneous negative characterisation of the other (the out-group; Them). This is achieved through emphasising (or what is called *foregrounding*) the positive traits, actions or beliefs said to characterise Us and de-emphasising (or *backgrounding*) the negative ones; conversely, negative traits, actions or beliefs said to characterise Them are foregrounded whilst positive traits and so on about Them are backgrounded.

Ideology: Meanings that contribute to the production and reproduction of unequal power relations. As Thomson (1990) has put it, ideology is 'meaning in the service of power'.

Indexical reference: An utterance whose meaning varies according to the context in which it is uttered. For example, *I* refers to (points to, or *indexes*) the person speaking; *now* indexes the time of the utterance; *here* indexes the place of the utterance; and so on. So, despite *I* being 'the same word' if you say it or if your Mum says it, because the context of the utterance changes, the content of the word also changes. Therefore, in order to successfully, or at least fully, interpret an indexical, the hearer must know who the speaker was, and the time and place of the utterance.

Inductive argument: A process of plausible reasoning, in which the premises of an argument support the conclusion, but do not ensure it. Inductive arguments often rely upon forms of generalisation, extrapolation and interpretation. Academics working within the pragma-dialectic model of argumentation maintain that there are three inductive argument schemes: symptomatic arguments, comparison arguments and causal arguments.

Interpersonal function: One of the three major functions of language use, posited by Systemic Functional Linguistics. In addition to the ideational and textual functions, language also serves to express a speaker's attitude to what they're saying and to communicate the speaker's perceived relation to the hearer (i.e. their relative social status, how close or familiar they are, the degree of friendliness and so on).

Intransitive verb: A verb that takes a subject but not an object. For example, *sleep*, *die* and *run* are all intransitive. Intransitive verbs can be used to elide agency for negative processes, by limiting a clause to representing the *effect* of an event (e.g. '18 Iraqis *died*') rather than the process that brought about this effect (e.g. 'A British bomb *killed* 18 Iraqis').

Logocentric analysis: A term that Alan Luke (and originally Derrida) has applied to discourse analysis that is overly preoccupied with the intricacies of 'the text', rather than with the wider social, political and historic contexts that bound and situate communication and the extent to which these material realities are reflected in, or are contradicted by, the claims of the text.

Logos: One of the three modes of rhetorical proof suggested by Aristotle. In the words of Aristotle, a logetic strategy is achieved through 'the proof, or apparent proof, provided by the words of the speech itself' (1356a 2–5). In short, we are more likely to be persuaded by someone who presents reasons (or premises) to support their standpoint. This can occur in a variety of ways, which can be grouped into deductive and inductive argument schemes.

Materialist philosophy: Starts from an assumption of basic reality: the world exists; it exists outside of, prior to and independent of us; and it is this material existence (and specifically our social relations) that determines our consciousness.

Methodology: The study of research methods or the theory that supports a particular research method.

Modality: Referring to judgements, comment and attitude in text and talk and is indicated through the use of modal verbs (such as *may, could, should, will and must*), their negations (*may not, couldn't, shouldn't, will not* and *must not*) or through adverbs (*certainly*).

Narrative: Literally, a story. In more detail, Hinchman and Hinchman (1997) provisionally define narratives as 'discourses with a clear sequential order that connects events in a meaningful way for a definite audience and thus offer insights about the world and/or people's experiences of it' (cited in Elliott, 2005: 3).

Nominalisation: The transformation of a process (an action) into a noun (a name, or nominal). For example, 'An Israeli extremist killed Yitzhak Rabin' may be transformed in the nominalisation 'the killing of Yitzhak Rabin'. Nominalisations can occur for a variety of reasons: they tend to be shorter, and sometime concision is required; perhaps the details of the process or event are sufficiently well known that the full clause can be dispensed with; perhaps the full details of the process or event were provided earlier in the discourse, and hence do not need to be repeated; or perhaps the nominalisation is used to cover over some aspect of the process or event that is embarrassing or ideologically uncomfortable.

Noun: A fairly complex term but, as a rule of thumb, nouns are naming words. Nouns can be classified in a number of ways. There are proper nouns (e.g. John Richardson, Paris) and common nouns (e.g. girl, table). Further, nouns may be classified as count nouns – that is, nouns that can take the indefinite article 'a' or be made plural (e.g. a girl – twenty girls) and mass nouns, which cannot be numerated (e.g. furniture). Or nouns can also be grouped into concrete nouns (e.g. table) or abstract nouns (e.g. freedom).

Object: The entity (in other words, the person or thing) affected by a transitive verb. For instance, in the active sentence 'John kicked the ball', 'the ball' is the object; similarly, in the passive sentence 'The ball was kicked by John', 'the ball' is still the object.

Parallelism: A rhetorical scheme in which a set of words in successive phrases, clauses or sentences have the same or very similar grammatical structure. Corbett (1990: 463) has gone as far as to argue that parallelism 'is one of the basic principles of grammar and rhetoric'. For example, in his inaugural address, John F. Kennedy said: 'Let every nation know, whether it wishes us well or ill, that we shall *pay any price, bear any burden, meet any hardship, support any friend, oppose any foe* to assure the survival and the success of liberty.' Parallelism is often accompanied by anaphora and antithesis.

Pathos: One of the three modes of rhetorical proof suggested by Aristotle. Pathos is a mode of proof that operates through the audience, and is specifically used in a rhetorical argument to move the audience from one emotional state to another in order to make them more receptive to the arguer's standpoint. As Hill (1983: 26) states, Aristotle's theory of pathos demands the audience 'should not be abandoned to any chance pathe, or states of feeling, that might overtake them, but should be brought into the appropriate pathos by the speaker'.

Pragmatics: The study of language from the point of view of its users. Pragmatics starts from the observation that people do not always say what they mean and do not always mean what they say. To understand what it is that someone is 'saying' we have to take the context of the utterance into account. For example, if someone came up to you with an unlit cigarette in their mouth and said 'Do you have your lighter?', you could correctly answer 'no'. But it would usually be deemed inappropriate to just say 'yes' without *giving* this person a light, since it wasn't just a question, but also a *request*. On the other hand, there are instances in which this utterance could simply be a question. For example, if you've just left someone's house and your friend asked 'Do you have your lighter?', they may not be asking for a light. Given this, the most widely used shorthand definitions of pragmatics are the study of 'meaning in use' or 'meaning in context'.

Predicational strategies: Predication is 'the process and result of linguistically assigning qualities to persons, animals, objects, events, actions and social phenomena' (Reisigl & Wodak, 2001: 54). In other words, the ways that language use assigns size, shape, colour, beauty, value and many other qualities to people, places, ideas, objects and so on.

Preposition: Used to modify verb phrases and noun phrases, providing extra details on the time, place or the manner in which the action described in the process occurred; they are marked by a preposition (e.g. 'as', 'in', 'on', 'to', 'amid' and many others) and an object (e.g. '*as* we went', '*in* the box', '*amid* the chaos', etc.).

Presupposition: A taken-for-granted, implicit claim embedded within the explicit meaning of a text or utterance.

Prolepsis: A rhetorical scheme, in which a speaker includes – and argues against – the anticipated objections of an antagonist, who may be present, absent or even imagined. Often, this occurs indirectly – in other words, the speaker does not signal that they are responding to counter arguments – through simply addressing certain objections 'without necessarily attributing these concerns to a specific person or group' (Jasinski, 2001: 555).

Referential strategies: In essence, this refers to the way that people are named and the social values attached to such a choice. The manner in which social actors are named identifies not only the group(s) that they are associated with (or at least the groups that the speaker/writer *wants* them to be associated with); it can also signal the relationship between the namer and the named.

Scalar implicature: Part of Grice's theory of implicature, which has come to be regarded as a central part of contemporary linguistic pragmatics. Scalar implicature relates to what is called the maxim of quantity: you should make your contribution as informative as is required. Using a quantity indicator, the choice of what is called a 'weak term' implies the rejection of a stronger term on the same scale. In other words, 'some' implies 'not all'; similarly 'none' implies 'not some'. So we may say 'some lesbians play football' and this implies that I did not have sufficient evidence to claim that 'all lesbians play football'.

Scheme: A rhetorical figure of speech involving 'a deviation from the ordinary pattern or arrangement of words' (Corbett, 1990: 426). Examples include alliteration, parallelism and prolepsis.

Symptomatic argument: An inductive argument based on a relation of concomitance, association or connection. According to van Eemeren and Grootendorst (1992: 97), the argument 'is presented as if it is an expression, a phenomenon, a sign or some other kind of symptom of what is stated in the standpoint'. In other words, an individual example is taken to illustrate a wider pattern, issue or trend.

Syntax: The study of the rules that (depending on the theoretical approach) may structure or govern the construction of language. All theories of syntax have a position on: the classes of words in a language (i.e. nouns, verbs, etc.); the rules for their combination, which are usually defined in some explicit sense of patterns of acceptability (grammatical) and unacceptability (ungrammatical); and explanations on the relationships between form and content (or, more formally, between syntactic form and semantic meaning).

Textual function: One of the three major functions of language use, posited by Systemic Functional Linguistics. In order to achieve the ideational and interpersonal functions (see above), language needs to be presented 'in coherent, adequate and appropriate texts' (Fowler *et al.*, 1979: 188).

Transitive verb: A verb that requires a subject and one or more objects to be grammatically correct. Take the verb 'to kick', for example; this could not be used in a clause in an active way without a subject (who did the kicking) and an object (that was kicked).

Transitivity: The basis of representation since it examines the relationships between participants and the roles they play in a described process. It concerns the 'who (or what) does what to whom (or what)?' Simpson (1993: 88) argues that in any process there are three components that can be changed: the *participants* (which also relates to strategies of reference and predication); the *process* (the verb process chosen, whether this is constructed in an active or passive voice, tense, etc.); and the *circumstances* (essentially the use and form of adverbial and prepositional phrases).

Trope: A rhetorical figure of speech in which words are used to mean something apart from their ordinary meaning. Examples include metaphor, metonym and irony.

Verb: The part of speech that refers to action, existence or a state of being. In English there are four principal types of verb process that a sentence can use. First, *verbal* processes, such as speaking, shouting or singing. Second, verbs can be *mental* processes such as thinking, dreaming and deciding. Third, *relational* processes of being, such as have, seem and be (or is), which involve a subject and an attribute (e.g. 'You are *x*'; 'I have *y*'). And fourth, *material* processes, which can be further divided into *transitive* verbs involving two or more participants – the subject and the object of the action (e.g., 'He kicked her', 'I pushed you'); and *intransitive* verbs with only one participant (e.g. 'She ran', 'Aristotle flew', etc.).

References

Aldridge, M. (2002) The Ties that Divide: Regional Press Campaigns, Community and Populism, a Paper presented at the PSA Media and Politics Research Group, Loughborough University, 10 January 2002.

Aldridge, M. (2003) The Ties that Divide: Regional Press Campaigns, Community and Populism. *Media, Culture and Society*, 25: 491–509.

Allan, S. (2004) *News Culture* (2nd edn). Buckingham: Open University Press.

Althusser, L. (1971) *Lenin and Philosophy*. New York: Monthly Review Press.

Aristotle (1962) *Poetics* (trans. James Hutton). New York: W.W. Norton.

Aristotle (1984) Rhetoric (trans. W. Rhys Roberts), in J. Barnes (ed.) *The Complete Works of Aristotle*, Vol. 2, pp. 2152–2269. Princeton University Press.

Atkin, A. (2000) Punishment and the Arsenault Case, *Sheffield Online Papers in Social Research*, 1(1), www.shef.ac.uk/socst/Shop/atkin.pdf (consulted 11 September 2005).

Atkin, A. and Richardson, J. E. (forthcoming) Arguing about Muslims: (Un)Reasonable argumentation in letters to the editor. *Text and Talk*.

Austin, J. L. (1962) *How to do Things with Words*. Oxford: Clarendon Press.

Bachrach, P. and Baratz, M. S. (1970) *Power and Poverty: Theory and Practice*. New York: Oxford University Press.

Bell, A. (1991) *The Language of News Media*. Oxford: Blackwell.

Belsey, A. and Chadwick, R. (1992) *Ethical Issues in Journalism and the Media*. London: Routledge.

Berelson, B. (1952) Content analysis in communications research, in B. Berelson and M. Janowitz (eds) (1966) *Reader in Public Opinion and Communication* (2nd edn), pp. 260–266. New York: The Free Press.

Blommaert, J. (1999) The debate is open, in J. Blommaert (ed.) *Language Ideological Debates*, pp. 1–38. Berlin, New York: Mouton de Gruyter.

Blommaert, J. (2005) *Discourse: A Critical Introduction*. Cambridge: Cambridge University Press.

Blumler, J. G. and Gurevitch, M. (1995) *The Crisis of Public Communication*. London: Routledge.

Blundy, A. (2004) *The Bad News Bible*. London: Review.

Bourdieu, P. (1991) *Language and Symbolic Power*, edited by J. B. Thompson, translated by G. Raymond. London: Polity Press.

Bromley, M. (1998) 'Watching the watchdogs?' The role of readers' letters in calling the press to account, in M. Bromley and H. Stephenson (eds) *Sex, Lies and Democracy*, pp. 147–162. London: Longman.

Brookes, R. (2002) *Representing Sport*. London: Arnold.

Brown, G. and Yule, G. (1983) *Discourse Analysis*. Cambridge: Cambridge University Press.

Butt, D. G., Lukin, A. and Matthiessen, C. M. I. M. (2005) Grammar – The First Covert Operation of War, *Discourse and Society*, 15(2–3): 291–320.

Callinicos, A. (1983) *Marxism and Philosophy*. Oxford: Oxford University Press.

Cameron, D. (1996) Style Policy and Style Politics: A Neglected Aspect of the Language of the News, *Media, Culture and Society*, 18: 315–333.

Cameron, D. (2001) *Working with Spoken Discourse*. London: Sage

Cardiff School of Journalism (2004) *Too Close for Comfort? The Role of Embedded Reporting during the 2003 Iraq War* (Summary Report: Prepared by Justin Lewis, Terry Threadgold, Rod Brookes, Nick Mosdell, Kirsten Brander, Sadie Clifford, Ehab Bessaiso and Zahera Harb).

Chatterjee, P. (2004) *Iraq Inc. A Profitable Occupation*. New York: Seven Stories Press.

Chokri, A. (2005) Reporting Global Terror: Editorial and Translation Challenges, Paper presented at *Global Terror: A Debate*, Centre for Translation and Comparative Cultural Studies, Aston University, 8 April 2005.

Chomsky, N. (1999) *The New Military Humanism: Lessons from Kosovo*. London: Pluto Press.

Chomsky, N. (2002) *Pirates and Emperors, Old and New: International Terrorism in the Real World*. London: Pluto Press.

Chomsky, N. (2005) Globalization and War, in G. Hubbard and D. Miller (eds) *Arguments Against G8*, pp. 19–43. London: Pluto Press.

Chouliaraki, L. and Fairclough, N. (1999) *Discourse in Late Modernity: Rethinking Critical Discourse Analysis*. Edinburgh: Edinburgh University Press.

Clark, K. (1992) The linguistics of blame, in M. Toolan (ed.) *Language, Text, and Context*, pp. 208–224. London: Routledge.

Collins, J. and Glover, R. (2002) *Collateral Language: A User's Guide to America's New War*. New York: New York University Press.

Condit, C. M. (1989) The rhetorical limits of polysemy, in J. L. Lucaites, C. M. Condit and S. Caudill (eds) (1999) *Contemporary Rhetorical Theory: A Reader*, pp. 494–511. New York: The Guilford Press.

Conley, T. M. (1984) The Enthymeme in Perspective. *Quarterly Journal of Speech*, 70: 168–187.

Corbett, E. P. J. (1990) *Classical Rhetoric for the Modern Student* (3rd edn). Oxford: Oxford University Press.

Cotter, C. (2001) Discourse and media, in D. Schiffrin, D. Tannen and H. E. Hamilton (eds) *The Handbook of Discourse Analysis*, pp. 416–436. Oxford: Blackwell.

Cottle, S. (2000) Rethinking News Access, *Journalism Studies*, 1(3): 427–448.

Coward, R. and Ellis, J. (1977) *Language and Materialism: Developments in the Semiology and the Theory of the Subject*. London: Routledge and Kegan Paul.

Cox, R. W. (2004) Beyond Empire and Terror: Critical Reflections on the Political Economy of World Order, *New Political Economy*, 9(3): 307–323.

Cunningham, B. (2004) Across the Great Divide: Class, *Columbia Journalism Review*, May/June 2004: 31–38.

Curran, J. and Seaton, J. (1997) *Power without Responsibility: The Press and Broadcasting in Britain*. London: Methuen.

Curtis, M. (2003) *Web of Deceit: Britain's Real Role in the World*. London: Vintage.

Curtis, M. (2004) *Unpeople: Britain's Secret Human Rights Abuses*. London: Vintage.

Dahl, R. A. (1961) *Who Governs? Democracy and Power in an American City*. New Haven: Yale University Press.

Deacon, D., Pickering, M., Golding, P. and Murdock, G. (1999) *Researching Communications: A Practical Guide to Methods in Media and Cultural Analysis*. London: Arnold.

Delin, J. (2000) *The Language of Everyday Life*. London: Sage.

DeWerth-Pallmeyer, D. (1997) *The Audience in the News*. Mahwah: LEA.

Dor, D. (2003) On Newspaper Headlines as Relevance Optimisers, *Journal of Pragmatics*, 35: 695–721.

Dunlevy, M. (1998) Objectivity, in M. Breen (ed.) *Journalism: Theory and Practice*, pp. 119–138. Paddington, NSW: Macleay Press.

Eagleton, T. (1981) *Walter Benjamin, or Towards a Revolutionary Criticism*. London: NLB.

Eagleton, T. (2002) *Marxism and Literary Criticism*. London: Routledge.

Ehrenreich, B. (1989) *Fear of Falling: The Inner Life of the Middle Class*. New York: HarperCollins.

Ehrenreich, B. (1995) The silenced majority: Why the average working person has disappeared from American media and culture, in G. Dines and J. M. Humez (eds) *Gender, Race and Class in Media: A Text-Reader*, pp. 40–42. London: Sage.

Ehrenreich, B. and Russell Hochschild, A. (eds) (2003) *Global Woman: Nannies, Maids, and Sex Workers in the New Economy*. New York: Metropolitan Books.

Elliott, J. (2005) *Using Narrative in Social Research*. London: Sage.

Ellul, J. (1965) *Propaganda: The Formation of Men's Attitudes*. New York: Random House Inc.

Essed, P. J. M. (1991) *Understanding Everyday Racism: An Interdisciplinary Approach*. Newbury Park, CA: Sage.

Fairclough, N. (1992) *Discourse and Social Change*. Cambridge: Polity Press.

Fairclough, N. (1995a) *Media Discourse*. London: Arnold.

Fairclough, N. (1995b) *Critical Discourse Analysis: The Critical Study of Language*. London: Longman.

Fairclough, N. (2000) *New Labour New Language?* London: Routledge.

Fairclough, N. (2003) *Analysing Discourse: Textual Analysis for Social Research*. London: Routledge.

Fairclough, N. and Wodak, R. (1997) Critical Discourse Analysis: An overview, in T. A. van Dijk (ed.) *Discourse Studies: A Multidisciplinary Introduction*, Vol. 2, pp. 67–97. London: Sage.

Fortenbaugh, W. W. (1996) Aristotle's accounts of persuasion through character, in C. L. Johnstone (ed.) *Theory, Text, Context: Issues in Greek Rhetoric and Oratory*, pp. 147–168. New York: SUNY Press.

Foss, S. K. (1996) *Rhetorical Criticism: Exploration and Practice*. Prospect Heights, IL: Waveland.

Foucault, M. (1972) *The Archaeology of Knowledge and the Discourse on Language*. New York: Pantheon.

Fowler, R. (1991) *Language in the News: Discourse and Ideology in the Press*. London: Routledge.

Fowler, R., Hodge, R., Kress, G. and Trew, T. (1979) *Language and Control*. London: Routledge and Kegan Paul.

Franklin, B. (1997) *Newszak and the News Media*. London: Arnold.

Franklin, B. (1998) *Tough on Soundbites, Tough on the Causes of Soundbites*, www.catalyst-trust.co.uk/pub3.html, accessed 11 September 2005.

Franklin, B. (2004) *Packaging Politics: Political Communications in Britain's Media Democracy* (2nd edn). London: Arnold.

Franklin, B. (2005) McJournalism: the local press and the McDonaldization thesis, in S. Allan (ed.) *Journalism: Critical Issues*, pp. 137–150. Maidenhead: OU Press.

Franklin, B., Hamer, M., Hanna, M., Kinsey, M. and Richardson, J. E. (2005) *Key Concepts in Journalism Studies*, London: Sage.

Freedman, D. (2003) The Daily Mirror and the war on Iraq, in A. R. Biressi and H. A. Nunn (eds) *Mediactive, 3: Media War*, pp. 95–108. London: Barefoot Publications.

Frost, C. (2004) The Press Complaints Commission: A Study of Ten Years of Adjudications of Press Complaints, *Journalism Studies* 5(1): 101–114.

Fukayama, F. (1992) *The End of History and the Last Man*. London: Penguin.

Gallie, W. B. (1955) Essentially Contestable Concepts, *Proceedings of the Aristotelian Society*, 56, 167–198.

Gallup, G. (1958) *A Guide to Public Opinion*. Princeton: Princeton University Press.

Galtung, J. and Ruge, M. (1965) Structuring and selecting news in S. Cohen and J. Young (eds) (1973) *The Manufacture of News: Social Problems, Deviance and the News Media*, pp. 62–72. London: Constable.

Gandy, O. H. (2000) Race, ethnicity and the segmentation of media markets, in J. Curran and M. Gurevitch (eds) *Mass Media and Society* (3rd edn), pp. 44–69. London: Arnold.

Gandy, O. N. (1982) *Beyond Agenda Setting: Information Subsidies and Public Policy*. New York: Ablex.

Gee, J. P. (1990) *Social Linguistics and Literacies: Ideology in Discourses*. London: The Falmer Press.

Gee, J. P. (1999) *An Introduction to Discourse Analysis: Theory and Method*. London: Routledge.

Gerbner, G. (1958) On content analysis and critical research in mass communication, in L. A. Dexter and D. Manning (eds) (1964) *People, Society and Mass Communications*, pp. 476–500. New York: Free Press.

Gerbner, G. (1991) Symbolic functions of violence and terror, in R. Picard and Y. Alexander (eds) *In the Camera's Eye: News Coverage of Terrorist Events*, pp. 3–10. Washington DC: Brassey's Inc.

Gillespie, M. (1995) *Television, Ethnicity and Cultural Change*. London: Routledge.

Gitlin, T. (1979) Prime-time Ideology: The Hegemonic Process in Television Entertainment, *Social Problems*, 26: 251–266.

Glasgow Media Group (2000) *Viewing the World: A Study of British Television Coverage of Developing Countries*, available at www.dfid.gov.uk/pubs/files/viewworldsum.pdf, accessed 6 April 2005.

Gramsci, A. (1971) *Selections from the Prison Notebooks*, trans Q. Hoare and G. N. Smith. London: Lawrence & Wishart.

Gregory, L. and Hutchins, B. (2004) Everyday Editorial Practices and the Public Sphere: Analyzing the Letters to the Editor Page of a Regional Newspaper, *Media International Australia Incorporating Culture and Policy*, 112: 186–200.

Grey, D. L. and Brown, T. R. (1970) Letters to the Editor: Hazy Reflections of Public Opinion. *Journalism Quarterly*, 47: 450–456.

Hackett, R. (1984) Decline of a Paradigm? Bias and Objectivity in News Media Studies, *Critical Studies in Mass Communication*, 1(3): 229–259.

Hall, S. (1980) Encoding/Decoding, in P. Marris and S. Thornham (eds) (1996) *Media Studies: A Reader*, pp. 51–61. Edinburgh: Edinburgh University Press.

Hall, S. (1982) The rediscovery of ideology: Return of the repressed in media studies, in Gurevitch *et al.* (eds) *Culture, Society and the Media*, pp. 56–90. London: Methuen.

Hall, S., Critcher, C., Jefferson, T., Clarke, J. and Robert, B. (1978) *Policing the Crisis: Mugging, the State and Law and Order*. London: Macmillan.

Halliday, F. (2006) Anti-Arab prejudice in the UK: The BBC response, in E. Poole and J. E. Richardson (eds) *Muslims and the News Media*, pp. 24–34. London: I. B. Tauris.

Hamblin, C. L. (1970) *Fallacies*. London: Methuen.

Hansen, H. V. and Pinto, R. C. (eds) (1995) *Fallacies: Classical and Contemporary Readings*. Pennsylvania: Pennsylvania State University Press.

Harcup, T. (2002) Journalists and Ethics: The Quest for a Collective Voice, *Journalism Studies* 3(1): 101–114.

Harcup, T. and O'Neill, D. (2001) What is News? Galtung and Ruge revisited. *Journalism Studies*, 2(2): 261–280.

Harris, S. (1991) Evasive action: How politicians respond to questions in political interviews, in P. Scannell (ed.) *Broadcast Talk*. London: Sage.

Hartley, J. (1992) *The Politics of Pictures: The Creation of the Public in the Age of Public Media*. London: Routledge.

Herman, E. S. (1992) *Beyond Hypocrisy: Decoding the News in an age of Propaganda*. Boston, MA: South End Press.

Herman, E. S. (2002) The Cruise Missile Left: Aligning with Power. *Z Magazine*, 15(11), available at http://zmagsite.zmag.org/Nov2002/Herman1102.htm, accessed 23 August 2005.

Herman, E. S. and Chomsky, N. (1994) *Manufacturing Consent*. London: Vintage.

Hetherington, A. (1985) *News, Newspapers and Television*. London: Macmillan.

Hill, F. I. (1983) The Rhetoric of Aristotle, in J. J. Murphy (ed.) *A Synoptic History of Classical Rhetoric*, pp. 19–76. David, CA: Hermagoras Press.

Hubbard, G. and Miller, D. (2005) *Arguments Against G8*. London: Pluto Press.

Iarovici, E. and Amel, R. (1989) The Strategy of the Headline, *Semiotica*, 77(4): 441–459.

Iggers, J. (1999) *Good News, Bad News: Journalism Ethics and the Public Interest*. Boulder: Westview Press.

Jackson, I. (1971) *The Provincial Press and the Community*. Manchester: Manchester University Press.

Jasinski, J. (2001) *Sourcebook on Rhetoric*. Thousand Oaks, CA: Sage.

Joll, J. (1977) *Gramsci*. London: Fontana.

Jones, P. E. (2001) Cognitive linguistics and marxist approach to ideology, in R. Dirven, B. Hawkins and E. Sandikcioglu (eds) *Language and Ideology. Volume 1: Theoretical Cognitive Approaches*, pp. 227–251. Amsterdam: John Benjamins.

Jones, P. E. and Collins, C. (forthcoming) Political Analysis Versus 'Critical Discourse Analysis' in the Treatment of Ideology. *Atlantic Journal of Communication*.

Jowett, G. S. and O'Donnell, V. (1992) *Propaganda and Persuasion*. London: Sage.

Jucker, A. H. (1992) *Social Stylistics: Syntactic Variation in British Newspapers*. Berlin: Mouton de Gruyer.

Kelso, P. and Byrne, C. (2003) Readers join Attack on Sun over Coverage of Bruno Breakdown, *Guardian*, 24 September 2003.

Kieran, M. (1998) Objectivity, impartiality and good journalism, in M. Kieran (ed.) *Media Ethics*, pp. 23–36. London: Routledge.

Kitzinger, C. and Frith, H. (1999) Just say no? The Use of Conversational Analysis in Developing a Feminist Perspective on Sexual Refusal. *Discourse and Society*, 10(3): 293–316.

Klein, N. (2004) You asked for my evidence, Mr Ambassador. Here it is, *Guardian*, 4 December 2004, available at www.guardian.co.uk/comment/story/0,,1366278,00.html, accessed 5 September 2005.

Knightly, P. (2000) *The First Casualty: The War Correspondent as Hero and Myth-maker from the Crimea to Kosovo*. London: Prion.

Kress, G. (1983) Linguistic and ideological transformations in news reporting, in H. Davis and P. Walton (eds) *Language, Image, Media*, pp. 120–138. Oxford: Blackwell.

Kress, G. (1994) Text and grammar as explanation, in U. H. Meinhoff and K. Richardson (eds) *Text, Discourse and Context: Representations of Poverty in Britain*, pp. 24–46. London: Longman.

Lakoff, G. (1991) *Metaphor and War: the Metaphor System Used to Justify the War in the Gulf*, http://lists.village.virginia.edu/sixties/HTML_docs/Texts/Scholarly/Lakoff_Gulf_Metaphor_1.html, accessed 28 June 2005.

Larson, R. P. (2004) Anatomy of a bonding: An embedded reporter's account of the bonding process with the soldiers, in Y. R. Kamalipour and N. Snow (eds) *War, Media and Propaganda: A Global Perspective*, pp. 125–130. Lanham: Rowman and Littlefield Publishers Inc.

Lasswell, H. D. (1949) Why be Quantitative?, in B. Berelson and M. Janowitz (eds) (1966) *Reader in Public Opinion and Communication* (2nd edn), pp. 247–259. New York: The Free Press.

Leitch, V. B. (1983) *Deconstructive Criticism: An Advanced Introduction*. New York: Columbia University Press.

Lewis, J. and Brookes, R. (2004) Reporting the War on British television, in D. Miller (ed.) *Tell Me Lies: Propaganda and Media Distortion in the Attack on Iraq*, pp. 132–143. London: Pluto Press.

Lindlof, T. R. (1995) *Qualitative Communication Research Methods*. London: Sage.

Lockyer, S. and Pickering, M. (2001) Dear Shit-shovelers: Humour, Censure and the Discourse of Complaint. *Discourse and Society*, 12(5): 633–651.

Luke, A. (2002) Beyond Science and Ideology Critique: Developments in Critical Discourse Analysis, *Annual Review of Applied Linguistics*, 22: 96–110.

Lukes, S. (1974) *Power: A Radical View*. London: Macmillan Press.

Lule, J. (2004) War and its Metaphors: News Language and the Prelude to War in Iraq, 2003. *Journalism Studies*, 5(2): 179–190.

Lynch, J. (2003) Reporting Iraq – what went right? What went wrong? In A. R. Biressi and H. A. Nunn (eds) *Mediactive, 3: Media War*, pp. 109–126. London: Barefoot Publications.

Lynn, N. and Lea, S. (2003) 'A phantom menace and the new Apartheid': The Social Construction of Asylum Seekers in the United Kingdom. *Discourse and Society*, 14(4): 425–452.

MacManus, J. H. (1994) *Market-driven Journalism: let the Citizen Beware?* Thousand Oaks/London: Sage.

Mahajan, R. (2003) Responding to Colin Powell, *CommonDreams.org* 7 February 2003, http://www.commondreams.org/views03/0207-03.htm, accessed 25 August 2005.

Manning, P. (2001) *News and News Sources: A Critical Introduction*. London: Sage.

Marsh, D. and Marshall, N. (2004) *The Guardian Stylebook*. London: Guardian Books.

Martin, W. (1986) *Recent Theories of Narrative*. Ithaca, NY: Cornell University Press.

Marx, K. (1998 [1848]) Manifesto of the Communist Party (trans. T. Carver), in M. Cowling (ed.) *The Communist Manifesto: New Interpretations*, pp. 14–37. Edinburgh: Edinburgh University Press.

Marx, K. and Engels, F. (1974) *The German Ideology* (edited by C. J. Arthur). London: Lawrence and Wishart.

McKerrow, R. E. (1989) Critical Rhetoric: Theory and praxis, in J. L. Lucaites, C. M. Condit and S. Caudill (eds) (1999) *Contemporary Rhetorical Theory: A Reader*, pp. 441–463. New York: The Guilford Press.

McLellan, D. (1986) *Ideology*. Minneapolis: University of Minnesota Press.

McNair, B. (2005) The emerging chaos of global news culture, in S. Allan (ed.) *Journalism: Critical Issues*, pp. 151–167. Maidenhead: OU Press.

McQuail, D. (1994) *Mass Communication Theory: An Introduction* (3rd edn). London: Sage.

Mey, J. (2001) *Pragmatics: An Introduction*. Oxford: Blackwell.

Miller, D. (2003) Embed with the Enemy, *CounterCurrents.org* 4 April 2003, http://www.countercurrents.org/iraq-miller040403.htm, accessed 30 August 2005.

Mills, S. (1995) *Feminist Stylistics*. London: Routledge.

Molotch, H. and Lester, M. (1974) News as Purposive Behaviour: On the Strategic Use of Routine Events, Accidents and Scandals, *American Sociological Review*, 39: 101–112.

Montgomery, M., Durant, A., Fabb, N., Furniss, T. and Mills, S. (2000) *Ways of Reading: Advanced Reading Skills for Students of English Literature*. London: Routledge.

Moon, D. G. and Rolison, G. L. (1998) Communication of classism, in M. L. Hecht (ed.) *Communicating Prejudice*, pp. 122–135. Thousand Oaks: Sage.

Morrison, A. and Love, A. (1996) A Discourse of Disillusionment: Letters to the editor in Two Zimbabwean Magazines after Independence. *Discourse and Society*, 7(1): 39–75.

Munt, S. (2000) Introduction, in S. Munt (ed.) *Cultural Studies and the Working Class*, pp. 1–16. London: Cassell.

Murdock, G. (2000) Reconstructing the ruined tower: Contemporary communications and questions of class, in J. Curran and M. Gurevitch (eds) *Mass Media and Society* (3rd edn), pp. 7–26. London: Arnold.

Murdock, G. and Golding, P. (1977) Capitalism, communication and class relations, in J. Curran, M. Gurevitch and J. Woolacott (eds) *Mass Communication and Society*, pp. 12–43. London: Edward Arnold.

Negrine, R. (1997) Just the News Please, *The World Today*, 53(4): 97–98.

Nohrstedt, S. A., Kaitatzi-Whitlock, S., Ottosen, R. and Riegert, K. (2000) From the Persian Gulf to Kosovo – War Journalism and Propaganda, *European Journal of Communication*, 15(3): 383–404.

O'Byrne, D. J. (2003) The discourse of human rights and the neo-conservative discourse of war, in A. R. Biressi and H. A. Nunn (eds) *Mediactive, 3: Media War*, pp. 13–22. London: Barefoot Publications.

Ochs, E. (1997) Narrative, in T. A. van Dijk (ed.) *Discourse as Structure and Process*, pp. 185–207. London: Sage.

Okrent, D. (2004) Weapons of Mass Destruction? Or Mass Distraction? New York Times, 30 May 2004, http://www.antidepressantsfacts.com/times-editors-7.htm, accessed 11 September 2005.

O'Neill, J. (1992) Journalism in the market place, in A. Belsey and R. Chadwick (eds) *Ethical Issues in Journalism and the Media*, pp. 15–32. London: Routledge.

Orwell, G. (2004 [1946]) Politics and the English Language, *Why I Write*, pp. 102–120. London: Penguin Books.

Pêcheux, M. (1994) The Mechanism of Ideological (Mis)Recognition, in S. Žižek (ed.) *Mapping Ideology*, pp. 141–151. London: Verso.

Perelman, Ch. (1979) *The New Rhetoric and the Humanities*. Dordrecht: Reidel.

Perelman, Ch. and Olbrechts-Tyteca, L. (1969) *The New Rhetoric: A Treatise on Argumentation*, translated by J. Wilkinson and P. Weaver. Notre Dame: University of Notre Dame Press.

Petley, J. (2006) Still no redress from the PCC, in E. Poole and J. E. Richardson (eds) *Muslims and the News Media*, pp. 53–62. London: I.B. Tauris.

Phillips, L. and Jørgensen, M. W. (2002) *Discourse Analysis as Theory and Method*. London: Sage.

Plunkett, J. (2003) News Chiefs to Stop Staff Entering Iraq, *Broadcast*, 28 March 2003.

Reah, D. (2002) *The Language of Newspapers*. London: Routledge.

Reese, S. D. (1990) The News Paradigm and the Ideology of Objectivity: A Socialist at the Wall Street Journal, in D. Berkowitz (ed.) (1997) *Social Meanings of News*, pp. 420–440. London: Sage.

Reisigl, M. and Wodak, R. (2001) *Discourse and Discrimination: Rhetorics of Racism and Anti-Semitism*. London: Routledge.

Renfro, P. C. (1979) Bias in selection of 'letters to the editor'. *Journalism Quarterly*, 56: 822–826.

Richardson, J. E. (2001a) 'Now is the time to put an end to all this.' Argumentative discourse theory and letters to the editor. *Discourse and Society*, 12(2): 143–168.

Richardson, J. E. (2001b) British Muslims in the Broadsheet Press: A Challenge to Cultural Hegemony?, *Journalism Studies*, 2(2): 221–242.

Richardson, J. E. (2004) *(Mis)Representing Islam: The Racism and Rhetoric of the British Broadsheet Press*. Amsterdam: John Benjamins.

Richardson, J. E. (2006) Who gets to speak? A Study of Sources in the Broadsheet Press, in E. Poole and J. E. Richardson (eds) *Muslims and the News Media*, pp. 103–115. London: I.B. Tauris.

Richardson, J. E. and Franklin, B. (2003) 'Dear Editor': Race, Readers' Letters and the Local Press. *Political Quarterly*, 74(2): 184–192.

Richardson, J. E. and Franklin, B. (2004) Letters of Intent: Election Campaigning and Orchestrated Public Debate in Local Newspapers' Letters to the Editor. *Political Communication*, 21(4): 459–478.

Ross, K. (1998) Making race matter: An overview, in B. Franklin and D. Murphy (eds.) *Making the Local News: Local Journalism in Context*, pp. 228–240. London: Routledge.

Sanders, K. (2003) *Ethics and Journalism*. London: Sage.

Schement, J. (1998) Through Americans: Minorities and the new media, in A. Garmer (ed.) *Investing in Diversity: Advancing Opportunities for Minorities and the Media*, pp. 87–124. Washington DC: Aspen Institute.

Schiffrin, D. (1994) *Approaches to Discourse*. Oxford: Blackwell.

Shaikh, A. (1986) Capital as a social relation, in J. Eatwell, M. Milgate and P. Newman (eds). *The New Palgrave: A Dictionary of Economic Theory and Doctrine*, pp. 72–78. London: Macmillan.

Simpson, P. (1993) *Language, Ideology and Point of View*. London & New York: Routledge.

Slisli, F. (2000) The western media and the Algerian crisis, *Race and Class*, 41(3): 43–57.

Snoeck Henkemans, F. (2002) Clues for reconstructing symptomatic argumentation, in F. H. van Eemeren (ed.) *Advances in Pragma-Dialectics*, pp. 197–214. Amsterdam: Sic Sat.

Snow, N. (2004) Brainscrubbing: The failures of US public diplomacy after 9/11, in D. Miller (ed.) *Tell Me Lies: Propaganda and Media Distortion in the Attack on Iraq*, pp. 52–62. London: Pluto Press.

Sontag, S. (1990) *Illness as Metaphor and AIDS and its Metaphors*. New York: Doubleday.

Sreberny, A. (2000) Media and diasporic consciousness: An exploration among Iranians in London, in S. Cottle (ed.) *Ethnic Minorities and the Media*, pp. 179–196. Buckingham: OU Press.

Taylor, P. M. (1995) *Munitions of the Mind: A History of Propaganda from the Ancient World to the Present Era*. Manchester: Manchester University Press.

Taylor, P. M. (2003) 'We Know Where You Are': Psychological Operations Media During *Enduring Freedom*, in D. Thussu and D. Freedman (eds) *War and The Media: Reporting Conflict 24/7*, pp. 101–113. London: Sage.

Temple, M. (2004) *The Local Press and Political Apathy: Carry on Campaigning*. A paper presented to the PSA Annual Conference, University of Lincoln, 6–8 April 2004. http://www.psa.ac.uk/cps/2004/Temple.pdf, accessed 11 September 2005.

Thomson, A. (1996) *Critical Reasoning: A Practical Introduction*. London: Routledge.

Thomson, J. B. (1990) *Ideology and Modern Culture*. Cambridge: Polity Press.

Titscher, S., Meyer, M., Wodak, R. and Vetter, E. (2000) *Methods of Text and Discourse Analysis*. London: Sage.

Tomlin, R. S., Forrest, L., Pu, M. M. and Kim, M. H. (1997) Discourse semantics, in T. A. van Dijk (ed.) *Discourse as Structure and Process*, pp. 63–111. London: Sage.

Toynbee, P. (2003) Mothers for sale, *Guardian*, July 19 2003, http://books.guardian.co.uk/review/story/0,,1000234,00.html, accessed 11 September 2005.

Trew, T. (1979a) Theory and ideology at work, in R. Fowler, R. Hodge, G. Kress, and T. Trew (eds) *Language and Control*, pp. 94–116. London: Routledge and Kegan Paul.

Trew, T. (1979b) 'What the papers say': linguistic variation and ideological difference, in R. Fowler, R. Hodge, G. Kress, and T. Trew (eds) *Language and Control*, pp. 117–156. London: Routledge and Kegan Paul.

Tuchman, G. (1972) Objectivity as Strategic Ritual, in *American Journal of Sociology*, 77: 660–679.

Tuchman, G. (1978) *Making News*. New York: The Free Press.

Tuchman, G. (1983) Consciousness Industries and the Production of Culture, *Journal of Communication*, 33: 330–341.

Tunstall, J. (1971) *Journalists at Work*. London: Constable.

van Dijk, T. A. (1988) *News as Discourse*. Hillsdale, NJ: Lawrence Erlbaum.

van Dijk, T. A. (1991) *Racism and the Press*. London: Routledge.

van Dijk, T. A. (1993) *Elite Discourse and Racism*. Newbury Park, CA.: Sage.

van Dijk, T. A. (1996) Discourse, opinions and ideologies, in C. Schaffner and H. Kelly-Holmes (eds) *Discourse and Ideologies*, pp. 7–37. Clevedon: Multilingual Matters Ltd.

van Dijk, T. A. (1997a) *Discourse Studies: A Multidisciplinary Introduction. Vol. 1: Discourse as Structure and Process*. London: Sage.

van Dijk, T. A. (1997b) *Discourse Studies: A Multidisciplinary Introduction. Vol. 2: Discourse as Social Interaction*. London: Sage.

van Dijk, T. A. (1998) *Ideology: A Multidisciplinary Approach*. London: Sage.

van Dijk, T. A. (1999) *Discourse and Racism*, www.hum.uva.nl/teun/dis-rac.htm, accessed 31 January 2000.

van Dijk, T. A. (2001) Multidisciplinary CDA: A plea for diversity, in R. Wodak and M. Meyer (eds), *Methods of Critical Discourse Analysis*, pp. 95–120. London: Sage.

van Eemeren, F. H. and Grootendorst, R. (1987) Fallacies in Pragma-Dialectical Perspective, *Argumentation*, 1: 283–301.

van Eemeren, F. H. and Grootendorst, R. (1992) *Argumentation, Communication and Fallacies: A Pragma-Dialectical Perspective*. Hillsdale, NJ: Lawrence Erlbaum.

van Eemeren, F. H. and Grootendorst, R. (1994a). Rationale for a pragma-dialectical perspective, in F. H. van Eemeren and R. Grootendorst (eds) *Studies in Pragma-Dialectics*, pp. 11–28. Amsterdam: Sic Sat.

van Eemeren, F. H. and Grootendorst, R. (1994b) Relevance reviewed: the case of 'argumentum ad hominum', in F. H. van Eemeren and R. Grootendorst (eds) *Studies in Pragma-Dialectics*, pp. 51–68. Amsterdam: Sic Sat.

van Eemeren, F. H. and Grootendorst, R. (2004) *A Systematic Theory of Argumentation*. Cambridge: Cambridge University Press.

van Eemeren, F. H., Grootendoorst, R., Jackson, S., and Jacobs, S. (1997) Argumentation, in T. A. van Dijk (ed.) *Discourse as Structure and Process. Discourse Studies: A Multidisciplinary Introduction*, pp. 208–229. London: Sage.

van Eemeren, F. H., Grootendorst, R. and Snoeck Henkemans, F. (2002) *Argumentation: Analysis, Evaluation, Presentation*. Mahwah, NJ: Lawrence Erlbaum Associates.

van Eemeren, F. H., Garssen, B. and Meuffels, B. (2003) The conventional validity of the pragma-dialectical freedom rule, in van Eemeren, Blair, Willard and Snoeck Henkemans (eds) *Prooceedings of the Fifth*

Conference of the International Society for the Study of Argumentation, pp. 275–280. Amsterdam: ISSA.

van Eemeren, F. H., Grootendorst, R., Snoeck Henkemans, F., Blair, J. A., Johnson, R. H., Krabbe, E. C.W., Plantin, Ch., Walton, D. N., Willard, C. A., Woods, J. and Zarefsky, D. (1996) *Fundamentals of Argumentation Theory: A Handbook of Historical Backgrounds and Contemporary Developments*. Mahwah, NJ: Lawrence Erlbaum.

van Leeuwen, T. (1996) The representation of social actors, in C. R. Caldas-Coulthard and M. Coulthard (eds) *Texts and Practices: Readings in Critical Discourse Analysis*, pp. 32–70. London: Routledge.

Verschueren, J. (1985) *International News Reporting: Metapragmatic Metaphors and the U-2*. Amsterdam: John Benjamins.

Vološinov (1973 [1929]) *Marxism and the Philosophy of Language* (trans. L. Matejka and I. R. Titunik). Cambridge, MA: Harvard University Press.

Wahl-Jorgensen, K. (2001) Letters to the Editor as a Forum for Public Deliberation: Modes of Publicity and Democratic Debate. *Critical Studies in Mass Communications*, 18(3): 303–320.

Wahl-Jorgensen, K. (2002) Understanding the Conditions for Public Discourse: Four Rules for Selecting Letters to the Editor. *Journalism Studies*, 3(1): 69–81.

Walsh, J. (ed.) (1995) *The Gulf War Did Not Happen: Politics, Culture and Warfare Post-Vietnam*. Aldershot: Arena.

Walton, D. N. (1989) *Informal Logic: A Handbook for Critical Argumentation*, Cambridge: Cambridge University Press.

Wayne, M. (2003) *Marxism and Media Studies: Key Concepts and Contemporary Trends*. London: Pluto Press.

Webster, F. (2003) Information warfare in an Age of Globalization, in D. Thussu and D. Freedman (eds). *War and the Media*, pp. 57–69. London: Sage.

Weiss, G. and Wodak, R. (2003) *Critical Discourse Analysis: Theory and Interdisciplinarity*. London: Palgrave.

Welch, D. (1993) *The Third Reich: Politics and Propaganda*. London & New York: Routledge.

Westergaard, J. (1977) Power, class and the media, in J. Curran, M. Gurevitch and J. Woolacott (eds) *Mass Communication and Society*, pp. 95–115. London: Edward Arnold.

Wetherell, M. and Potter, J. (1992) *Mapping the Language of Racism: Discourse and the Legitimation of Exploitation*. Hempstead: Harvester Wheatsheaf.

White, H. (1981) The value of narrativity in the representation of meaning, in W. J. T. Mitchell (ed.) *On Narrative*. Chicago: Chicago University Press.

Widdowson, H. G. (2004) *Text, Context, Pretext: Critical Issues for Discourse Analysis*. Oxford: Blackwell Publishing.

Wober, J. M. (2004) Top people write to *The Times, British Journalism Review*, 15(2): 49–54.

Wodak, R. (1996) *Disorders of Discourse*. London: Longman.

Wodak, R. (2001) What CDA is about – a summary of its history, important concepts and its developments, in R. Wodak and M. Meyer (eds) *Methods of Critical Discourse Analysis*, pp. 1–13. London: Sage.

Wodak, R. (2002) Fragmented identities: Redefining and recontextualizing national identity, in P. Chilton and C. Schäffner (eds) *Politics as Text and Talk: Analytic Approaches to Political Discourse*, pp. 143–169. Amsterdam: John Benjamins.

Wodak, R. and Meyer, M. (eds) (2001) *Methods of Critical Discourse Analysis*. London: Sage.

Wodak, R., De Cillia, R., Reisigl, M. and Liebhart, K. (1999) *The Discursive Construction of National Identity*. Edinburgh: Edinburgh University Press.

Woods, L. A. and Kroger, R. O. (2000) *Doing Discourse Analysis: Methods for Studying Action in Talk and Text*. Thousand Oaks, CA: Sage.

Worcester, R. M. (1998) Demographics and values: What the British public reads and what it thinks about its newspapers, in M. Bromley and H. Stephenson (eds) *Sex, Lies and Democracy*, pp. 39–48. London: Longman.

Index

Note: Where Tables or Figures appear on pages unconnected with their subject matter they are indicated by an italic page reference.